DATE DUE

GAYLORD			PRINTED IN U.S.A.

From Personal

to Professional

Management

David E. Shepard

*Virginia Western
Community College*

Holbrook Press, Inc.

Boston

Printed in the United States of America

Library of Congress Cataloging in Publication Data

Shepard, David.
    From personal to professional management.
    Bibliography: p.
    Includes index.
    1. Management   I. Title.
HD31.S444   658.4   76-919
ISBN 0-205-04992-3

To Annie,

David,

Mark,

Scott,

Amy,

and John

Contents

Preface   xiii

Part 1   Introduction to Management

1   What Is Management?   3

*A Manager Is   Happiness is a Job?   Professional
Managers   Planning   Organizing   Activating
Controlling   For Discussion   Case 1-1 The Puzzled
Paperboy   Case 2-2 The Inventory Clerk Turnover*

2   Decision Making and Case Presentation   19

*Bases for Decisions   For Discussion   Case 2-1 Yourself
Case 2-2 The All Over Forty*

**3   Management History and Current Schools of
Thought   33**

*Ancient Systems   Scientific Management   The Gantt Chart
Administrative Emphasis   Human Relations School   The
Quantitative School   The Systems Approach   Summary
For Discussion   Case 3-1 The Lamenting Mentor   Case 3-2
The Growing Concern for the Growing Concern*

4   Management Roles and Activities   51

*A Manager's Systems   Activities for Various Levels of Managers
Figurehead   Liaison   Umpire   Information Center   Control
Center and Communicator   Final Decider   Chief Spokesman
Negotiator   Resource Allocator   Trainer   Coordinator and
Leader   Roles and Functions   Activities and Functions*

*For Discussion   Case 4-1 The Blinkedy Blank Lighting
Company   Case 4-2 The Assurance to the Insurance Man*

Part   2   Planning

5   Management Goals and Objectives   67

*Defining Goals and Objectives   Objectives as Motivators
Management by Objectives   Types of Goals   Communication of
Goals and Objectives   For Discussion   Case 5-1 The Easy Election
Case 5-2 The Wondering Mrs. Watson*

6   Planning to Reach Goals   81

*Steps in Planning   Who Plans?   Time Span in Planning
No Planning   Why Plans Fail   To Write or Not to Write   Group
Planning   Dissemination of Plans   For Discussion   Case 6-1
The Disagreeable Agreement   Case 6-2 The Rattled Mr. Randle*

7   Classifying Plans   97

*Goals and Objectives   Other Types of Plans   Policy   Precedence
as Policy   Strategies   Procedures   Rules   Single-Purpose Plans
Budgets   For Discussion   Case 7-1 The Sitter Who Upset the
Sittee   Case 7-2 Little Lying Laura*

8   Creativity and Innovation   115

*Who Can Create?   Overcoming Subordinates' Obstacles   Other
Creative Blocks   The Creative Process   Altering Forms
Brainstorming   Personal Objective Aids   For Discussion
Case 8-1 Getting Stuck with the Sticks   Case 8-2 The F.I.N.K.
Bank Think Tank*

9   Selling Ideas   129

*Idea Evaluation   Familiarizing Oneself with the Idea   Qualifying
the Audience   Getting the Attention of the Audience*

Presenting the Main Idea   Asking for Action   Overcoming Objections from the Audience   For Discussion   Case 9-1 Plugging Up the Holes in the Doughnut Plan   Case 9-2 The Young Presenters

Part 3   Organizing

10   Organizational Structure   147

Unity of Command   Line and Staff   Chain of Command Forms of Organization   Types of Assistants   Problems of Staff Personnel   Formal and Informal Organization   Departmentation For Discussion   Case 10-1 Righting the Wrong Boss   Case 10-2 The Cascade of Confidential Claims

11   Organization Concepts   171

A Job   Authority   Responsibility   Obligations   Delegation and Decentralization   Span of Control   Dynamic Organization For Discussion   Case 11-1 The Quarterback Quota   Case 11-2 The Busted Ratebuster

Part 4   Activating

12   Staffing the Organization   189

Recruiting   Screening   The Interview   Evaluating the Applicants Selecting   Induction   Training   Compensation   For Discussion Case 12-1 The Unstaffed Staff   Case 12-2 The Growing Concern for the Growing Concern (B)

13   Motivation and Morale   207

Motivation   The History of Motivation   What Are Man's Needs? Motivators and Satisfiers   X's and Y's   Other Motivational Theories Summary   Morale   For Discussion   Case 13-1 The Elected-Rejected Course   Case 13-2 The Splitting Seamstress

14   Direction and Discipline   225

*Leadership Influences   Styles   Discipline   Rules   Initial
Reaction to Rule Violations   Disciplinary Actions   Some Guides
for Discipline   For Discussion   Case 14-1 Counselor's Counselors
Case 14-2 The Search for a Research Leader*

15   Communication and the Lack of It   245

*The Process of Communication   Human Relations in Communications
The Process in Detail   Communication Barriers   Overcoming
Communication Barriers   The Grapevine   Communications
Summary   For Discussion   Case 15-1 The Moving to Higher
Education   Case 15-2 The Show Biz Whiz*

Part   5   Control

16   Examining the Control Function   265

*Bases of Standards   Areas of Control   Control Points   Types of
Control   Problems with Control   Maintaining Control   For
Discussion   Case 16-1 The Charismatic Character   Case 16-2 The
Perplexing Promotee*

17   Business Ethics   285

*Ethics Defined   Happiness Seekers   Responsibility to Many Publics
The Magnitude of the Manager's Decisions   Legalism   The System
Conflict of Interest   Apathy and Experts   Other Areas of Ethical
Conflict   Situationalism   For Discussion   Case 17-1 The Boozed
Accused   Case 17-2 The Right Bookkeeper in the Wrong Company*

Part   6   The Future

18   What's Ahead?   303

*The Ad-hocracy   Multi-national Matrix Organizations   More and
Less Risks   Professionalized Management   Managerial Orientation*

Mobile Managers   Rising Levels of Achievement   Growth or Nongrowth   Life Will Be Better   For Discussion   Case 18-1 The Church That Change Built   Case 18-2 The Disappearing Cavity

Glossary of Management Terms   315

Bibliography   327

Index   329

Preface

I have written this book with the intention of helping students make the transition from the management of personal assets, such as time, money, and physical and mental abilities, to the management of a professional situation—using men, money, materials, and machines to achieve a goal. This book was also written for those who possess limited managerial experience, the employee who wants to reach a position of leadership, or the newly appointed manager who has good working experience but little formal training.

At the beginning of each chapter are learning objectives, brief descriptions of specific material which the student will encounter, and hopefully master, as a result of studying that particular section of the book. At the conclusion of each chapter are two case studies. One case presents a familiar situation, to which the student will be able to relate; the second case depicts a professional situation. Both sets of circumstances require leadership, communication, motivation, and other managerial abilities necessary to accomplish the goals. The transition from the personal to the professional situation should facilitate the students' understanding of the basic framework of management.

The first part of this book is an introduction to management. The next four parts deal specifically with the functions of management: planning, organizing, activating, and controlling. The sixth part is a look toward the future. At the end of the book is to be found a glossary of concise definitions of terms used in the field of management and a bibliography suggesting additional readings in various business books.

D.E.S.

part 1

_____

introduction to management

At the conclusion of this chapter,
you should be able to—

- Explain what a manager is and what he or she does.

- Contrast a personal manager and a professional manager.

- Recognize and discuss common characteristics of various organizations.

- Compare managers with other professionals in your community.

- List, with several examples in all categories, the functions of management.

1

What Is Management?

So you want to be a manager, you want to study management.

"No!" you say. You are only reading and studying management because it is required in your program, or because your parents want you to be a businessman, or because you had to take something and this is it—but certainly not because you want to be a manager.

Or, "yes!" you say, you do want to study management. Your supervisor told you that you're going to be the next foreman in the shop and you want to be prepared. Or, you're already the head cashier and your girls squabble all the time and you want to know how to handle the situation. Or, you're a veteran who is trying to catch up for those years in the military, and you hope this will open the door to management for you. Or you're a housewife and you want to know if you can apply business management solutions to your home management problems. Or maybe you're a manager who does things because they "feel right" and you want to know the formal approach.

Regardless of why you are a student of management, whether for positive or negative reasons, and despite your feelings toward management and managers at this time, we should begin our discussion by defining that person—the manager—and his or her work.

A MANAGER IS . . .

A manager directs the efforts and outputs of machines, materials, money, himself and others toward the accomplishment of a set goal, within certain constraints or limitations. Management is the performance of those functions: planning, organizing, activating and controlling, that leads to the accomplishment of objectives through human and other resources. The term *management* also refers to the group of people who control the activities of a business organization.

This is a broad definition and you might be tempted to say, "That couldn't be right because even I might fit that description, and I'm not a manager."

Yes, you are. You are a personal manager. The greatest difference between you and a professional manager is that he accomplishes objectives through others. You accomplish goals by doing the work yourself. While you are in school, you are directing your own personal efforts: spending your money for tuition, books, a typewriter, a car; using the machinery at your disposal; allocating your time and space resources; and directing all these inputs toward the goal of earning a degree, graduating. You are a personal manager, managing your own affairs.

You didn't start life managing your own affairs. For the first several years everything you did was controlled by your parents, your teachers, your coaches, and maybe an employer. As you grew older, you started wanting to make more and more of your own decisions; you wanted to control your own destiny. You reasoned that you were more capable this year than last because you had more knowledge, more experience, more skills and, more practice making decisions.

Chris Argyris,[1] a management theorist, suggests that you would be moving from immaturity to maturity, from a passive to an active state, from dependence to independence. You are becoming capable of behaving in many ways. You are developing deep and strong interests and are moving to higher positions of control over others as well as yourself. Argyris suggests that you are "healthy" if you are developing in this way, and any control that impedes your progress might stunt your maturity.

You have fought, maybe you still fight your guardians for the right to manage your personal affairs, and you now fit somewhere on a scale of zero to one hundred with 0 percent representing those for whom all decisions are being made, and 100 percent representing those who are completely independent, making all their own decisions.

Most often, your position on the scale will reflect, to some extent, your earnings or personal finances. If you are not working, living at home, completely dependent on your family for food, housing, tuition, books, transportation, clothes, and all other necessities, then there is a good chance that you eat what is provided, sleep where told, attend a school and study a course prescribed by someone else, drive the car or ride a bus as dictated by another, and maybe compromise your clothing, hairstyle, and possibly even your personality.

However, if you are working and on your own, then you can live where you want, go where you choose, stay as long as you wish, wear what you like, and drive the car that best suits your lifestyle. So it would seem that a job represents independence, and independence represents freedom. In this sense, it can be said that work is a blessing.

HAPPINESS IS A JOB?

Is it true then? Is work the panacea? the cure all? No, certainly not. All one must do is observe those who are working to find support for Charles A. Reich's statement that "the majority of adults in this country hate their work."[2] Why? They hate their work because they resent their managers, the work, and the system itself. For example, your salary may enable you to buy the kind of clothes you want, but you cannot wear these same clothes to work. Therefore, the job gives you satisfaction; yet, the job itself may subject you to harassment, boredom, and a general feeling of disenchantment and even despair.

Such a situation illustrates two of the greatest challenges facing managers today: (1) to provide opportunities for the employee to get satisfaction from the work he is doing and not just money for the time he is on the job, and (2) to create entwining goals so that the success of the company will be a result of the total of the successes of the employees—mutually beneficial goals for the employer as well as the employee.

The success of the student after graduation is shared by all who contributed to his growth and education. We can see this in television interviews with former "managers" of successful people—the second grade teacher, scout leaders, and coaches. However, at this point, it is hard for the assembly-line worker in a Detroit auto plant to feel a share of success for every automobile produced. Not everyone is happy with his or her job, and managers can, to some extent, alleviate this dissatisfaction by fostering congenial working conditions.

PROFESSIONAL MANAGERS

Do you know someone who makes his or her living as a manager of some kind? The supervisor of a department store, the superintendent of schools, the mill superintendent, the attendant who runs the service station, the sheriff, and even the swimming pool director are managers. There are others. Doctors, dentists, and attorneys, for example, are professionals, but not managers because they accomplish results primarily through their own efforts with help from their subordinates, rather than through the efforts of the subordinates alone. Let's examine the roles of some of these managers. Let's see what the pool director, the school superintendent, and a department store supervisor have in common.

Most community swimming pools are owned by stockholders (some may be members as well) who make all the major decisions regarding the pool. In a school system, the taxpayers of a particular district finance the schools, and they make the decisions concerning those schools. In business, the owners are the stockholders and they make the decisions regarding the welfare of that business. (See Figure 1.1.)

The pool members cannot make all the decisions all the time because, oftentimes, a majority of them will not be available. Therefore, they elect a board of directors to represent them. And the taxpayers (busy earning money so they can be taxpayers) elect a school committee or a city council that will appoint a school committee. Stockholders of a corporation act in the same manner when they elect a board of directors.

The pool board hires a pool director, the school board employs a superintendent of schools, and the board of directors of a corporation elects a president, or a general manager, or someone to head the organization. They are professional managers. These are people who are paid to manage. They are given such titles as director, administrator, superintendent, president, foreperson, supervisor, and general manager.

The pool director is told by his employers, "Here is your pool, manage it." The school superintendent is told, "Here is your school system, educate our youth." The

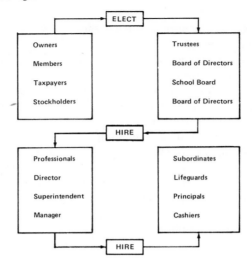

FIGURE 1.1   Typical structure of professionally managed organizations.

business manager is told, "This is your store" or "Here is your factory, make a profit."

It would seem that the schools, pools, and businesses have very much in common. They do. The director, the superintendent, and the business manager will now begin the process of management. That process is the same for each of them and is comprised of four functions: planning, organizing, activating, and controlling. Let's briefly preview these functions and see how they apply to the managers under consideration realizing that these functions are a continuous process, and that our managers will be engaged in various functions depending upon the project with which he is dealing. (See Figures 1.2 and 1.3.)

PLANNING

Innovation is the part of planning which seeks and applies new ideas and concepts to a given situation. Innovation is preceded by creativity. It is the function of a manager to transform new ideas into a goal, or a plan to accomplish a goal. The manager himself need not be the originator of ideas, but can get ideas from many sources. His managerial function is to provide an environment in which these ideas might be transformed into new, workable methods or innovations.

For example, in the case of the pool director, let us suppose a young swimmer says, "Let's form a junior swimming team and compete with the other teams in the area." It is then up to the director to determine how this idea might be implemented to achieve a predetermined goal. Probably, in this case, that goal would be to provide a place to swim, relax, and socialize with other pool members and their families. If the director feels this idea will not achieve the goal, she will discard it in favor of other ideas that can be applied.

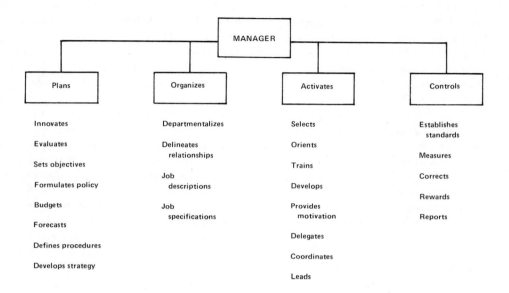

FIGURE 1.2   The functions of management.

	Pool Director	School Superintendent	Business Manager
Planning			
Organizing			
Activating			
Controlling			

FIGURE 1.3   Management functions common to all professional managers.

The school superintendent must also consider a variety of ideas: "Let's have an ungraded primary department." "Let's have kindergarten throughout the system." "Let's have modular scheduling in the high school." He must decide if such ideas can be applied to the existing situation in his school district. If so, he innovates. If not, he discards. The manager of a business has the same barrage of ideas. "Let's stay open on Sunday instead of working Mondays." "Let's have a four-day work week." "Let's sell pork and beans." He, too, must consider some application for these ideas, or discard them.

Out of a hundred ideas reaching the pool director, the superintendent, or the business manager, perhaps a few will be applicable. It is here that the manager reaches a second step of the planning process—giving the innovation a critical evaluation to determine how it will relate to overall objectives. At this point, a manager makes a "go" or "no go" decision. At this point the manager decides whether to commit energies and resources to the implementation of this new idea or not.

For example, the pool director might say, "If we form a junior swim team, it would be enjoyable for those team members, but it might upset the other members who want the pool available to them at all times, because we would have to restrict the use of the pool during practice and meet periods. Since many of our members will be upset, I reject this idea."

The school superintendent, reviewing some new ideas, might say, "The idea of a kindergarten is commendable and acceptable and would enhance our system. Yet the community, as a whole, would benefit more by building a vocational school. Since there is a shortage of money, I reject the kindergarten idea."

The business manager might say, "Although selling pork and beans might bring more money into our company, it would also distort our public image, and although this is a good idea, I reject it."

What if these decision makers decided to accept the innovation. What would occur then? A definite commitment to proceed to the next phase of planning (setting objectives) would occur, and objectives would be set for the company as a whole and for the individuals connected with the company. In the beginning, ideas are the basis of objectives. But once objectives are adopted, new ideas become the means of reaching those objectives. (Chapter 5 deals extensively in this area of setting objectives.) However, planning does not stop with setting goals. The planner must make forecasts about the conditions of the company, about conditions of the country in general, the competition, what might happen to the customer, how the government will act, and so on. The planner must also develop strategies by which the company and the individuals within the company can reach these objectives. In the area of financial management, the planner must also develop budgets to accomplish these objectives. He will set a program or a step by step way by which an objective might be met. He must also develop procedures in an effort to meet these goals.

Let's consider one of our managers and try to determine how she would plan. The pool director might set as an objective ". . . that our preschool children are taught to swim and to respect, but not fear the water, to participate in group activities."

To accomplish this, she might first make a forecast of how many children will be involved in the beginners class. Then she can estimate the number of teachers to be hired, the amount of space and time necessary, the needed supplies, and she can begin to develop a budget. Once she has developed a budget, she must try to evolve a method of securing enough money to support the expenses she foresees. This would influence her tuition policy: whether or not she planned to get most of the money from the parents of the children, or, whether she would obtain partly from them, and have this program supported by the entire membership.

After the financial aspects had been taken care of, she might concentrate then on programs and procedures and adopt a certain book or method of teaching, or she may develop a management-by-objectives attitude and review the total objectives of the program with her teacher or teachers, allowing them to develop their own methods of attaining the objectives.

ORGANIZING

Let's stick with our pool director in organizing this preschool swimming class. She has arrived at a method of determining how many teachers she needs. Now she has to begin to structure the school and the people who will be involved in the school. She must write a job description from which the pool director would establish a list of criteria indicating the necessary qualifications for an applicant to be considered for the job. We might read these specifications in the help wanted advertising column: *"Swimming instructor, capable of teaching preschool children. Experience preferred, but not necessary. Salary competitive. Must have Red Cross certificate. Send resume to ———."*

The pool director would also have to delineate the relationships between herself, the new instructor, and the students, the parents, the board of directors, and the general membership of the pool. For example, should a parent, dissatisfied with the training her child is receiving, go straight to the teacher and complain, or should she go to the pool director who in turn would forward her complaint to the teacher, or should a complaint be made through the board of directors if the parent feels that the teacher is not responding to the needs of the kindergarten children? Should the pool director herself be empowered to hire this instructor, or would the hiring be done (after the recommendation of the pool director) by the board of directors? Should the board review all candidates and make a final recommendation to the pool director who would have the final approval of the teacher? If there were two or more teachers, then who would be responsible to the others? Decisions on all these questions should be made by the pool director, the manager, before she proceeds to the next function—activating.

ACTIVATING

Activating is setting plans and organizational procedures into motion. It is at this stage that the organization, the office, or the job we have planned is staffed. Then, we start a new employee moving toward the goal that has been set forth. Staffing involves the selection of the new employee according to the job description and job specification.

Once the choice has been made from among the applicants, the new employee must undergo a period of orientation which will acquaint him or her with the policies, procedures, and goals of the company. If the methods to be used are unclear or completely foreign, then, the new employee must be trained, and his or her potential developed fully. At this point we would begin to delegate authority and responsibility to our new employee, who, in turn, would delegate to subordinates at some point in the future.

Management must provide motivational opportunities so the new employee will strive to attain the corporate goals as personal goals are reached through the work performed. Management must stimulate him or her to work hard, to be imaginative and inventive, and to earn and deserve promotions and raises.

The school superintendent has to hire a new principal. He has set minimum educational qualifications, minimum experience requirements. Several likely candidates may be selected through a screening process, and after reviewing these men and women in view of the goals to be accomplished, one is chosen. From the new person he expects the school to have discipline, the teachers to be motivated, to work diligently, morale to be high, both student and faculty. He expects a learning process to take place. He wants healthy children with good attendance records.

The superintendent tells the principal that she can expect the superintendent to help her in any way, even send her back to school, if necessary, to train for this job. He tells the new principal that she can expect aid from the superintendent's office in curriculum and discipline areas, in personnel, and other staff matters. The principal now has to select other people, faculty, custodial force, kitchen workers, and aides, and delegate to each of these people certain responsibilities and authority so they may help reach the goals set forth by the superintendent. It will be up to the principal to motivate and stimulate these workers toward the school objectives.

CONTROLLING

The final step in the managerial process is control. What we are concerned with now is the comparison of the actual results with what was proposed and planned. We will, in all probability, experience a gap, between the actual and the anticipated. If our objectives are financial in nature, we will be able to state this gap in terms of dollars. (We expected sales to be $1,250,000. but sales were only $1,125,000., a gap of $125,000. Why?) If our goals have been stated in other ways, then we must make our comparisons appropriately.

To make this comparison, we must be able to measure what a man or woman, or departments have done as compared to what we expected them to do. If we expected a job to be done within a certain number of hours, or if we expected a certain ratio of attendance, or if we expected a certain amount of turnover, stated in terms of percentages or numbers, or if we wanted sales to reach a particular point, then we compare what actually happened with what was anticipated. Once we make the comparison, then we must act. We often see newspaper articles, or hear that a community pool has reached a membership of 500, far exceeding the goals and expectations, or the Bath Run Elementary School has 68 less students than had been predicted, and therefore, two teachers will be transferred to another school, or sales of 2.8 million dollars were termed "disappointing" by the manager of a local furniture manufacturing company who had hoped to top three million dollars.

Control without corrective action or reward is ineffective. If the anticipated results were realized, then we must reward that individual, or those people, or the department responsible. If, however, the goals were not met, then, conversely, we must find the reason and take corrective action. We must determine who or what was responsible for the failure. Then, we must take appropriate action to insure that future strategies will result in anticipated goals. If our goals were unrealistic, they must be reconsidered. If necessary, those responsible might be retrained or even replaced.

If the sales manager employs six salesmen, and two of these did not measure up to the projected sales goals, then the manager must take corrective action. He might revise the goal and lower the quota. He might train the people unable to meet the goal to be more effective. He might transfer these people to another product line which they might be better able to sell. He might change their geographical area, or, as indicated earlier, he might terminate these people, and hire some new salespeople who have a greater potential for meeting company objectives. Control is the preliminary function to planning in the continuous process.

In conclusion, there are four functions of management—planning, organization, activating, and controlling. In this chapter they were discussed only briefly, but we will analyze each of them in the chapters to come.

FOR DISCUSSION

1. *What are the four functions of management? Relate these to a professional management position with which you are familiar.*
2. *What is the difference between a professional manager and other professionals in your community?*
3. *How do you think the majority of adults in this country feel about their work? Do they like it or dislike it? Why?*
4. *What kind of a rating would you give your present or former manager (supervisor, boss, foreman)? Why?*
5. *Is it possible for a clergyman not to be a manager?*
6. *Discuss the organization of your school. Compare it with other organizations with which you are familiar.*

ENDNOTES

1. Chris Argyris, *Personality and Organization* (New York: Harper and Row, 1957).
2. Charles A. Reich, *The Greening of America* (New York: Random House, 1970), p. 296.

A Note about the Cases

At the conclusion of each chapter are two cases, one dealing with a familiar non-business situation, the other with a business situation. Chapter 2 discusses decision making and case presentation at length, but in these first cases you are asked only to answer the guide questions found at the end of each case. Then, as you read Chapter 2, compare your solutions and methods of arriving at those solutions with those provided in the text.

CASE 1–1

The Puzzled Paperboy

"You're going to get some help on your paper route or else . . ." Mrs. Martin told her young son Jeff. "We're all getting tired of being kept right here seven days a week so you can deliver papers. We haven't been to Grandma's for months. Our last visit lasted only a few hours. And I want to go to the beach, and I am not going to make the round trip in one day."

"Well I've had three helpers and none of them worked out," said Jeff.

"And why not?" his mother asked.

"You know why. Jack wanted to split the route with me instead of working for me. Terry wanted more money after two days, and Bobby wouldn't work when we had supplements. Besides, he wanted me to supply him with a bicycle."

"I've told you before, Jeff, you've got to get these things straightened out in the beginning. Everything should be written down. Then there wouldn't be all the misunderstandings."

"I think I'll just quit," Jeff said. "I'm getting tired of delivering newspapers anyway."

"Go on," said Mrs. Martin, "quit! Then, it won't be long until you're roaming the neighborhood looking for empty bottles so you can return them to collect the deposits. That route has been pretty good to you. Even if you got a helper you could probably still make fifteen dollars a week, and that's plenty considering your time and effort. Besides, who's going to feed tapes and records to that machine you bought? You needn't look for me to pass out five or ten dollars a week for you to spend on the top two hundred."

"Then I'll just keep going like I have been."

"Oh, no," Mrs. Martin said, "I just told you, you're going to find a helper, or give it up!"

"Can't you make up your mind? First, you say 'quit' and I agree. Then, you say 'don't quit.' Then, you say 'quit' again. I don't know what you want, and I'm not sure you do either."

"That's where you're wrong, my little friend," Mrs. Martin told Jeff, "because I've given this situation a lot of thought. First, I'd be very disappointed if you gave up the route. It's given you some independence, and some responsibility, and you've been able to buy some things we couldn't afford. That part is good. Second, for your independence, responsibility, and pocket money we've all had to give up our holidays—that's bad. I want

you to approach this matter as the general manager of the Jeff Martin
Newspaper Distribution Company. I want you to set goals that will keep
the good points and eliminate the bad. Then, I want you to figure out how
you can reach these goals. As far as a helper is concerned, you might
consider such things as how old, how big, how much to pay, raises, what
days to deliver, collect, or not, who furnishes the bicycle, how many customers, how to check on him, what hours he is to work, and so on. All these
questions should be answered before you approach anybody about working for you."

Jeff agreed to work on the problem, outlining his ideas, and thought his
older brother, Michael, a business student, would be able to help him
work out the details of his plan.

Jeff had 161 daily and Sunday subscribers. Four were daily subscribers. Three were Sunday subscribers only. From the daily and Sunday
subscribers he collected 70¢ and netted 19.5¢ per week each. From the
daily subscribers he collected 45¢ and netted 13.5¢. From the Sunday only
subscribers he collected 25¢ and netted 6.5¢. In addition to his regular
bill, due each Tuesday, he had to pay 25¢ a week for accident insurance
and 12¢ a week to be bonded. Both payments were compulsory. However,
it was more than offset by a bonus of 3¢ per week for each full subscriber.
This bonus was paid quarterly, and was contingent upon Jeff having few or
no complaints. Jeff thought he might consider giving up part of his bonus
for quality help but he could not make up his mind, nor had he given any
thought to other fringe benefits.

GUIDE QUESTIONS

As his older brother:

1. *What would you advise Jeff to do?*
2. *What figures would you use to support your recommendations?*
3. *What appears to be the cause of Jeff's problem?*

The Inventory Clerk Turnover

Charlie Hubbard, warehouse manager for the Wise Electrical Manufacturing Company, eased himself slowly down into the chair behind his cluttered desk.

"I'm getting too old for this business," he muttered to himself.

"Too old for what?" said George as he walked through the door. George Wise, son of the founder, was the general manager of the company.

"Too old to unpack all these boxes and climb ladders to stock the shelves," said Charlie. "I've been working my tail off, and I can't seem to get anybody to help me."

"That's why I'm down here, Charlie."

"You mean you're going to help me put this stock on the shelves?"

"No, Charlie," George said, "But I do want to talk to you about something. I've been going over some quarterly figures for our payroll, and I was quite upset that you had hired three new clerks, especially since only one was authorized. When I asked payroll about it, they said you didn't have three at any one time, but that they were hired in quick succession. What seems to be the problem?"

"Well, George, they're just not making them like they used to. These kids today just don't want to work. They want everything and they don't want to do anything. The first guy I hired for this job quit after three days. He told me the work was too hard. Told me I didn't tell him he would have to climb up and down these ladders, and unpack boxes, and do all that stuff. I don't know what he thought an inventory clerk should do.

The second guy didn't seem to mind the work but he wanted a raise after two weeks. I asked him what made him think he should get a raise in so short a time, and he said I had promised him a raise after he learned the work and he felt like he had learned everything. TWO WEEKS! I've been here thirty years and still don't know it all. Anyway, everybody knows you don't get a raise until after three months on the job. So, he quit, too.

And the third guy just didn't have it. He just couldn't cut it. He could barely read, and couldn't write legibly, or even count. I had to follow him around, checking on everything he did. Finally, I told him to get out of here, I'd rather do the work myself, and that's what I'm doing. I'm saving the company a lot of money, but I'm about breaking my back doing it."

"I appreciate your efforts, Charlie," George said, "But I'm not sure you are saving us any money."

"What do you mean? We're authorized to employ two men in this department. I'm doing all the work myself and the work is getting done. How come I'm not saving the company money?"

"This turnover problem is costing us more than you think. I've made some quick calculations and it seems to me you've spent hundreds of dollars hiring a receiving clerk and we still don't have one. You ran twelve days of display ads. I assume you attracted twenty or thirty people to the company in response to the ad. Think of the time spent interviewing those prospects!

Now, once you found the ones you wanted, you spent hours training them. In addition to your time, other people in the company have had to spend time with them. Twenty-five dollars apiece for their physical examination. The payroll people and the personnel office have been involved. We had to put them on the workman's compensation insurance program. One of them became our responsibility for unemployment compensation. Bill Thomas told me that production, at least his department, was shut down twice because of outages in raw materials. Said you told him it was because of one of those new guys you hired."

"That's exactly what I told him," Charlie said. "One of those guys screwed up royally. According to his calculations, we had several boxes of switches, but when production called for them, we didn't have a one. I just can't seem to be able to get the right guy to help me."

"Maybe that's your problem, Charlie. Maybe you're looking for someone just to help you stock, but I don't think that's really what you need. I want you to manage the warehouse, not do all the work yourself. We've given you the responsibility for the warehouse and the authority to do whatever you must, however you have to, to carry out this assignment. What I would like you to do is sit down and determine exactly what has to be done by the person you are going to hire. *Write a job description.* Then I want you to consider what kind of person might best fit that description. What kind of a background should he have? Should he be a college graduate or not? Should he have a driver's license? Do you want someone with experience? Exactly what do you want, Charlie? And finally, I want you to decide exactly where this fellow could go if he turned out to be a good worker. How can he move up through our organization? Work on this right away, Charlie. Get someone to hold down the fort tomorrow afternoon at three, and come to my office so we can discuss your recommendations."

GUIDE QUESTIONS

1. *Is Charlie functioning as a manager? Why?*
2. *What is his problem? What seems to be the cause of his problem?*

3. What do you think an inventory clerk does, and what do you feel would be the minimum requirements for becoming one?

4. Based on your present knowledge, how far do you think an inventory clerk might advance within a company?

At the conclusion of this chapter,
you should be able to—

- **Determine the bases upon which most decisions are made.**

- **State the steps involved in decision making.**

- **Understand the use of cases in studying management.**

- **Know how to present your recommended solution to a case to your fellow students.**

2

Decision Making and Case Presentation

In the first chapter, several references were made to managerial decision making. A manager is judged by the results of the decisions he makes. Few managers make mostly poor or wrong decisions. Those who do tend not to remain in the ranks of management for very long. Conversely, some managers seldom make mistakes and these rise rapidly in the company ranks. Most managers make more right decisions than wrong ones; few have spectacular incidents; they rise in rank at a normal rate, are seldom fired, but generally do not reach the top corporate spots.

In the previous chapter, we said that all people are managers—at least personal managers—so it would follow that all people are decision makers, though not necessarily professional decision makers. In fact, you are constantly making decisions. In the morning you have to decide whether or not to get out of bed. When you finally sit up, do you light a cigarette, put on your slippers, or walk barefoot to the bathroom, or go get the paper first? What's for breakfast? What are you going to wear? Should you cut your first class? Have you done your homework? Which route should you take to school? By the time a student reaches his first class in the morning, he has made thirty, forty, fifty, or more decisions. (This factor alone may be responsible for the exhaustion exhibited by a number of early morning class members.)

BASES FOR DECISIONS

How do you solve problems? The two most common methods of solving them are: (1) making a decision based on your own former decisions or experiences, or (2) basing your decisions on what others have done or are doing. For example, if you get up in the morning and your wife or mother asks, "What do you want for breakfast?" you are likely to say, "Bacon and eggs over light, toast and coffee," because that is what you had yesterday and the day before, and the day before that. Or you might say, "I don't know. What's everybody else going to have?"

The response to the question, "What are we going to do Saturday night?" might easily be, "The same thing we did last Saturday night," or, "I don't know. What's everybody else going to do?"

As a general rule, as long as our previous experiences have been extremely gratifying, mildly pleasant, or even "not objectionable," we will continue to make similar decisions when confronted with similar situations. Many people have eaten the same breakfast day after day, month after month, even year after year with no variations, while others, upon seeing eggs over light for the third morning in a row, decide they want waffles or pancakes or even give up altogether on breakfast.

If you and your friends have had great times for four Saturday nights in succession at the bowling alley or drive-in theater, then you will look forward to going again. Yet, if you have gone somewhere alone for four Saturday nights in a row, trying to join a group, and you ended up being alone and frustrated, you might resort to another activity. You might go with a friend, or give up on that particular place, or stay at home and watch television. Staying at home watching TV may not be extremely gratifying, but it would not be objectionable or frustrating, and you might adopt this as your normal Saturday night habit and forget the nights out.

But what do you do when you are faced with a new situation and you have had no experience to draw on. Do you know anyone else who has had a similar experience, or made a comparable decision? How do you approach problems such as these? How do you find solutions to strange situations in which you find yourself?

At the end of Chapter 1 there were two cases, "The Case of the Puzzled Paperboy" and "The Case of the Inventory Clerk Turnover." The paperboy's situation is one in which you may have found yourself already. Maybe it was your little brother, or even your own child. If you have found yourself in such circumstances, you know it can be an agonizing barrier to a satisfactory way of life.

The turnover problem is a situation you might possibly find yourself in as a manager of a warehouse. This, too, might cause some anxiety on your part, and would require you to overcome a situation causing the trouble and ill feeling on the part of your boss. Could we find a solution to both of these problems by using the same method? Yes, we can and we might do so by following this plan:

1. Familiarize yourself with the situation and how it relates to the overall objectives.
2. Formulate a precise statement of the problem or main issue.
3. Develop reasonable alternative courses of action.
4. Analyze the alternatives, carrying the analysis to a logical conclusion.
5. Select the alternative most compatible with overall objectives.
6. Plan the implementation of the selected course of action. (Figure 2.1.)

Many successful managers have said that the best training they ever received on the way to the top was being placed in a position of authority, making decisions concerning the outcome of all situations related to that position, and being held accountable for those outcomes. Tossed into the water—sink or swim, so to speak. This was the real test of all their previous training. It would be much like a member of a first

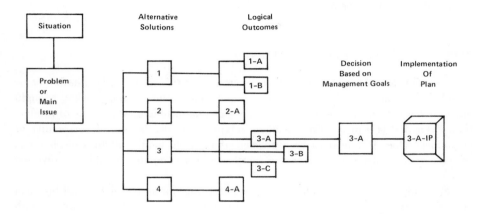

FIGURE 2.1 The six steps of decision making.

aid squad who practiced for months on a dummy, and finally worked under emergency conditions for the first time. At this instance, all his training would be put to use. He would have to analyze the situation, develop and compare alternative courses of action, select one, and then go to work.

A method that can be used to strengthen the student's decision making abilities and improve his or her presentation and ability to convince is the case method. In this method, the student is given a case study such as the "Case of the Puzzled Paperboy," and asked to devise a solution to the problem, and then demonstrate the plan to his or her classmates. It is highly improbable that all the classmates will discover the same solution. In many cases their solutions will be quite different to the one presented. It would be up to the student who discovered the initial solution to defend his decision against the arguments of his peers.

The preceding example would not be unlike a situation that might arise in a meeting of the board of directors of the community pool, when one of the directors would want to initiate Friday night dances, or at a school-board meeting when a member would want to change from a graded to an ungraded primary system, or in a business situation when a member of the board of directors would want to divert a portion of the profits to an educational or environmental project. Each of these initiators would have to present a convincing argument based on thorough analysis, and be able to defend it against those members who prefer alternative plans, or would prefer no changes at all. In many graduate schools of business administration this case method is used exclusively. It is assumed that any background work necessary for making decisions on cases will be done independently by the student. Now, let us consider the six steps of decision making.

Familiarize Yourself with the Situation

At this point the manager might ask such questions as: Why has this situation come to light? In what general area is the problem or main issue? Who, or what, brought this to my attention? Is it a sales, finance, or personal problem, or an issue of production. Even if it is a production problem, might it not also be one of personality or personnel? Does it appear to be a problem that would lend itself to a mechanical, formula type of decision? Given the facts, would a computer be able to solve the problem?

Speaking of facts, it should become apparent to you as you delve into business problems, whether in a real situation or a case study, that you will never have enough facts. If all the facts were readily available and could be fitted neatly into a magic formula that would give the solution without any judgmental decision on the part of the manager, there would be little need for a manager. However, there is a movement in business now (which will be discussed later and in more detail) in which managers endeavor to quantify and formularize all business decisions, to attach numerical representations to all inputs in the decision-making process. While in many situations this is a valid method of solving problems, it does not lend itself to all problems. It is the responsibility of the decision maker, the manager, to determine when this method is suitable. It is also the responsibility of the same decision maker who has chosen to quantify the problem, that he or she reconvert those quantified solutions into the original terms. For example, the manager must remember that the reduction of traffic deaths from 541 to 519 on a Labor Day weekend represents an improvement, but the 519 deaths are not merely numbers, but 519 lives lost. The manager must also decide if he should try to solve the problem and make the decision by himself, or should he seek a group decision. The answer may become more apparent when the second step is considered.

Formulate a Precise Statement of the Issue

The most important point of the second step of decision making is: DO NOT TREAT SYMPTOMS. Examine the causes and decide what changes might alleviate the problem.

For example, the major part of a doctor's work is the diagnosis. In many cases, once the diagnosis has been made, there is usually only one positive course of action. In some illnesses, there might be several methods of treatment available to the physician, and he or she would have to choose the alternative that training and experience indicate would offer the best results. If a patient went to a doctor and said, "Every time I get ready to take a test, I break out in a rash," the doctor probably would not prescribe an ointment for the rash, but would try to help overcome the patient's fear of tests. In this manner, the doctor would solve the problem instead of treating the symptoms.

A similar application might be made to business situations. When a highly qualified person is given a boring and repetitive task, and after a short time says he is going to quit the job, a raise of fifteen cents an hour will not solve the problem. The raise might make the worker happy for a while, but soon will be just as disillusioned with the work as before. In such a situation, the whole wage structure might be altered to the disadvantage of the company, without any real benefits due to this management decision.

In the "Case of the Puzzled Paperboy," was it the fact that there were no available helpers that made the situation difficult for the paperboy to overcome, or his mother to accept? If you were Michael, the paperboy's older brother, you might say the problem is that your mother wants a day off. Or you might say Jeff needs another helper, or the problem is that Jeff doesn't know what he is doing. If you say any of these things, then you would not have made a precise statement of the problem. You would have reached backward to define the situation causing the problem. You would have to say that mother is upset because there are no days off. There are no days off because Jeff has no helpers to deliver the papers. Jeff doesn't have a helper because he had three and they soon quit because of misunderstandings with Jeff. The misunderstandings occurred due to a lack of a precise definition of what the job entailed.

You then might reconsider the problem. If Jeff defines the position of helper, and writes down the description, he should be able to determine the necessary characteristics of the person to fill the position. If he finds a qualified person who will take the job, then that person is likely to stay on the job and learn the route. Then Jeff could rely on him and take a vacation day. If Jeff takes the day off, he and the rest of his family can go on an overnight trip to Grandma's. If they do, then Jeff's mother will be happy.

Thus, in the final analysis, the lack of a precise job description coupled with not defining the desired characteristics of the person needed to fill that position are the causes of the puzzled paperboy's problem. We should use this same method to determine the cause of the inventory-clerk-turnover problem.

Develop Reasonable Alternative Courses of Action

If there is but one course of action available to the decision maker, then there is no decision to be made. We have to assume, then, that making a decision involves choosing between alternatives.

One of those alternatives is to do nothing—to leave the situation as it is. In some cases this is valid, at least as a temporary solution to a problem. For example, the logical solution to a problem might be to hire three new people or buy three new machines, yet there is no money available to do either of these for at least thirty days.

Thus, the "solution" to the problem would be to do nothing. Doing nothing in many cases is the most logical answer. All changes upset personnel, particularly those who have held the same positions for a long time. Therefore, the manager should not make changes for the sake of changes alone, but should make only those changes that will result in a positive solution.

When proposing alternatives, the manager does not have to decide immediately whether the outcomes would be good and logical, but only possible. His analysis of the alternatives would come later. To solve the "Case of the Puzzled Paperboy," we might present the following reasonable alternatives:

1. Do nothing.
2. Write a job description and job specifications.
3. Request help from the route manager.
4. Give up the route.

There are many more logical alternatives that we might list, but we will limit ourselves to these and move on to the fourth step of decision making.

Analyze the Alternatives and Form a Logical Conclusion

In analyzing an alternative, we should ask the following question: If I do this, what will happen? How will the people involved react? Will the total process of the activity under consideration be enhanced or hurt? Would this alternative be an acceptable solution to the problem?

You might consider the decision acceptable to most of the people involved, but some might be hurt. Therefore, you would not want to adopt it unless it is a necessity. You might find that another alternative would not be acceptable under any circumstances, and you might find that some alternatives seem to satisfy all parties involved and would be adoptable under normal circumstances. Let's examine the alternatives proposed for the solution of the paperboy's problem.

1. Do Nothing If the paperboy does nothing and continues to deliver the papers seven days a week, the logical conclusion to this is that his mother and his family will be more and more upset and he will be forced to give up the paper route entirely. This would give the family an opportunity to visit Grandma occasionally, or take a vacation, but it would deprive the paperboy of his independence, his responsibility, and his extra money. This solution seems unacceptable considering the needs of the paperboy.

2. Write a Job Description and Job Specifications This would seem to be the first step to overcoming the problem. As we said before, once he develops a job description specification, Jeff would find it much easier to deal with a prospective assistant. He would know exactly what he could pay him, for which days and under various conditions, and he would know what kind of assistant he would be looking for, not accepting the first fellow to come along. If he found an assistant, he could hire him, train him, and teach him the route, and then begin to have vacation days, delegating his responsibilities to his assistant. This appears to be a good, logical, alternative solution to the problem.

3.   Request Help from the Route Manager   The route manager might be of great assistance if Jeff knows in advance the nature of the help he needs. The manager has had more experience with such problems and will aid in finding the solution. He may suggest that he and Jeff write a job description and specifications for an assistant carrier. This would be helpful to Jeff and he could tailor the standard job description to his particular needs. Analysis of this alternative indicates that it is a good preliminary alternative but number two would still be the backbone of the plan.

4.   Give Up the Route   As indicated, this alternative would deprive Jeff of independence and responsibility, and would have to be rejected as not being a suitable solution to the problem.

Once we have completed our evaluation of the alternatives, we move on to step five.

Select the Most Suitable Alternative

If we have done a good job of analyzing the alternatives, step five would be easier but not always predetermined. In the case of our puzzled paperboy, we probably would decide to make a job description and job specifications for the assistant carrier as indicated in alternative two, with or without the help of the route manager as in number three. In either case, the burden of accomplishing the solution is on Jeff, and he would have to begin the job of planning to overcome an unpleasant situation.

This is a relatively simple problem compared to many in business. There might be a limited amount of money available for three projects, each looking equally promising, but each of which would take all the money available. It would be up to the manager to use his judgment in this situation, and to assign values as well as risks to the alternatives. If, after the values and risks have been assessed, the alternatives still look equally promising, the decision maker would have to use his intuition or a hunch based on his history of decision making to come up with the final choice among the available alternatives.

The manager has fulfilled the first function of management. He has taken ideas from others, from himself, and his observations, and made innovations—that is, he has applied these ideas to a real situation. The innovations have become the alternative solutions to a problem. The decision maker then submits these alternative actions to analysis or evaluation, discarding those alternatives that seem least satisfactory, and accepting the alternative, which, in his judgment, offers the best chance for success.

This step is extremely critical in the management functions because the decision based on that manager's evaluation of all possible solutions becomes the basis of the management functions to follow: planning, organizing, activating, and controlling. It is also critical because it eliminates all those discarded alternatives, and they will not be considered again unless the chosen alternative proves to be wrong. This explains in part why many managers make good and workable decisions but not great ones, and therefore rise along a predictable line of ascension in the company, yet never reach the top management positions.

This also explains in part why there are no right or wrong answers to case problems. Many students, upon completion of a case problem, will demand from the discussion leader a right or wrong response to their presentation of a case and their eventual solution to that problem. It may be difficult for the leader to give a right or wrong answer, even if he is totally familiar with the case problem and with the solution. The fact remains that although a particular plan may be adopted, that plan is not necessarily the best plan, even though it proved satisfactory.

The student would be judged by the leader on the types of alternatives proposed and the logical analysis of them, the conclusions reached and the effectiveness of the presentation. If the student overlooked many pertinent aspects or solutions, or reached illogical conclusions, then the leader might also fault the solution for weaknesses in these areas. The leader might also fault the student for failure to show how the plan would be implemented.

Plan the Implementation of the Selected Course

This last process in decision making begins to test the validity of the decision. The whole concept of planning will be taken up later, but some of the questions that would be asked in this planning step are such things as: will the completion of this plan coincide with the objectives and goals of the overall company objectives? Will the strategy involved in carrying this alternative to its logical conclusion be in agreement with or in opposition to the strategic plans in other departments or in this department? Will the adopted program be within the confines of the budget set forth for this department, or for the whole company? Will the procedures for this plan deviate from our accepted procedures? Must we establish new procedures or abolish the plan? Do the boundaries of the policies set for the company include the policies necessary to carry out this plan?

What begins to show is the compatibility of the adopted proposal with the rest of the program. In the case of the puzzled paperboy, the implementation of the program might call for a payment of five dollars a day for an assistant. This would not be within the budget of the total situation because the paperboy himself would be working for nothing, or paying his assistant more than he is taking in, and he would lose money each week. Planning the implementation of this program under these circumstances would show that the selected alternative would be invalid and totally unacceptable if, in fact, a five dollar a day payment was necessary to attract the proper assistant. The entire situation would have to be restudied, and a new set of alternatives, or a review of the existing alternatives would have to be made. If no other logical solution is found, it is possible that Jeff would have to forgo his paper route.

There are other methods of testing an alternative in the planning stages. The decision maker might employ the services of a devil's advocate. This is a person who challenges all the decisions made by the decision maker, giving the decision maker an opportunity to rethink and reinforce his conclusions and enabling him to become more firmly entrenched in his position.

The manager who has made the decision might also give the facts to someone else, and ask that person to go through the decision-making process and come up with what he feels is the best solution. At this point, both decision makers would compare their solutions. If they do not agree, perhaps a composite solution might be hammered out between them.

Another method the decision maker might use would be to submit the facts to a group decision, and see whether the group decision would be compatible with the original decision.

Finally, he might present his solution, along with his analysis of the situation, to a committee for adoption. He should be prepared for any eventuality, because if the committee, which should be receptive to the adoption of a program, would turn him down, the chances for a second presentation would be remote. He would have suffered a setback which might be disastrous both to his company and to his personal career.

In conclusion, one might say that the necessity of making decisions—good decisions—is vital to the role and success of a manager. The use of case studies helps the student strengthen his decision-making abilities by exercising his decision-making muscles. Case studies will add to his business knowledge when he views many situations from a variety of industries. Case studies strengthen the student's ability to diagnose and identify the most pressing problem or main issue. Finally, presenting the results of his or her analysis and decision to peers for evaluation and adoption or rejection is the ultimate test of a student's decision-making potential.

FOR DISCUSSION

1. *Many people say management is decision making.*
   What do you say?
2. *We often hear that older people are "set in their ways".*
   Why would this seem to be true in light of the methods of
   solving problems? What implications would this have for
   you as a manager?
3. *What are the steps in decision making?*
4. *Define case method and state your reaction to this system*
   of management study.
5. *"If it works, it must be right." What are your comments?*
6. *Your car just "died" and you need another one. Determine*
   what kind you should buy employing the decision-making
   process.

CASE 2–1

Yourself

Consider yourself a case study. A student at Morristown Community College, you have certain assets and liabilities, some special qualifications along with some unique limitations. You may have many obligations or maybe none at all, no debts or perhaps you are very much in debt. You have likes, dislikes, prejudices, wants, needs, and desires, potentials that you must weigh against opportunities in those fields, and a general knowledge of the environment in which you live.

You must make a decision concerning your longterm objectives and goals, listing possible alternative courses of action. Analyze each of these, listing the good and bad features of them, and finally, make a choice. Once you have arrived at a choice, a decision, document a method of implementation of this choice listing some checkpoints or benchmarks, that will guide you over the next few years.

The All Over Forty

During the week of Thanksgiving, the production foreman of Miner Manufacturing Company, Harold Carter, found himself with a holiday at hand and a rush order that had to be shipped by the end of the week. At the close of work on Tuesday, he called the production men together and told them about the situation.

"It's a hot one, men, for Trojan Metals, and as most of you know, they're our best customers. We can't mess up with them. I know a lot of you already have planned your Thanksgiving day, and I don't want to spoil it, but I do want to get enough of you over here on Saturday to finish up the job."

Ten of the fourteen men in the production department volunteered for the Saturday work, came in as promised, completed the Trojan job and got it shipped. "It's good to have a bunch of guys like I've got," Carter told his wife that night at supper. "When I've got a job to get out, I can count on them."

The following Friday, payday for the previous week, Carter noticed his men gathering in little groups after he had passed out the checks. He hesitated for a while and finally asked one of the older men what seemed to be the trouble.

"How come we didn't get paid time and a half for working Saturday?" he asked.

"I don't know," Carter said, "Maybe the bookkeeper made an error."

"Well, if she's wrong, she's wrong for everybody. The guys who didn't work Saturday got five days pay and those that did work only got six."

"I'll check into it," Carter told him and went on upstairs to the office.

"I didn't make a mistake," Cindy Stevenson, the bookkeeper, told Carter, "I asked the boss what to do about it and he said 'pay them a straight six days'."

Carter was about to argue with Cindy when the boss came out of his office, greeted Carter, and asked how everything was going in production.

"I was just telling Cindy that the men are upset because they didn't get time and a half for working Saturday," Carter said.

"Why?" asked the boss, "They didn't work Thanksgiving. That's a holiday we just paid them for. They just weren't thinking right. Go back and explain it to them. They'll understand. We'll pay overtime if people work more than forty hours, but not in a situation like this. That would be like paying a guy time and a half for a holiday. It's bad enough to pay straight time and not get any production, much less time and a half for nothing."

"Well," Carter said, "I was kinda looking at it from the men's point of view. They did come in on Saturday, and they helped me out of a tight spot."

"Look, Carter," the boss said, "If you try to look at everything from the men's point of view, you're going to get into a lot of trouble. You're management now and it's up to you to carry out policy. Now get down there and straighten those guys out."

Carter closed the office door behind him and slowly walked back to the production department trying to figure how to break the news to his men.

GUIDE QUESTIONS

1. *What is Carter's problem?*
2. *Can you explain why a supervisor is sometimes called the "man in the middle?"*
3. *Will the decisions of the boss have far reaching implications? Explain.*
4. *How might the state of the economy affect Carter's reaction?*

At the conclusion of this chapter,
you should be able to—

- Discuss scientific management, some of its contributors, and current implications.
- Make use of a Gantt chart.
- Compare a behavioralist manager with a scientific manager.
- Understand a systems approach to management.
- Give specific applications for quantitative decision-making techniques.

3

Management History and Current Schools of Thought

Although there are some isolated examples of management systems and concepts to be found throughout history, most of what we know as management today has had its beginnings in the nineteenth century.

As a matter of fact, most of the writers of management theory and texts are still alive and still writing. "But," you might say, "didn't the Greeks and Romans and other civilized cultures organize their empires and armies as we do today?"

ANCIENT SYSTEMS

Yes, the ancients did have organizations similar to some that exist today. Even the Bible alludes to practices enabling leaders such as Moses to accomplish great works through departmentalization, decentralization, and the use of a staff. For instance, in the Bible in Chapter 18 of Exodus, Jethro says to his son-in-law, Moses:

> "You are not acting wisely, you will surely wear yourself out . . . look among all the people for able and God-fearing men, trustworthy men who hate dishonest gain, and set them as officers over groups of thousands, of hundreds, of fifties, and of tens."

Students of management history must remember, too, that throughout history, or at least until the Industrial Revolution, all the civilized world was run by institutions such as the church, the military, or by a monarch, who assumed that God gave him or her power to direct the activities of all his or her subjects. Everyone worked for the state, the church, the lord, except for a few who were proprietors in the present-day sense. These were the men who ran the pubs, the inns, the stables, blacksmith shops, and other small, service businesses.

In this system wealth was accumulated by decree rather than by good management and better efficiency, and power was held by threats and violent acts against those who opposed the rulers in power. Money and power were slow to change hands until the eighteenth century and the Industrial Revolution. A man born into one state in life, a prince or a pauper, would predictably die in that same state. Unlike today, a person in pre-Industrial Revolution times who acquired certain standards and values as a youth, would die holding fast to those same standards and values. Now we find that we can count on only one thing—change.

In the book *Future Shock*[1] the author depicts the history of mankind by dividing the past fifty thousand years into 800 equal parts, 800 lifetimes. For the first 650 lifetimes, men lived their lives in caves. Only in the last 70 lifetimes have men been able to communicate between historical ages. Only in the last six has there been a printed word. Man has been able to measure accurately in the last four lifetimes. The electric motor has been available to us for the last two lifetimes. And it is about this same length of time, two lifetimes, that there has been any move at all toward an evolvement of management principles. It is within this lifetime that almost all significant developments and writings in management have evolved.

Up until the nineteenth century, all recorded history shows that adherents to any management philosophy were followers of the school of custom. In this method, every student, every subordinate was taught by his master or superior to manage in a particular way. The student would then try to emulate his superior with the goal of maintaining the status quo, not changing one thing.

SCIENTIFIC MANAGEMENT

Moving from this school of custom toward, but not reaching the school of scientific management, we find a man named Charles Babbage, who in 1832 published a book titled *On the Economy of Machinery and Manufactures*.[2] Babbage's most significant contribution to management was his calling for the use of scientific inquiry to determine the most efficient use of resources. He suggested the use of time studies to set standards for a fair day's work. He also wanted management to standardize methods.

The "Father of Scientific Management" was Frederick W. Taylor whose work appeared in the early 1900s. It is assumed that Babbage influenced Taylor's studies, but it was Taylor himself who first delved deeply into scientific management.[3] While watching workers at the Midvale Steel Company, Taylor observed that the men were producing far less than their capabilities indicated that they might produce. Taylor disliked waste and inefficiency, and set about breaking down and studying each element of these workers' jobs. He wanted to make the men under him more efficient. He did not seek a sweat shop solution whereby every man was made to work to the very limits of his capacity, but he did seek a solution whereby management's needs might be served better, and the workers' capabilities used to a greater extent.

In the case of the now famous Pig Iron studies, Taylor determined that the optimum weight for a shovel load was 22 pounds. He also observed that the same shovels were used for all kinds of jobs requiring shoveling despite the fact that the shovelers were handling different materials. He therefore sought and obtained approval and proceeded to get shovels appropriately shaped for each kind of job. Pig

Iron handlers were trained to use the shovels, and their tonnage increased from 12½ to 47½ long tons per day—an increase in production of more than 300% per day. Taylor was able to have workers' wages improved from $1.15 to $1.85 per day. Not quite the 300% increase, but wages *were* better than before.

Taylor developed four scientific principles for management. They are as follows:

1. Develop a scientific method for each element of a man's work to replace the old rule of thumb method.
2. Select, train, teach and develop the workman according to scientific principle rather than allow him to train himself.
3. Cooperate with the men to insure that all the work being done is done in the way prescribed. This should include providing for increased earnings by those who follow the prescribed way.
4. Divide the work between management and workers so that those jobs that can best be done by management people will be taken by them.

In addition to setting standards for a day's work, Taylor also devised a piece-rate system based on accurate work standards. Under this system, the worker was given an opportunity to earn more than his standard daily pay by achieving better than standard results.

THE GANTT CHART

In that same decade, Henry L. Gantt, a disciple of Taylor who worked with him at Midvale, developed an incentive plan considered superior to Taylor's, and also conceived the Gantt Chart, still used extensively today in scheduling problems.[4]

The first chart, Figure 3.1, shows how a student might plan his career over a ten-year period. He could do this same planning for months or days if he felt this were necessary. As you can see, the student has planned to finish high school, attend college, then medical school, and finally internship before he becomes a doctor. Some of his summers he plans to work or travel, while others will be spent in research and work related to his goal of becoming a physician.

The chart could be stationary, having a top-to-bottom marker indicating the present period of time. Or, it could be a roll chart also having a top-to-bottom indicator, but the indicator would be stationary and the chart itself would move. You will note that planning is indispensable in using a Gantt chart, and the chart itself is essential in seeing that these plans are carried out as scheduled. When there is a deviation from the plan, it can be noted readily by observing the chart, and remedial action can be taken. For example, if the student should fail a quarter, he might forgo his summer at the beach, attend summer school, and be back on schedule in the fall.

Figure 3.2 is the same Gantt chart used for production. Notice that the time period is much shorter—one month in advance. Rather than have work, play, or study inputs, this production chart gives number codes for customer jobs. It notes the time the

April   May

Job Number	21	22	23	24	25	26	27	28	29	30	1	2	3
1482	Ship												
1471	Mat				Pro						I&R		Ship
1431	Pro				I&R	Ship							
1431-A	Production												
1431-B	Production									I&R		Ship	
1422	ED		Mat			Pro					I&R		Ship

KEY

ED	Engineering Drawings
Mat	Materials Requisition
Pro	Production
I&R	Inspection & Rework
Ship	Shipping

FIGURE 3.1   *Student's plan from high school through medical school.*

Activity	Year and Quarter									
	'74 1234	'75 1234	'76 1234	'77 1234	'78 1234	'79 1234	'80 1234	'81 1234	'82 1234	'83 1234
High Sch.										
Pre-Med.										
Med. Sch.										
Intern.										
Beach										
Social										
Practice										
Travel										
Research										

FIGURE 3.2   *Gantt chart in production.*

engineering drawings should be ready, the time the materials should be in the plant and available for use, the production time from beginning to end with a one day interruption in work when it goes from one machine to another, and finally a period for inspection and rework, packaging and shipping. If the chart is kept up to date, even with a very heavy work load, it is possible for the production department personnel to know the status of any job at any time. Also, members of other departments such as purchasing, sales, or accounting, concerned with work in process, can see at a glance what state the work is in in relation to its scheduled completion. In actual production, any departure from this plan, any delay of machine availability, on raw materials, or anything else that would cause a delay would be noted with some type of distress signal so that everyone would be aware that this job was behind, and all possible means would be used to get it back on schedule.

In the 1910s, Frank Gilbreth and his wife Lillian first used time and motion studies to discover the one best way to do every job. He was concerned both with increasing productivity and with improving health and safety measures for the worker. Lillian Gilbreth also did independent study after the death of her husband, and pioneered in personnel management, developing techniques of scientific selection, placement, and training.

ADMINISTRATIVE EMPHASIS

In 1916, Henri Fayol, a French mining engineer and business executive, contributed much to management theory in his first published work.[5] His most important theory set forth a division of managerial functions, dividing management into five categories: (1) planning, (2) organizing, (3) commanding, (4) coordinating, and (5) controlling. Since Fayol first developed his classification of management activities, many other writers have used these same classifications, or other classifications, which add or take away one or more of Fayol's functions. In addition to these functions, Fayol proposed fourteen principles of management, many of which are still significant today and are discussed at various places in this book.

Max Weber, a German sociologist and a contemporary of Taylor and Fayol, is credited with the idea of bureaucracy as a means of controlling human beings.[6] Bureaucracy is a method of professional management as opposed to owner management, the prevailing form of business at that time. The fundamentals of this method had been used for centuries, but Weber was the first to describe it fully. In his bureaucracy, he established a hierarchical system of control. He also advocated division of labor, scientific selection of personnel, and a career potential for every employee based on seniority and achievement.

There were other contributors to these scientific and administrative schools, and their ideas were based primarily on applying scientific and organizational methods to work and workers, the work itself being of prime importance. An observer might have the impression that the workers were mere tools, means to an end, that they existed because nothing had been invented to take their places. Other management thinkers who came along later began to concentrate on man as a person, for whom work was done. Furthermore, these behavioralists believed that work could be a means of satisfying company objectives as well as personal objectives for the individual worker.

HUMAN RELATIONS SCHOOL

Some of the first studies concerning the human relations school of management were conducted in the 1920s and 1930s by Elton Mayo and his associates, F.J. Roethlisberger and William J. Dickson of the Graduate School of Business Administration at Harvard.[7] These researchers were working on a project, conceived by Mayo, to measure the effects of noise, light, rest periods, and other factors on the production rate of workers. The studies were conducted in the Hawthorne plant of the Western Electric Company in Chicago, and are now referred to as the "Hawthorne Studies."

The program was devised to prove a relationship existed between work produced and the physical conditions of the work environment. The researchers theorized that if the work environment was poor, then the person working in that environment would experience fatigue and monotony, causing production to fall off. Shortly after the project began, it was found that the output they were expecting was not going to materialize. They found that some of the participants were reacting contrary to what had been anticipated. In one experimental room, the lighting was increased several times and then reduced. It was expected that productivity would go down with the reduction of lighting, but instead of going down, it went up. Prompted by the results of this study, the researchers conducted extensive interviews with the Hawthorne workers to determine what did affect productivity.

The results of their studies showed that workers reacted not only to physical conditions but to psychological ones. They also found that sociological conditions affected workers. Workers reacted to peer pressure, setting norms for daily work that might or might not agree with the norms established by management. Groups restricted their production to what was considered a proper day's work. Why? One reason given was that if they worked too hard, it would put some of them out of work. Another said if they worked hard enough to produce what the company decided they should produce, then the company would raise the standard production rate. Some workers even worked slower than they normally would because they felt if they worked fast then the slower men would get a hard time from the foreperson.

By scientific management, a foreperson might determine that 6,000 units a day would be standard. But, by observing social pressures and group norms, the individual worker set a standard rate of producing 5,000 units a day. The behavioral philosophy prevailed over the scientific.

Roethlisberger and Dickson developed the following norms of behavior from their studies at the Hawthorne plant:

1. If you turn out too much work, you are a rate-buster.
2. If you do too little work, you are a chiseler.

3. You should not tell your supervisor anything that would harm an associate, or you are a squealer.
4. If you are a person with some position, you should not act superior.

The Hawthorne studies showed us that the attitude of the worker can be just as important or more important than the scientific methods or the machinery used in production. If a worker does not want to do the work, or the social norms prevent him from doing what is expected by the company, then the company will have to take some corrective action to provide motivation for that individual or the group as a whole.

Shortly after the publication of the Roethlisberger and Dickson findings in *Management and the Worker,* James D. Mooney[8] and Alan C. Reiley published a book titled *Onward Industry,* in which they expounded four principles: (a) The scalar or chain of command principle based on delegation of authority and responsibility to each level in the organization. (b) The function principle based on specialization of work. (c) The staff principle which gives rise to the advice and support activities rendered by staff to the main function of the organization. (d) The coordinative principle which calls for unity of action toward a common purpose.

We might note that in this context the word staff does not have the meaning that many readers would give it. This will be discussed later. For now, we will consider line personnel as those people directly related to the output of the product or service. Staff people are those persons who give support and advice to the line people. Staff is not an activity engaged in by all those members of the "general's team." It is merely an advisory, or auxiliary, service that provides help to the main operating divisions.

Ralph C. Davis, a university professor who also began writing in the 1930s, proposed the notion of a business plan.[9] As the starting point, planning begins with objectives. Davis defined these as profit, service, and social objectives. Many recent papers and books have been devoted to the management by objective (MBO) concept or the later concept of management for results—concepts that allow the worker to determine how he will realize a particular goal.

A vice-president of the New Jersey Bell Telephone Company, Chester I. Barnard, put much of the scientific school behavioral schools of management together. He suggested that management had a responsibility to create a system in which both the company, management, and the workers could all satisfy their objectives. To do this he said that managers had to be good with both human and technical skills. Barnard's book, *The Functions of the Executive,*[10] published in 1938, reflects the state of the art of management when the United States entered World War II, in 1941. Many new concepts of management were conceived during this war as men were called upon to solve problems that had never before confronted military and civilian organizations.

THE QUANTITATIVE SCHOOL

During and since World War II, continued progress in scientific management coupled with the invention of the computer, at least in its commercial state, has resulted in much activity in the area of quantitative analysis. This branch of scientific management deals with the quantification of all decision inputs, with the final decision narrowed down to a quantitative output. Mathematics is the language of the quantitative analyst, and the behavioral aspects of the people involved in the decision take on their quantitative appearances by the risk that they pose in either doing or not doing the work which they are expected to do.

The manager constructs a model, an abstract symbol, usually a formula, which shows the entire situation and the interrelationships of all factors to all others under consideration. For instance, in an application of the linear programming technique, the manager of the grocery section of a food store might be confronted with a problem of what sizes, brands, and quantities of canned soup to display on a ten-foot section of shelving. Since the space is limited, including a can of one brand of soup, excludes the display of another, satisfying the condition of having a linear or straight line relationship where trade-offs can occur. A second condition of a linear problem would be that the result being sought would be the optimization of a situation, in this case, the greatest profit, although in other cases it might be the least cost, the shortest time, or the most sales. A third condition, that there are some restrictions or "constraints" would also be taken into consideration. These might include such limitations as the amount of profit per can, maximum numbers which could be sold, or the number of times the section could be serviced by a stock clerk.

This technique of quantitative methods for arriving at solutions is sometimes called operations research and is taught under that same heading. In addition to linear programming problems, there are other types of quantitative methods such as the Monte Carlo theory, which is a form of simulation and which includes the probability or the odds of one drawing the right card to fill an inside straight in poker, or a crapshooter making his point.

There are also problems of queuing, the British term for lining up. This is a situation where one might analyze the cost of having people stand in line for an airplane ticket, or to check out at a supermarket counter, or the cost of materials waiting to be processed.

There is another method of arriving at solutions in this mathematical, quantitative method through gaming, a form of simulation which involves the use of strategies. The participants find out what an opponent has done, and use a particular strategy to overcome the opponent's advantage or his move toward a particular direction. Gaming is used in college, graduate schools, and seminars, as well as in actual business situations, to find solutions.

We will not go into these particular mathematical, quantitative methods of arriving at decisions, except in mentioning them briefly here.

THE SYSTEMS APPROACH

Perhaps the most recent innovation in management is the systems approach: the viewing of a company, a department, or the people within these divisions as only parts of larger and more complex systems, and also of smaller, simpler systems.

The manager at any level manages a system, composed of inputs, a processor, outputs, and feedback. The inputs might be raw materials and manpower that, through various machining processes, are transformed into finished goods to be sold to another system. The acceptance or rejection from that other system is the manager's feedback that he will use to alter the components of his system if necessary.

You can view yourself as a personal systems manager. You eat an abundance of food (the input). You do lots of physical work and play (the processor). Your body is firm and well developed (the output). When you stand in front of the mirror and you're pleased, or when others look at you admiringly (feedback), you decide to continue just as you have been doing. If your mirror inspection revealed a little extra fat around the waist, or if those admiring glances cease, then maybe you should decide to cut down on the input, or speed up the processor to make the output acceptable. (See Figure 3.3.)

As a personal systems manager, you would have to regard yourself as a part of many systems. If you were only involved in one system, if you lounged in your den twenty-four hours a day and never come out, then maybe a few extra pounds wouldn't make any difference, but what if you're a member of the swimming team (another system), if you're someone's mate (another system), or if you're running for an office (yet another system)?

You can see that what you do as a personal manager even to your own body can

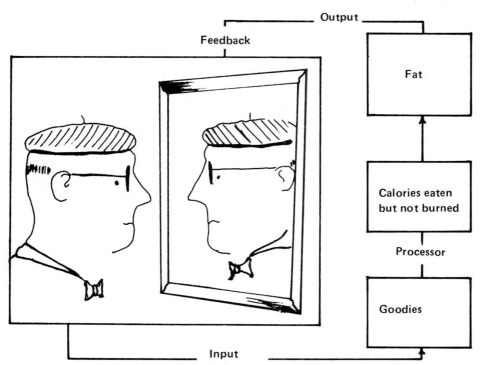

FIGURE 3.3   An example of the personal systems cycle

easily affect many other systems. All the other systems will give you feedback so that you can make adjustments to the components of your personal system, if necessary, to achieve the feedback you want. (See Figure 3.4.) The professional manager would also view his system as one which interacts with many other systems.

For example, in the systems approach the manager would be aware that the job for his subordinates, just as for himself, would only be one of many systems in which they are involved. While the job would be of major importance most of the time, there would be occasions when the job would take a secondary position because of some problem. If the manager does not view the situation from this perspective, then he might take action that would be detrimental to the employee, the company, or both.

The professional manager should be looking for feedback from all those systems with which his or her system interacts, adjusting the components of the system to achieve the most harmonious, satisfying combination of input, process, and output for all systems including the personal one.

The systems approach to management has grown, and will continue to grow, as the people in business become better educated and more aware. The old adage, "Mine is not to reason why, mine is but to do or die" is practically dead. Both managers and workers do want to know what they are doing, why they are doing it, who or what their work affects, and how it affects them.

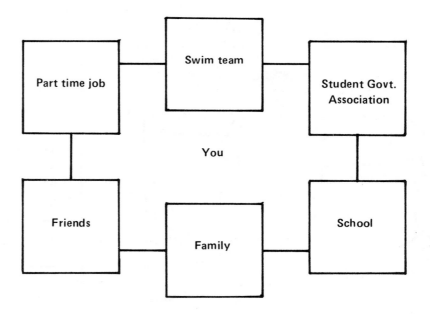

FIGURE 3.4 *An example of the personal systems interaction*

The concept of systems requires everyone involved to be more aware of the relationships within that system and between it and those systems with which it interacts. It requires them to enlarge their viewpoints. They no longer simply make a tire, but they make an item that could save lives, that might be criticized by Ralph Nader, that depletes natural resources, that provides profits, and that goes flat and is repaired at a service station. The tire isn't born in the process, nor does it die there; it passes through one system and into another.

The people in the systems approach are not only workers, stockholders, and customers, but mothers with sick children, brothers who want meaningful work, elderly widows who need their dividends to buy food, and the teenage girl next door who should not have a flat tire on a dark, rainy night. The systems approach requires involvement.

SUMMARY

And so we moved from the Classical, to the scientific, to the human relations, the quantitative, and finally to the systems approach to management. This does not imply that all managers rejected the Classical and adopted the scientific form at the turn of the century. Nor does it mean that all managers now use a systems approach to management. It simply means that the general emphasis at a given time by the practitioners, researchers, and writers was on that form of management described.

FOR DISCUSSION

1. *Why should we even consider the history of professional management since the history is so short?*

2. *Taylor's "scientific method" has made life better for all of us, both producers and consumers. Comment on this statement.*

3. *How might you make use of a Gantt chart?*

4. *From your present knowledge of management, what would you add to or take from Fayol's managerial functions?*

5. *Is bureaucracy bad?*

6. *Using the Hawthorne studies as the basis for your answer, would it have been possible for Taylor's redesigned shovels to have produced no noticeable increase in the total amount of pig iron handled per worker per day?*

7. *Does the computer, through quantitative analysis, replace the manager as the chief decision maker?*

ENDNOTES

1. Alvin Toffler, *Future Shock* (New York: Random House, 1970).

2. Charles Babbage, *On the Economy of Machinery and Manufacturers* (London: C. Knight, 1835).

3. Frederick W. Taylor, *Scientific Management* (New York: Harper and Row, 1947).

4. George Filipetti, *Management in Transition*, rev. ed. (Homewood, Ill.: Richard D. Irwin, 1935).

5. Henri Fayol, *General and Industrial Management* (London: Sir Isaac Pitman & Sons, 1949) first published in France in 1916.

6. Max Weber, *The Theory of Social and Economic Organization* (New York: The Free Press, 1947).

7. F. J. Roethlisberger and William J. Dickson, *Management and the Worker* (Cambridge, Mass.: Harvard University Press, 1939).

8. James D. Mooney, *The Principles of Organization* (New York: Harper and Brothers, 1947).

9. Ralph C. Davis, *Fundamentals of Top Management* (New York: Harper and Row, Publishers, 1951).

10. Chester I. Barnard, *The Functions of the Executive* (Cambridge, Mass.: Harvard University Press, 1938).

CASE 3–1

The Lamenting Mentor

Coach Harold Miller had not been prepared for the bombardment he had just gotten from the Monday Afternoon Club (MAC) quarterback session. He had expected some questions regarding his strategy of the previous Saturday, but he had felt the group would be more sympathetic to his plan.

The MAC's were members of the junior and senior classes of Central College who met with the coaches of all sports to review films, ask questions, find out what the game plans were, and determine how they had worked.

During the Saturday game with State College, Central had been ahead by just six points in the third quarter when Miller put in his second line of defense, which had held pretty well until there was a mix up in signals. A short pass over the heads of the rushing linemen allowed a State player to practically walk into the endzone. The touchdown and a subsequent extra point put State ahead. Central was never able to catch up. The game ended 21 to 20 and spoiled Central's unbeaten record.

"Now, we'll be lucky if we can get into the conference playoffs," a student said. "One more loss and we're doomed. Why did you put those guys in there when you did? Why didn't you wait until we had a bigger lead?"

"I put them in because I wanted the second string to get some actual time under the gun," said Miller, "To perform in a real, tough situation, so that they'll be ready next year with a good backlog of experience. The only way to teach a guy to play football is to put him in charge under fire, and let him make a few mistakes."

"Maybe it was you who made the mistake," said another student. "If we don't get in the championships this year, maybe you won't have to worry about what kind of a team we have next year."

An uneasy silence followed this statement because it came from the son of a wealthy, influential citizen of the community who had himself been a football player for Central, and who was now a member of Central's President's Athletic Advisory Committee.

The session broke and Miller drove home thinking about what the student had said. He thought of the time he had spent at Central. He thought about his family and about the Quarterback Club meeting scheduled for 7:00.

"Maybe I'm lucky to get it from the kids first," he thought, "Now maybe I can change my explanation and come up with a different reason for send-

45

ing in the second line. From talking with these kids, I get the feeling that their fathers are out for blood."

GUIDE QUESTIONS

1. *Do you think Coach Miller is accomplishing the goals of a college football coach?*
2. *What would be the implications of a systems approach to coaching football?*
3. *What alternatives did Coach Miller have rather than put in his second line defense?*
4. *How would you advise him to approach the committee?*

Growing Concern for the Growing Concern, Part 1

Roy Martin, president of Prepared Paper Products, Inc., recently made the biggest business decision of his life when he decided to move from a safe, comfortable situation to a life of mergers, acquisitions, and the big time. He had already agreed, in general terms, to acquire another paper products plant in South Carolina. Though somewhat removed from his current operating state of Maryland, he was preparing to go to the South Carolina office and hammer out a binding agreement.

One thing worried Martin about his own plant. He would be away for at least a week, possibly two, and he did not know who should be left in charge. If this were a case where Martin would be gone only this time, then the company would be run as a team effort by several men who reported directly to Martin. However, this might be only a prelude to many weeks of being absent from the plant, and Martin felt that he must reach a definite decision about a reliable person. He decided to appoint an executive vice-president, a person who would be the operating head of the company in Maryland.

There were several people in Martin's organization from whom he might choose. Also, there were some "outsiders" who might be suitable for the job.

First, there was Edith Swikert, assistant to Martin and in charge of public relations for the company. Edith had done a good job of building a public image for the company. She wrote press releases, wangled speaking engagements for Martin, wrote his speeches, and, in general, paved the way for the first public stock issue of Prepared Paper Products. The stock issue was successful and Martin gave much of the credit to Edith. However, she had had very little supervisory experience, always acting as a staff member in an isolated capacity. She knew the business well, but had not operated at all in a situation where she had authority over others.

The personnel director, Pete Rossen, was another staff member who had had little supervisory experience. The only direct orders he had given were those to his secretary and his assistant in charge of interviewing and testing. Rossen had staffed the entire company and had a good eye for men and women who were trustworthy and loyal to the company. There had been very limited turnover in Paper Products personnel and Martin felt Rossen was largely responsible. Rossen used fairly sophisticated methods of testing and interviewing candidates for positions. He kept up with the latest techniques in personnel management, and he made sure Paper Products was even with, or ahead of, all local industries regarding fringe benefits and wages.

Controller Harold Gentry had a degree in accounting and a flair for finance. He had been able to sway the local bankers and the Small Business Administration (SBA) representatives to grant Paper Products a sizable loan when it was desperately needed, when the company had shown great promise and little money. The initial loan had been repaid and several additional loans had been made to Paper Products by the same financiers. Martin credited Gentry for the close rapport between the company and the SBA. He was a conscientious accountant, but his chief liability was that he was not a man of vision, but rather a man who waited until all the figures were in before he did the counting; a man who waited for others to do the planning before he presented the plans to the financial world.

The production superintendent, Marshall Jones, had little academic preparation for the job, but had been in production some thirty years. He resigned his former position and had come to Paper Products when Martin was just beginning to get the company started, six years ago. He got along well with his men and seemed to be able to motivate the production force when the squeeze was on. Quite often, Jones got involved with the details of production and had been observed, on occasion, repairing machines in the plant. He told Martin one time that the head man in the production department had to know more about production, the machines, the raw materials, and everything else. He had proven his ability time after time.

Steve Marsh, the sales manager, was quite the opposite kind of fellow. He believed that a manager should manage men but should not do any of the work that the men, the salesmen in his case, were supposed to do. In fact, Steve had never done much selling, but had a degree in marketing, and did have the theory necessary for the job. He had set up a compensation plan for the salesmen that included a basic salary and a commission for sales in excess of the quota. He did not call the men in for periodic sales meetings. He felt that helping each man set a realistic quota for himself was important, and that the men themselves could devise means of selling the products. When he did conduct an occasional conference, it was more a meeting to discuss new products, to point out the good and bad qualities of the products, and to brainstorm to discover the many appeals the salesmen might use to sell these products.

In addition to the in house prospects, Martin had been approached by Barry Scott, the general manager of a small competing firm. Scott told Martin he wanted to make a change because there was no future or room for advancement with his present company. The company was wholly owned by a family that wanted it for a source of steady income, having no desire to expand into other fields or acquire companies. Martin knew Scott had been successful in all areas of the small company, and he had been able to provide the owners with a steady and reliable, though not spectacular return on their investment.

Martin thought of each man individually, weighing pros and cons carefully to determine which one might be the best candidate for the position of vice-president.

GUIDE QUESTIONS

1. *What goals do you feel Martin has for his company?*
2. *How would knowing the goals and management philosophy help in choosing an executive vice-president?*
3. *What do you think is meant by the term "line" and "staff" in the case and how might this influence Martin's decision?*
4. *What are the good and bad features of promoting from within and of going outside the company to fill the vice-president's job?*

*At the conclusion of this chapter,
you should be able to—*

- **Recognize differences between the activities and duration of activities at various levels of management**
- **Describe some of the roles a manager assumes.**
- **Correlate managerial functions with managerial roles.**

4

Managerial Roles and Activities

In the last chapter we said that an analysis of systems in which you are involved would show that you are part of many different systems—school, work, athletics, political and social groups, family, and church—but we stopped at that point without defining the roles you would occupy as a member of any one system.

As a member of a family, you might be a sister, a daughter, a mother, a wife, a partner, a provider, a disciplinarian, a comforter, an interceder, and so on, depending on the situation. As a student you could be either an active or a passive participant, a researcher, a friend, a classmate, a tutor, a bridge partner, a photographer, a cheerleader, an advisor, a carpool driver, a roommate or any of dozens more.

If we define a student as one who studies something or a person enrolled in a school, or, if we define a mother as a woman who has borne a child or a female parent, we would be correct, but we still would not be conveying a precise description of a student or a mother, unless we speak of the roles assumed within that system.

Likewise, we would be correct if we said a manager is a person who plans, organizes, activates and controls. Yet we could not portray him with any accuracy without referring to the roles he or she assumes within that system.

A MANAGER'S SYSTEMS

A manager as well as a student, is involved in many systems, but primarily those of family and work. In the home, the manager is a father or a mother, mate, mechanic, cook, painter, philosopher, accountant, nurse, disciplinarian, coach and so on. But these activities, these roles, make him indistinguishable from his neighbors who wave to him from their backyards as they go about filling identical roles.

To a lesser degree in terms of time and commitment, the manager probably belongs to a fraternal organization, a civic club, a country club, a religious group, a political group, and to several social groups. A top manager might be a member of the board of directors of a bank, the Chamber of Commerce, a charitable organization, the Retail Merchants, or hold an elective political office, while an entry level manager would hold similar but lower ranking positions. But what we really want to know is what roles a manager assumes within the work system?

ACTIVITIES FOR VARIOUS LEVELS OF MANAGERS

We would find, through study or by observation, that a manager spends most of his time talking, face to face, or on the telephone or to a recording machine. He accomplishes most of what he does through others by talking and communicating. So it would stand to reason that an effective manager would also be an effective communicator and a persuasive talker.

To whom would our manager talk? The manager talks to subordinates, peers, superiors, suppliers, customers, friends, even enemies, bankers, directors, social contacts, business contacts, secretary, and to many other people, and for each person to whom he speaks, the manager will assume a different role.

At this point, we should reflect on some of the differences between top managers (presidents, general managers, board chairmen) and entry-level managers (foremen, supervisors, department heads). Entry-level managerial roles, generally, are confined to the organization itself, and they will seldom deal with people outside of the company. Top managers will spend much of their time interacting, interfacing with other external systems—customers, suppliers, business organizations, government representatives and others. Middle managers might have both internal and external contacts.

Top managers meet for substantial periods of time with their contacts and they are likely to have the meetings arranged in advance. Both the top manager and his or her secretary plan the agenda. The foreman makes up his own calendar because he probably won't have a secretary and his meetings will be much more spontaneous and last for short periods of time, only a minute or two. At the beginning of a shift, the foreman might meet individually with ten or more subordinates, give them instructions and have them working on jobs within about fifteen minutes. Long meetings for foremen and supervisors are usually those meetings called by their superiors (a staff meeting or supervisors meeting). Those meetings which they arrange are for short periods.

Top and middle managers will have better opportunities to have "alone" time because they are more likely to have private offices and have someone to screen out unwanted or untimely calls and visitors. Entry-level managers seldom have offices (more often, a desk in the work area) and must make themselves available for all interruptions to keep from having any lost sales or production.

A final difference which we might observe is that top managers will have greater emphasis on the first two functions of management—planning and organizing—while the entry-level manager will be much more concerned with activating and controlling subordinates. With these differences in mind, let's look at some of the roles a manager might play.

FIGUREHEAD

A manager might assume the role of a figurehead. For instance, there are people with elementary school children who have problems with their teachers either in learning or in discipline and these people will not go to the teacher to try to solve their problem. They look for the head of the organization, either the principal or the superintendent. In any general school system, the superintendent would be the head, the figurehead, and these people would go directly to him for a solution to their problem. The problem would eventually go back to the child's teacher who would have to be the one to make the decision on how to work out the problem, but nevertheless, the figurehead, the superintendent in this case, would still have to be involved in the thing and would be a receiver and a transmitter of information. This action would take up part of his managerial time.

The foreman of the spinning room must be present at the retirement dinner for one of his subordinates. It would not look right if he neglected to attend even though he had little in common, or was at odds with his subordinate. The supervisor must approve many things for the record even though he has nothing to do with decisions that require his authorization. Visitors are introduced to department heads who, in turn, conduct the tour of their departments in a manner which they deem most appropriate. And finally, top managers of local industries, businesses, and governments are included on many lists as *the* figureheads representing the power structure of that community.

LIAISON

The school superintendent would also act as a liaison between the school board, those elected members from the community, and the actual working members of the school system—the principals, the staff, the teachers, aides, and the custodial and maintenance workers. He would tell the school board (the board of directors) what has been happening in the system, what is expected to happen, how much it will cost, and such information as that. The members would in turn ask him to do certain things, make studies and recommendations, evaluate the system, and conduct other managerial functions. These school board members also act as figureheads and they, too, are called by parents. They pass this information on to the superintendent who talks to the teacher who finally gets things straightened out.

But this principal, this manager, is not only a liaison between the working school personnel and the school board, he is also the leader of these paid employees. He has to help formulate policy, give instructions to his people, motivate them, hire them, promote them, fire them when necessary, and do all things a leader would do.

The foreman is often called the man in the middle because of his role. The workers, the rank and file, regard him as their leader, their liaison with top management. When the workers have problems, they expect their foreman to bring these problems to top management and get decisions favoring the workers and remedy the situation. Top management, on the other hand, expects the foreman to be management's representative to the men, communicating and implementing policy decisions made at a higher level. Often the different views of this same role are conflicting and leave the foreman with a "damned if I do and damned if I don't" decision.

UMPIRE

The manager must also act as an umpire deciding who is right in many situations when several of his subordinates disagree on a method of accomplishing a particular goal. He, alone, would probably know all the ramifications, all the consequences, of seeking a particular goal and those people involved in this situation which needed an umpire might be looking at the problem from a selfish point of view or from a narrow perspective which may or may not be in line with the overall corporate objectives.

Grievances, filed by the workers, go to the foreman and on up to the plant manager for decisions. The department head makes a decision about who gets to go to lunch from twelve to one, who has to go at eleven and who has to hang on until one before they can go to eat.

INFORMATION CENTER

The manager must also be the information center for all information flowing to and from him. He knows more about his organization, department, or section than any other person. He receives inputs from all levels of the organization, both requested data and inputs from those who feel he should be aware of certain bits of information. The information might be factual, it may be studied, compiled information, it might be rumors or information from secret informers. Nevertheless, the manager is the focal point of all information flowing upward. The only time he would be unaware of things happening in the organization, would be when people withhold information from him intentionally because it might reflect poorly on them or their specific responsibility in the organization. However, if this information is of a significant nature, then the poor performance, the reason for not giving the boss the information to begin with, would show up when someone reported the initial poor performance had caused something else to go wrong.

CONTROL CENTER AND COMMUNICATOR

The manager, acting as a control center, can take plans from staff people, for instance, and require line people to carry them out, since staff people cannot directly require line members of the organization to exclude any actions regardless of how appropriate these actions might seem. Staff people have no direct authority over line personnel.

In his job of chief communicator, the manager must evaluate all bits of information coming to him and send on to subordinates, superiors, customers, peers and so on, all information he feels will be of value to them.

FINAL DECIDER

Within his area of control, the whole organization or one small department, the manager is the final decider, the chief decision maker. This may be a role of deciding who gets the promotion, who will be hired, which company will get the business, which products will be bought and sold, which machine will be purchased, and many other decisions relating to the overall good of the company. As a matter of fact, if the manager is unwilling to delegate responsibility and authority, he will make all the decisions which are to be made. Quite often, this renders the company helpless in cases where he is unavailable to make the decision or is reluctant to do so.

CHIEF SPOKESMAN

The manager acts as the chief spokesman for the corporation, the school system, the grinding department, the labor gang, the shoe department, or whatever the operation. If it is a corporation, all news releases will bear his name and stamp of authority. All charitable contributions will be made by him. The manager will be required to act as a spokesman in situations external to the organization. He will be the representative to and a member of the Chamber of Commerce, the Retail Merchants Association, the National Education Association, or any one of a thousand associations to which his organization might belong. In any case, he would be acting as a spokesman for his organization and in many cases he will act as a spokesman for his given field or industry. Many civic organizations have members who are representative of the merchants, the clergy, industry, education, and so on, who, within the committee structure would be acting for the industry as a whole.

Much of the responsibility the manager has as a spokesman would be much like that of a figurehead except that a figurehead might not have direct responsibility for the organization he would be representing. For instance, the Queen of England is the figurehead leader of the country, but the prime minister is the spokesman for the country, the person who could commit England to certain positions in international situations.

The foreman would act as a spokesman for his department in estimating deadlines, costs or general feelings concerning certain topics. The chief of the secretarial pool would say when her subordinates would be available for duty or when work might be scheduled. She would be counted upon to determine manpower needs and budget requests for her department.

NEGOTIATOR

While the manager might act as an umpire within his organization, he might act as a negotiator between his company and another. This might be a selling situation, a buying situation, a trade or a settlement. For instance, he might act as a negotiator in a contract settlement between labor and management, between his company and a national union. He would have the final approval on management's side. He may not be involved directly in the negotiations, for strategic reasons, but he would have a spokesman who would be carrying his message to the conference table, and in effect, the manager would be the final negotiator.

Within a company, departmental managers, foremen and other managerial people will negotiate for the most desirable personnel, the greatest amount of money, the newest machinery for their departments, and try to get the best for themselves and their subordinates. There is a built-in conflict within all companies which leads managers of departments to try and get the choice assets to be used for the benefit of their departments, toward accomplishing the corporate goals.

RESOURCE ALLOCATOR

This brings up another area in which a manager might act, and that is the function of a resource allocator. It is possible that the general manager would be the final resource allocator, but each manager, from the top to the foreman, does allocate certain resources—the best and or worst machines, the best and or worst jobs, the highest and lowest increases in pay. This would mean that managers—many lower-level managers—might be negotiating with a general manager for a particular resource. So now we have managers, all within the same company, having different roles at the same time. We also have an ambiguity of managerial functions in that the manager being trained, might also be training one of his subordinates. This leads to another field where managers must function. This is the field where he acts as a trainer and a teacher.

TRAINER

Every manager is responsible for training his subordinates whether he personally does the job or not. Any person, whether promoted or newly hired, regardless of previous training or experience, must be taught certain details concerning his job. This might entail formal training sessions away from the place of work, special sessions at the work place, or supervised on-the-job training. Most major businesses now have continuous training programs for all personnel, not just those newly hired, because techniques, methods, and concepts are continually changing and managers must keep up with these changes. Many managers, particularly those at the lower levels of management, feel that a subordinate should not be taught the job of his superior. The superior should not teach the subordinate everything he knows because the subordinate then might take his superior's job. This attitude comes from a lack of security of the superior, either in his ability to function on that job, or in his capability of assuming a higher position. For most managers, this principle would be a hindrance. More aggressive people feel that a subordinate should be taught the manager's job just as soon as the manager has mastered the job. The reason for this is that when an opportunity comes for the superior to advance, he already has a subordinate trained to take his place. In the short term, even when the manager is not a candidate for a higher position, he has a person to take his place when he goes on a trip in behalf of his superiors, or acts as a company representative in some other area which would take him away from his immediate position.

COORDINATOR AND LEADER

Probably the most important job a manager has, that job which is most discussed and looked upon, is his job of coordinating his subordinates and leading them to meeting a particular goal of that department or company. If he cannot do this, if he cannot lead his men, if he cannot motivate them and keep their morale up, coordinate their endeavors to accomplish whatever it is that they must accomplish, enforce company rules, regulations, and policy, then he will fail as a manager, simply because the goal will not be realized. The gap between what was proposed and what actually happened would be too great to keep this man on as a manager. Again, if a manager cannot coordinate and lead his subordinates, he will have a terrible time acting as an umpire, or a spokesman, or a developer of men, or in any of the other functions in which he would have to assume.

ROLES AND FUNCTIONS

If the manager acts in all these capacities and wears a different hat every few minutes, if he acts as a spokesman, a figurehead, as a coordinator, teacher, and motivator, then what about innovating, planning, controlling and all that? Why don't we study how to make speeches, how to get elected to the presidency of the Chamber of Commerce, and these things?

We do study many of these things in a basic manner. For instance, when our industrialist was negotiating with the union representative, he was following a plan which he had made as a result of a decision-making process. Negotiating without some previous plan is not negotiating at all, just as sailing around in the ocean until land is sighted is not really navigating. In both cases, the spokesman, that is the negotiator or the navigator, would simply be "satisficing," accepting less than ideal. One might get a contract and the other might find land, but neither of them would achieve a predetermined goal. If the navigator had been headed toward England, and had hit land in Spain, he certainly could not consider that a great success story, nor could the negotiator, who acceded to all the demands of the union without achieving anything for the company, be given any laurels for his "accomplishments." Therefore, planning is essential *before* any action. The negotiating is the action, but the planning, the procedures, and the policies were determined beforehand.

The spokesman for the company is only stating publicly something that has occurred prior to his statement. That is, he is announcing a decision made by a policy-level group, for instance, the adoption of a new product, the opening of a new territory or plant, the stand the company would take in the forthcoming bargaining session, or some other announcement which would be made, again, as a result of planning. Or, the spokesman might make an announcement of a decision which has occurred in the organizing stage such as the splitting of an existing unit into two separate sections, or in the directing phase where the company has added a new personnel manager or promoted someone to a vice-presidency. He might be acting as a spokesman for the control function of management when he announces the financial results of the previous year's planning and production activities.

Earlier, we discussed the manager acting as a communications center, receiving and dispensing information and suppressing those items which he felt would not be of value to certain people. Again, the manager must know the policy of the company, the goals and procedures which have been adopted, before he can decide if these facts are of any value, before evaluating the input he receives.

While it is apparent that a manager does act as a leader, a spokesman, a negotiator, an umpire and so on, it should also be apparent that without the basic functions of management—planning, organizing, activating and controlling, the manager could not act as the chief in any of these roles.

ACTIVITIES AND FUNCTIONS

We also might look at this from another point of view. If the manager spends 20 percent of his time on the telephone, then should the major emphasis of his managerial training be devoted to telephone manners and procedures, rather than the general functions of management? It would seem that the chief spokesman for the company, the store, or the school would have to know something about telephone manners before he should be allowed to spend much of his time talking to various people. We should realize, however, that this spokesman must know what he is talking about. For instance, the hardware store manager might want to be careful with his telephone manners when he is talking with a colleague about a particular brand of handsaws, but what is most critical is his awareness of the product, its uses, potential sales, and his ability to express his point of view, as well as being receptive to the point of view of his colleague.

We might spend some time instructing a manager in basic psychology, because as you might have observed, and as we have said, the manager spends most of his time dealing with people—communicating by telephone, in person, or by letter. Therefore, we should and will spend time talking about what motivates people, what does not motivate them, what they want to hear and what they would rather not hear. An awareness of human behavior is fundamental to being a successful manager. Machines can be bought. Money is available to anyone with a good idea. The chief ingredient to the success or failure of any venture—church, school, business, or other—is the attitude of the people who belong to the group. If they want it to succeed, it will succeed. If they lose interest, it will fail.

In all decision making and in all the cases which we will be considering in this book, we must be aware constantly of the people involved. How will the decision to fire or to promote affect those people and the rest of the members of the group? We must determine the long-range effects of any action before we take that action.

FOR DISCUSSION

1. *Name and give examples of at least five managerial roles.*
2. *Would a course entitled, "The Psychological Aspects of Business," be a good course for a manager? Why?*
3. *What type of situation might inhibit the upward flow of information?*
4. *Compare the functions of management with the roles a manager must assume.*
5. *Act out a management role with class members deciding which role was taken and commenting on the effectiveness of the role playing.*

The Blinkedy Blank Lighting Company

Jerry Harding, a student in the industrial management certificate program at Nicholson Community College, was elected production manager of the Blinkedy Blank Lighting Company, a psychedelic lamp manufacturer. The entire work force of Blinkedy Blank was composed of students.

To finance the initial expenses, the group had voted to sell shares of stock to themselves, their families, and other members of the Nicholson student body. The stock was sold for $3.00 a share. The holder of each share of stock was issued a warrant—an option to buy a finished lamp for $3.00. The selling price for the finished lamps was to be $4.00. Thus, the holders of the warrants could use them to buy lamps, or sell them to other lamp purchasers at a negotiated price, probably somewhat less than $1.00.

The sale of one hundred shares brought in $300.00, which was deposited in a two-signature bank account, and the purchasing agent was empowered by the executive committee to begin buying the needed materials. The final product was to resemble Figure 1.

To operate, the lamp is plugged in and flashers cause the bulbs to flash at irregular intervals, providing multicolor illumination.

Harding had been assured by the purchasing agent that all materials would be available to him the following week. Ten workers would be available to him the first week, twenty the second and third weeks, and ten the fourth week, when all the lamps were to be completed and delivered. Sales were to be made throughout the production cycle with the greatest sales

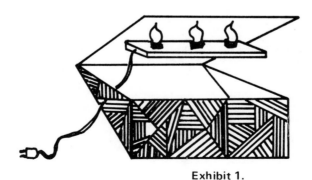

Exhibit 1.

FIGURE 1

effort at the completion of the project. Harding and his assistant, Philip Rogers, began organizing the flow of work and assigning the workers to jobs.

GUIDE QUESTIONS

1. *Would the term "student" amply describe Harding's role at Nicholson? Why?*
2. *In the case, is Harding a manager? Why?*
3. *What roles does Harding assume?*
4. *What factors might complicate the scheduling process?*

Assurance to the Insurance Man

The Universal Insurance Company of America is a full line insurance company whose largest volume is auto and life insurance with a recent concentration in the mutual fund. The sales department is separate from claims, and the national sales organization is set up as follows:

PRESIDENT

Regional Vice President (RVP)

District Sales Manager (DSM)

Area Sales Manager (ASM)

Local Sales Manager (LSM)

Agents

Regions are the Southwest, the Middle Atlantic, the Northeast and so on. District sales managers supervise sales in one state in the heavily populated regions and two or more states in the sparsely populated areas. There are usually three to five area sales managers within a district, each having charge of fifteen local sales managers, who have ten to twenty sales agents working under them.

Pete Golightly, an ASM in western North Carolina, found himself in a position of coming face to face with an agent Golightly had instructed his LSM to fire. The LSM did as directed whereupon the agent sought and was given permission to go to the ASM to appeal his case. The confrontation was something Golightly would have liked to avoid, but he could not. In preparing for the encounter, he reconsidered the case.

Joe Weatherby, the discharged agent, had been with Universal for fifteen years. He had come to the company on a part-time basis, and had continued on that basis until the date of his departure. His present job, the result of his most recent of many promotions in the department, was assistant postmaster, and many of Weatherby's insurance clients were postal employees.

What brought Weatherby under the scrutiny of company management was a matter of sales, or more specifically, that of production. Golightly was one of three ASMs in North Carolina. The total sales in his area was more than in either of the other areas in the state. Golightly had been satisfied with the sales and so had his former DSM. However, his former district sales manager retired and a new DSM replaced him—a new man with new objectives. He was interested not only in total sales, but in sales per salesman. He wanted only proven salesmen in his territory, men who could produce. In this category, Golightly came up short.

A quick analysis of the situation showed Golightly had sixteen full-time salesmen and fifteen part-timers, all poor producers when compared with the full-timers. Golightly had inherited all the part-timers from his predecessor. The other ASMs in the district had about the same percentage of poor producers but no part-time salesmen.

In coming to grips with this problem, Golightly decided he would have to eliminate part-time positions. He would not fire his part-time agents outright, but would give them a thirty day notice in which time they could quit their regular jobs and come with Universal full-time, or give up their part-time positions.

Weatherby's answer to his LSM was, "No." He could not give up his present position.

"I came to Universal fifteen years ago as a part-time man. That was my agreement at that time and I've stuck to my bargain. I feel I've done pretty well for Universal, too. After all, I'm getting about $7,500 a year in commissions and renewals, and you have to sell to get that kind of money."

In addition to the $7,500, Weatherby made about $16,000 a year in the post office job.

"In less than two years, I'll have thirty years in with the government and I'll only be sixty," Weatherby told his LSM, "At that time, I plan to devote my full efforts to selling for Universal. Right now, though, I can't quit. I'd be throwing away a $700-a-month pension. Just let me stay like I am for two more years."

The LSM told Weatherby that the company would pay him one year's commissions, $7,500, for his existing insurance as severance pay, but that he, the LSM, was not empowered to make exception to Mr. Golightly's new policy. Weatherby immediately asked for an appointment with Golightly telling the LSM that people wanted to buy insurance from older, mature men and that he, Weatherby, was just reaching his prime. In addition, he said, he had been assured all along by company representatives that he could sell part-time until he retired. To fire him now would be a breach of contract.

GUIDE QUESTIONS

1. *What are some of the alternatives Golightly might consider?*
2. *Should Golightly give his answer to Weatherby immediately?*
3. *What are some of the pros and cons to part-time employees in a business?*
4. *Why do you think the new DSM wanted more sales per salesman?*
5. *Evaluate Weatherby's statement, "people want to buy insurance from older, mature men."*

part 2

_____

planning

At the conclusion of this chapter,
you should be able to—

- Explain the difference between goals and objectives.

- List several categories of long term goals.

- Identify organizations whose goals are not to make a profit or even survive.

- Understand the value of setting goals and objectives.

5

Management Goals and Objectives

In Chapter 2 we analyzed the method and the principles involved in decision making. This was not a new method, or one you had never used. It was simply a structured look at a process we all use in making decisions. The more we are aware of this process, the more we observe the principles of decision making, and the more objective and analytical we are, the better will be our decisions. We should take a fresh look at things, and not continue to do things as we have in the past because we have always done them that way, or because everyone else is doing them that way, and base our decisions on what could, or would, be the best results of our current thinking, then we will be ahead of our competitors.

All managers, even personal managers, have certain functions that they perform. They get ideas, sift through the many in search of the best ones, plan and set objectives, activate the plan, and finally, exercise control over all activities by measuring results against objectives.

DEFINING GOALS AND OBJECTIVES

In this chapter we will discuss the importance of setting objectives or goals. First we might reflect on the fact that although these two terms are often used interchangeably, they do not have quite the same meaning. A goal is a broad aim or end toward which a person, or members of an organization, might strive; an objective is a short-range aim, a specific end to be accomplished through a particular amount of effort. In this context, the successful completion of many objectives would lead to the accomplishment of a goal.

A problem develops when we find that a goal for one person becomes an objective for another. The profitable operation of the dough department may be the goal of that department head, but it is only one of many objectives for the general manager of the pizza plant who must have many profitable departments to realize the goal of a profitable company. In the final analysis, the categorization of a desired end as to whether it is a goal or an objective will depend on the perspective of the viewer, how that end result relates to him or her.

Nonbusiness Goals

Before we get into the topic of setting business objectives, let us consider the goal of the football team at your former high school. The goal might be stated simply: To win as many games as possible, preferably all of them, while observing standards of fair play.

Now let us examine this goal from the point of view of various participants who decided to adopt this objective. First, look at the goal from the point of view of the school principal. He or she would like to win the games because it focuses attention on the school, builds good school spirit among the students and faculty, brings more revenue to the school athletic fund, and provides the opportunity to bathe in the glory of being the principal of the winning team's school. The school goal has been accomplished and one of the principal's personal objectives has also been accomplished.

Now let us look at the goal from the coach's point of view. He, too, would be happy for the team to win all its games. He would have great spirit among the players, the community supporters would be happy, his job prospects would be enhanced so he could stay at this school for more years, or possibly go to another school which would offer him a higher salary, and give him better facilities and a more select group of students to train. He would now be the "molder of young men," "the builder of the winning team." His goal will have been realized.

What about the ballplayers themselves, how do they react to winning? They are happy, they have team spirit. Each of them basks in glory and many of them, because of the publicity which accompanies winning, are receiving athletic scholarships to go to college. Some of the teammates are heroes, leaders of their own groups, and, in some instances, have a much wider choice of girl friends than they would have as losers.

The community leaders recognize the victors, have banquets for them, give them awards and honors. Everybody loves a winner.

Even the cheerleaders find it much easier to cheer for a winning team. The stands are filled with eager fans, happy to cheer the team on. Even timid and sophisticated adults can be drawn into a cheer for the old team, if the old team is on its way to glory. The band plays better, the horns toot louder, the marchers stand straighter, and the drums beat harder when the team is winning the game. Even after the game is over and the lights have been turned out on the field, the locker room cleared, and the parking lots empty, we continue to hear automobile horns blaring in the night because the driver's can't get over that feeling of winning, of accomplishing the goal.

In this example all participants from principal to student, from player to fan, know, support, and encourage the goal of the football team. All efforts by all groups are directed toward winning. The cheerleaders cheer for the team. The fans clap for their team and jeer at opponents. The coach unveils his winning strategy, and all the players work in unison to attain a goal. Individuals combine their own objectives with the goals of the team. Everyone's efforts are directed toward winning.

Let's look at another example of objectives in your personal life. Your father has a two-week vacation coming to him. He asks you to think about the possibility of a trip and come up with some ideas for him to consider. You might evaluate his idea of a trip and say, "No, time would be better spent painting the house, or working in the yard or garden, or relaxing around home. How about fishing and some other, home-based, leisure activities."

However, if you do decide a trip would be in order, then you must set an objective and define the scope of the trip. Suppose you live in Washington, D.C. After considering several alternatives, you tell your father, "Within the period of time allotted to you by your company, we will leave Washington and have as our destination Orlando, Florida and a visit to Disney World. We will stop at other places of interest as we go to and return from Florida."

Now that you have defined the objective, all other planning will be directed toward accomplishing that objective. For instance, you begin to pinpoint the time your father should request his vacation. You narrow the time to that which you would expect to have the best weather in Florida or to coincide with some other event on the way to or from your objective. You also begin to establish short-range objectives, the daily destinations, and side tours which would be of interest to everyone. You establish the mode of travel and the type of accommodation. Will you fly, take a bus or train, or will you drive? Will you stay in a hotel, a motel, or a tent? Will you visit relatives, or possibly rent a motor home and combine your method of conveyance with your accommodations and your restaurants? Whatever your steps would be, it certainly becomes clear that all plans you make will have to intertwine with the main objectives of the vacation trip.

Company Goals

How could these same efforts and the same spirit be directed toward company goals? What kind of goals would a company set? Who would set these goals? Management goals are those corporate aims, clearly defined and understood by all participants of the organization, toward which all efforts of these participants should be directed.

All long-term goals should be set by the board of directors and the chief executive of the corporation. This gives the company a united sense of direction and prevents, to a great extent, factionalism among the departments of the corporation. That is, it gives managers and other workers common goals and prevents them from working in opposition to that common goal in favor of a more immediate and personal goal.

In addition to uniting the participants behind a common cause, goals are of the utmost importance in measuring company results—the control function of management. If you don't know where you are going, you can't possibly know when you reach your destination. If you don't know what you expect a man to do, then you can't know whether or not he did it, if he did it well, or if he did enough of it, too little, or none at all. You cannot judge a man's behavior unless you have objectives you expect him to reach.

It is relatively easy for you to see how personal goals and objectives can be set and reached in a short period of time. But, how about business goals for the average individual? Does everyone who goes to work in the business world get to set his or her own goals? Very definitely not. He or she may set personal goals, but it is doubtful that he or she will be asked, or even allowed, to set the objectives of the company. This is one reason people go into business for themselves. The entrepreneur, regardless of how small the business may be, does get this opportunity to set goals and shape policy to make these goals a reality. A man might say, "I'm going to open a little restaurant and sporting goods shop down on the north fork of the Rivanna River so I can serve my fisherman buddies, their friends, and anyone else. Also, I can make a living while doing something that I enjoy doing."

Most people going into business as employees are confronted with objectives that have already been set, probably many years ago by the company's founders. Since that time, objectives have been changed by the different boards of directors in response to external forces necessitating such changes. Or, the board may be reacting to changes in ownership, to government policies, world economic conditions, or by many other things. Policies and objectives still exist, however, and everyone within that company should know that they exist and should direct his or her work to making these goals realities.

OBJECTIVES AS MOTIVATORS

We all work better with objectives in mind and with knowing the *why* of our work. For instance, a city water and sewage foreman took his crew to an open field and told them to dig a three-foot hole and call him. They dug the hole and called him. He came over, looked in it, shook his head and said, "Fill it up." They did. The foreman then pointed to another place and said, "Dig me another hole here."

They dug the second hole and called the foreman. He came, looked at it, shook his head and said, "Fill it up." Again, they did. He pointed to another place and told them to dig another three-foot hole. They did as directed the third time, but when the foreman shook his head, said, "Fill it up," and pointed to another place, they shook their heads and said, "No."

"We're not going to keep digging these holes for nothing," one of the men said.

"But there is a reason," the foreman explained. "An old sewer line went through this property some years ago, but the line isn't indicated anywhere on our maps. Now we have to find it by trial and error and that's what we're trying to do now."

With a purpose and an objective in mind, the men went back to work. After digging a few more holes, they found the sewer line.

A specific business goal might be ". . . employees of this company will be paid at or above the minimum wage as agreed upon. They will be paid accurately and promptly. They will share in the prosperity of this company." What are some of the implications of this goal? For one thing, it means the people involved in payroll or personnel, the managers or board members concerned with wages and salaries, will be compelled to observe legal restrictions concerning minimum hourly wages and premium payments for hours worked overtime. It would mean some specific method or procedure of computing and writing checks would be formulated and enacted. It would mean the employers would be paid on schedule. They could expect to receive their checks at a predetermined hour and day. Also, it would mean that some group or individual members of the management team would be considering methods of sharing the company's profits. These methods might include such things as profit sharing, bonuses, piece work, and additional fringe benefits such as stock options and stock purchase plans. The good feature about this system is that all employees would be working toward the some goals. We wouldn't have some of the supervisors worrying about how to beat the employees out of the minimum wage, or find ways to circumvent overtime pay premiums and trying not to pay any fringe benefits, or to give all the profits to the stockholders and none to the employees.

In working on a plan to pay people, the managers could anticipate problems that would arise as the company grows larger. First one person and then several people would make up the payroll. At some point in the future, a computer would be necessary to process the time, hours and money necessary for scheduled payment of employees. The expense of processing this payroll might become so great and there may be times when it would require many people to work on it on an overtime basis if a mechanized method was not approved. A manager could compute this, assign a risk factor to the probability that such expenses would occur, and he could make adjustments as needed.

MANAGEMENT BY OBJECTIVES

When a manager and subordinates both know the objectives of the company, he or she may assign to them the responsibility for setting their personal objectives, subject to approval. The manager should allow them to work out the methods by which they will reach their goals. This method of management by objectives presupposes that people work better if they have the opportunity to determine how they will accomplish a desired result. Quite often, workers set higher goals for themselves. Usually those goals are more ambitious than those which would be set for them by management. For instance, the sales manager might say he or she wanted each salesperson to sell at least $100,000 worth of mattresses and bedding next year. However, if the sales manager had asked each individual in the sales force how many could be sold, there is a likelihood that each salesperson would aspire to a goal higher than that suggested by the sales manager.

If the sales force were selling on a nonincentive basis, then it is highly possible that when they reached the $100,000 goal, or when they approached that goal, they would begin to slow down their efforts so that future goals would not be raised by a great percentage.

All objectives within the corporation—its departmental objectives and employee objectives—should support the main goals of the company. The objective of paying the employees on time each week would support a company goal of being a good corporate citizen to customers and employees who live in the community. Being a dependable employer and paying all employees on time will help the merchants within the community have more dependable customers, who in turn, will make the merchants more dependable. Even this objective of paying the employees can be more specific. It might be stated in the objective that each employee will be paid on Friday of each week or every other week or twice a month, or whatever policy might be adopted.

The person who has the responsibility for seeing to it that the employees of this company are paid should also have the authority to hire the number of people necessary to accomplish this objective. He or she should be allowed to spend the money for the machinery and the supplies necessary to realize the objective. Also, he or she can only be held responsible for those things he or she can control. If this were a company with many branches and the branch manager, in working up the payroll, had to send the raw figures to a central plant for processing, and the central plant computer broke down, then it would not be the responsibility of the branch payroll manager if the payroll were late. But this has to do with the delegation of authority and responsibility which we will talk about later.

TYPES OF GOALS

There are many kinds of goals that a corporation might undertake. Probably the first of these would be business goals and probably the first of these business objectives would be to make a profit. It might be argued, and often is, that the making of a profit is a result of the rendering of a satisfactory service or an acceptable product at a competitive price, and therefore, profit is not an objective, but a result of the accomplishment of an objective. It is a prize or a reward. However, most companies would say that profit is fundamental to the well being and continued existence of the company.

In addition to making a profit, the goal might dictate that this profit will be returned to the stockholders as a return on their investment in the company, or that part of this profit would be returned and part would be reinvested in the company. The goal might also state that this profit should result only after the employees have been paid a fair wage, after the customers have been satisfied. Of course, all corporate taxes will have been paid before profits can be distributed.

Many students who are new to the study of management will feel that profits of corporations are too high. Studies have been conducted among students concerning their attitudes toward profits. Most of these studies show that the students feel that corporations' profits are 50, 75 or even 100 percent of their investments each year and up to 33 percent on sales. This is not true nor even remotely realistic under today's competitive circumstances. At one time, Winn-Dixie, a grocery chain, distributed bags that said "Here's what happens to the dollar you spend at Winn-Dixie." It was claimed that net profit was 2¢ on a dollar. The bag inscription further exclaimed, "If you give your son 25¢ to go to our store, to buy a $10.00 order for you, he has made more on the order than Winn-Dixie."

Managerial goals can also be for the good of the community and for society in general. Goals in this area might be such things as clean air and water (this not only helps the public relations program of the company, it also fills the legal requirements). Other social objectives might be being an equal opportunity employer, promoting good citizenship practices among the employees, giving incentives to employees who engage in civic activities such as donating blood, being a member of city council, or working on community chest drives.

Another field in which businesses set goals is in contributing to nonprofit organizations. Some companies set aside a percentage of their profits to be divided among a number of charitable, educational, religious, and political institutions.

Nonprofit Goals

We might mention here that while we give great emphasis to profits in most businesses, there are those organizations which do not seek to make a profit, nor do they make sales in the normal course of business. They are agencies such as governmental institutions, schools (both of which are supported by taxes, gifts or tuition), and churches, that receive their income from collections, donations, and bequests. Most of their money is spent to accomplish a certain goal such as education, salvation, self-actualization, a healthy mind and body, or a goal more intangible than a satisfied customer.

Probably the reader does not know what he or she wants out of life. That is, you do not have personal goals and objectives. Nor have you established policies, constraints, or restraints to see that you accomplish your goal. This is not unusual. If questioned about it, you would possibly say "You can't establish any objectives or goals because you don't know what's going to happen tomorrow, or next month, or next year, so you can't possibly set goals for the next twenty or forty years." This same attitude also prevails in some businesses. For example, a manager might say, "I can't set goals because I don't know what's going to happen next month." Some people even avoid establishing budgets because they say, "If we establish budgets, we can't stick to them, so why establish them?"

The idea in long-term personal planning toward objectives or in corporate planning for objectives, is that even if day-to-day circumstances do not go as anticipated (for example, a blowout in Oklahoma would delay a cross-country trip) the individual or corporation can always go back to the path after the unforeseen circumstance is overcome, or, if the company or individual cannot get back to the right path, then he or she can alter objectives in light of the new prevailing circumstance. For instance, if a person wanted to render a service to mankind in the health field and decided to become a doctor, and, if, upon applying to a medical school, found that he or she would be unable to get into that school, then he or she could alter the program by becoming a nurse or going into some other allied health field that would enable him or her to reach the long-term objective.

If a business projects sales of fifty million over the next year, and it appears the fifty million goal will not be met, then the company officials can take steps to bring their expenses in line with the actual results of their sales.

COMMUNICATION OF GOALS AND OBJECTIVES

One other thing we might bear in mind about goals and objectives is that it is necessary for all members of the team or company to be aware of the objectives. Too often, a complaint of top management is that "he is one of the top guys in this company and he ought to know our objectives." Too many times, however, no one has ever taken it upon himself to explain these objectives, nor written them down for all to study, and therefore several managers, supervisors and many employees are all at odds trying to accomplish some mythical objective for the corporation. Usually this objective takes on the personal flavor of that individual trying to accomplish it, rather than the goal management intended for everyone to strive toward.

The person who is just taking a job at any level, from the lowest to the highest, should try to make him- or herself aware of the company goals, the policies that lead toward the accomplishment of those goals, and try to see if those policies and goals coincide with his personal goals and objectives. If they do not and there is no way that they can coincide, then that person should not take the job to begin with because it is impossible to work unreservedly toward something to which he is opposed, or if he tries, he betrays himself and becomes a very inefficient, ineffective employee.

Jobs should be structured so people taking them can realize their own personal goals while working toward the total corporate objectives.

Long- and Short-Term Goals

Goals and objectives, like plans, tend to fall into categories of short-term, intermediate, and long-term aims with the short-term goals having the most specific objectives and long-term aims being the most general. Short-term goals are those that will be attained within one year. Intermediate goals are to be reached in more than one but less than five years. Long-term goals are those that will be attained in five or more years.

The most important long-term goal is survival. You might say that making a profit is the same as survival, but that is not necessarily true. Many institutions are unconcerned with making profits, paying dividends, and those things associated with profit-making companies, but are interested nevertheless in continued life. For instance, governmental groups, political parties, churches, schools, social and fraternal organizations, and others all have the goal of survival, but not the goal of profit.

Some profit-oriented companies will accept not making profits initially or during periods of economic lulls as long as the long-term goal of survival is not endangered.

There are some businesses that do not have survival as a long-term goal. These are companies whose specific goals are the accomplishment of particular missions. Once the missions are accomplished, the reason for existence disappears. Examples of this are political campaigns—the candidate wins or loses. In either case he or she does not need the organization any longer.

Profit-oriented companies usually are concerned with the distribution of profits as a second, long-term goal. Most companies propose to give investors a "fair" return on their investment and allocate remaining profits to corporate projects to maintain the stability and growth of the company.

Growth is a third, general objective for most companies, primarily because businessmen feel that if they are not expanding, then they are going backward. Some few companies do not wish to grow beyond a certain point because the existing owners might lose control, because the market might become saturated with the product, or because continued growth might encourage competition. But, most companies, governments, political parties, clubs, and organizations want to grow.

Along with these goals of survival, growth, and making profits, companies seek to satisfy social objectives—to pay fair wages, to satisfy customers, to overcome pollution problems, to provide opportunities for youth.

Short-range objectives, sometimes considered benchmarks for long-term goals, tend to be more specific. They might be written as follows:

1. Increase sales 5 percent per year for the next two fiscal years.
2. Cut production costs 2 percent through increased efficiency.
3. Increase inventory turnover from 10 to 12 times by holding a constant inventory with increasing sales.
4. Increase average wages by 6 percent per year with top producers getting 10 percent and marginal employees 3 percent (in addition to cost of living adjustments).
5. Add two new profitable products to the company's line each year.
6. Fill a minimum of 75 percent of management vacancies through internal promotion.

Short-term objectives can be company-wide, plant-wide, departmental or even six-month individual goals set through a conference with subordinates and supervisors. These objectives are specific and for a limited duration, but they are entwined with the corporate, long-term goals. For example:

Corporate long-term goal	Survival, make a reasonable profit.
Corporate short-term goal	Cut production costs 2% over next year to maintain 10% return on investment.
Departmental goal	Improve production efficiency by 7%.
Individual machinist's goal	Cut scrap losses by 10% over next year.

We will conclude this chapter by saying that for goals to be sound, they should be: (1) specific; (2) measurable in dollars, time, percentages, numbers, or some units, (3) obtainable in terms of accomplishment and authority, (4) challenging to the participants, (5) limited in time and scope, (6) specific in expected results, and (7) communicated within the company.

FOR DISCUSSION

1. *What are some reasons for having corporate goals?*
2. *Is everyone in the company or business encouraged to help set the corporate goals?*
3. *What is management by objectives (MBO)? Do you believe in it?*
4. *What are some characteristics of sound objectives?*
5. *Profit is the basic objective of all managers. Comment on this statement.*
6. *Discuss what you think are the long-term goals and the short-term objectives of your school.*

The Easy Election

"Well, Buddy, we got your name on the ballot," said Steve Babbage to his second-year classmate Harold Robinson. "Now, all we have to do is get you elected."

The ballot referred to was that for the election of the officers for the Student Government Association (SGA) of Freemont Community College. Robinson had been nominated for the presidency and was competing against three others: the quarterback of the winning Freemont Ferrets, an outspoken minority group leader who demanded equality as a part of the platform, and the incumbent president.

"You act as if the nomination was the hard part," Harold replied. "As much as I would like to win, I feel like the low man of a four-headed totem pole. Everyone else has something going for him—the top jock, the victim of discrimination, and the experienced officeholder. I don't have anythink going for me."

"Yes, you do," said Steve. "You have an organization behind you and that's more than any of the other candidates have. You have ten people who are willing to spend as much time as you need, and work as hard as you want them to to get you elected. All your opponents are acting as individuals and hoping something they've done in the past will get them elected. All you have to do is come up with a good plan which will use all our forces, and getting elected will be easy."

"Easy," thought Harold as he drove home that afternoon. "Getting elected will be easy *if* I come up with the right plan, but what do I know about planning?"

GUIDE QUESTIONS

1. *What should Harold's long range goal be? How could this be phrased in terms of problem solving as indicated in Chapter 2?*
2. *What are some specific objectives Harold would have to accomplish if he hopes to win?*
3. *Would having an organization really help him? Why?*

The Wondering Mrs. Watson

Several years ago, Mrs. Andrew (Minnie) Watson, a widow, invested $30,000 in a two-acre lot and a new fifty-foot multi-purpose building on the main street of Collinsville, a small suburban community. She started a day-care center for children from ages 2 through 10. The maximum capacity for this building is 40 children. Gross operating revenues at this level are approximately $28,000 annually. Mrs. Watson has been running at this maximum level for about a year now with a waiting list of applications.

Mrs. Watson enjoys her work with the children and takes much pride in the community response to her efforts to provide quality day care and training for her enrollees. She believes she could easily enroll another 40 children if she could have an addition built on to her existing facility. The enlargement would require a $10,000 capital expenditure by Mrs. Watson.

The market for a service of this type appears to be very favorable with growing interest being shown in government-financed projects. Labor costs and other necessary expenses due to strict governmental regulations on schools of this nature have kept Mrs. Watson's net profit at about 25 percent of her gross. This 25 percent includes her time—an average of 40 hours a week. This rate of profit is not expected to increase more than 5 percent to a total 30 percent net. She estimates it will take at least 5 years to pay off the $10,000 building loan as well as the balance of the original loan.

Realizing she someday may wish to withdraw her time and personal effort in this venture and hire a manager, Mrs. Watson has been considering investing $60,000 in a multi-unit apartment house instead of building the addition to the center. Other units could be added as capital permitted.

She had been assured by her banker that she could finance either or both of the projects without any cash outlay by using her valuable land as collateral.

By continuing to use the income from the school for living expenses and repaying her original loan, she could apply all the income from rentals toward repaying the $60,000 allowing for repair and other necessary expenses. This would take approximately eight years. She must consider the possibility of an increase in public housing and private owners flooding a booming market, thus affecting future profit expectations. Mrs. Watson wonders what she should do.

GUIDE QUESTIONS

1. *What do you think Mrs. Watson's long-term goal should be?*
2. *What alternatives would you recommend to best accomplish that goal? Why?*

At the conclusion of this chapter,
you should be able to—

- Identify the steps in planning.

- Explain which managers work on which plans.

- Give reasons why some managers oppose planning.

- List some causes for the failure of plans to materialize.

- State the pros and cons of writing plans.

- Describe situations in which group planning is advantageous or disadvantageous.

6

Planning to Reach Goals

Reading the preceding chapter and comparing it with the title of this chapter, it might appear that goals and objectives are not a part of planning. They are. In fact, goals are basic to planning, just as planning is basic to management. Once goals have been established by those responsible for planning, then, the planners can decide how they will accomplish the goals.

Planning is a mental effort. It is pre-action. It takes place before machines are ordered, before men are hired, before materials are purchased. Planning is looking to the future, foreseeing opportunities, anticipating problems, and shaping events. Planning is viewing alternative actions, from inception to conclusion, in a sequential, logical manner so that projects that appear destined for failure can be altered or arrested in the preliminary stages.

Planning is looking at the "big picture", seeing how all parts of a program fit together, so that there will be no great overreaction to what are actually minor problems in light of total objectives.

Formally defined, planning is a mental activity to devise and formulate steps necessary to accomplish predetermined objectives in spite of unforeseeable and uncontrollable events. Paraphrasing, we could say that planning is setting objectives, deciding what to do, and how to do it to accomplish these objectives.

Planning is not solely a top-management activity, although top management is most prominent when considering corporate objectives and programs. Planning is pervasive throughout an organization, just as it pervades one's personal life. For instance, if you choose politics as a career, you might decide that becoming an attorney will be one of your intermediate goals. You might ask yourself such questions as where am I now? What resources—mental, physical, motivational and financial—do I possess that would help me achieve this goal? What adverse circumstances must I overcome? Some obstacles to consider are: minimum grades for acceptance, limitations of class size at the law school, discriminatory policies at school or in legal practice, admission to the bar. What pathway, what channel must I pursue to meet my objectives? What steps must I take?

STEPS IN PLANNING

Planning is systematic. It is methodical and sequential. Let's look at the planning sequence to determine what steps a manager must follow to establish a framework for achieving a goal. For the following steps, the planner might be a top manager, a committee, many lower-level managers, or even rank and file workers, depending upon the type of organization.

1. The planner must evaluate his present circumstances. He or she must look not only for problems within the situation, but for opportunities as well. He or she must determine the relative position, how the company ranks in relation to others. For example, a supervisor might ask how a department ranks in relation to other departments. The planner must evaluate the assets, the strong points of the organization as it exists. He or she also must be realistic in stating weaknesses, and be cognizant of these as the planning progresses. If the planner does discover a problem or an opportunity, then he or she should clearly define it, state it as sharply and vividly as possible.

2. The planner must set specific, overall company goals, or review existing goals so that objectives for current planning will be within the range of corporate aims. The planner has to devise plans for each objective that will enhance the chances of success for the company and for the individuals involved in the company.

3. The planner must appraise and forecast unforeseeable and uncontrollable circumstances such as competition, government policy, supply and demand, the unions, availability of financial resources, and technological advances. Some of these circumstances might be defined as semicontrollable, but this would depend upon the company and or the individual department. Forecasts of such uncontrollable events might require the planner to predict what the economy would do over the next six months or six years, to predict what the union would ask for (or settle for) in the next bargaining session.

4. The planner must devise reasonable alternative courses of action in light of the inventory of raw materials. In this step, the planner must ascertain what would be available to the enterprise under different sets of circumstances and different courses of action. This provides flexibility. In a personal example, the planner might say, "I am making a hundred dollars a week now: if I decide to go to school and reduce my employment to part-time, what alternative sources of income are available to me?" A business planner might ask, "If we decide to double the capacity of this plant, is there enough manpower in this area to support the expansion?" Or, "If we attempt the expansion, can we finance without borrowing?" Or, "If we can't finance our expansion internally, can we attract outside loans and investments to facilitate the move?"

5. The planner must choose the alternative which, after an analysis of all courses of action, offers the most promise of achieving the objective. After the present position has been evaluated and projected, what can be expected from others not under his control. Then, a program can be adopted based on the accuracy of the predictions. He or she might also want to include the outline of an alternative strategy in case the predictions are wrong.

6. The planner must set forth details of the proposed action, stressing the principal

steps which must be taken to accomplish the objective. He or she should indicate the timing of the steps, both duration and sequence. Finally, the planner should note who is accountable for the successful completion of each step, and what resources that person will need to carry out the assignment.

7. The planner must devise a means of control or measurement of what was anticipated as the goal and what was actually accomplished. Control is also a comparison of progress along the way, comparing the anticipated with the actual, so that intermediate corrections might be made when necessary. If we anticipated an increase over last year's sales, then we could compare this year's income statements, month by month, with last year's statements, month by month, to see that we are on the way to accomplishing our goal. If we were not, how much are we missing the mark. Based on this knowledge, we could proceed to take necessary remedial action.

WHO PLANS?

We said earlier that everyone plans, but we should carry this one step further. All individuals do some planning, but the majority of all planning is done in quest of short-term goals, leaving the long-term goals to take care of themselves.

In a business enterprise, all managers do some planning. The higher the person's rank in management, the more planning he will do, and the more he will be concerned with forces outside the company. First-level managers, or supervisors, do a limited amount of planning, and most of this will be for the short-term achievements. However, the major portion of their time will be spent in activating subordinates, directing their actions, and controlling their activities. Planning for the first-level supervisor might take less than ten percent of his time; whereas, planning by the top manager might make up more than half of his work day.

For instance, top-management people might spend a considerable amount of time planning an evaluation system of the workers. This plan might include such things as the duration of evaluation periods, questions that should be asked of the worker, the method of evaluation (ranking or rating), the type of report to be submitted by the supervisor conducting the evaluation, possible recommendations to be made by the supervisor, and other related matters.

Once the plan has been completed and approved by other members of the management team, it would then be put into effect and become a part of the supervisor's work. By the time it has reached the first-line supervisor, the "what" has already been planned, the "how" has been planned, the "why" has been planned, the "who" and "how much" have been planned. The only thing left for the first-line supervisor to plan is the "when." He or she must plan a schedule of reviews for evaluating the workers. The evaluation procedure itself is a method of control for the first-line supervisor. He or she must compare what was expected of the employee, with what was achieved by him. The reasons for the gap, if there is a gap, must be determined, and recommendations made on how to reduce the gap in the future. First-line supervisors spend much more of their time in this control process, and in directing, than do top managers.

The control for the original planners, the higher-management people, would be that the supervisors conducted the proper number of evaluations of the workers for which they were being held accountable.

TIME SPAN OF PLANNING

As mentioned in the previous chapter, there are three general time spans in terms of planning: short-term planning which is less than one year, intermediate planning which is more than one year but less than five, and long-term planning which is for periods of more than five years. If we consider who plans in relation to time span, we will see a definite correlation between the time involved in planning and the person who plans.

The first-line supervisor seldom engages in intermediate or long-term planning. He or she is almost always confined to a short-term situation, possibly only hourly, daily, or weekly planning, and only seldom becoming involved in long-term planning. Top and middle managers are concerned more with intermediate and long-term planning. In making longer-range plans, managers often incorporate a series of short-range goals. For example, "By March 31, our sales should be at $300,000. On June 30, we should have reached $650,000 if we hope to maintain our projected growth." The planners would be interested in setting up sequential steps toward the accomplishment of long-term objectives, as opposed to the first-line supervisor whose short-term goals might be ends unto themselves.

When Neil Armstrong landed on the moon, he said, ". . . one small step for a man, one giant leap for mankind." In saying this, he was pointing out that while his immediate activity was to take one step, this single step was the culmination of the plans and activities of thousands of people who had invested time, money, and energy in the moon landing. The final goal was the accomplishment of the long-term goal, putting a man on the moon.

The baseball player looks at the results of each inning as progressive goals. Is the team ahead or behind? How wide is the gap? What are the chances of narrowing the gap? If the score is tied 4 to 4 in the last of the ninth, two men out, three and two count, and then the batter hits a home run which wins the game, his activity has just been one more step toward the achievement of an objective. Other activities prior to the home run might have altered the results. The catcher might have let a ball get by him, the left fielder might have dropped a fly ball, or a base runner might have tripped and fallen while rounding third base. But, the planner's plan to keep these things from happening included long hours of practice and coaching. In a competitive situation, one small mistake, one lapse, might cause the whole project to be lost.

NO PLANNING

If planning is a function of management, can it be assumed that all managers make detailed short-term, intermediate, and long-range plans? Absolutely not! We can see in our personal lives where we have failed to make plans, particularly the long-range variety. We can assume that managers also might make this mistake. In fact, managers even oppose planning for the following reasons:

1. Planning takes time away from other activities. Some managers feel they just cannot take the time from day-to-day activities to plan or to think things through to logical conclusions. Often, the reason they cannot take this time is that they are too busy "fighting fires," a term used to designate the immediate action necessary to deal with an unexpected condition or event. Many of these "fires" originate because there are no plans. Many of these fires are not really fires at all, but only minor deviations from what normally might be anticipated.

2. Planning is pre-action and not very exciting. Putting out fires, on the other hand is the essence of action. It makes men heroes. The man on the floor of the production area shouting commands to his subordinates, rushing around, maybe even jumping in and doing the work himself, certainly has the appearance of being a greater company "saviour" than the guy sitting in his office, staring at the ceiling and making notes on a yellow, legal pad.

3. The results of planning are too distant. The results of long-term planning are long in coming, and even when they do arrive, they may have been altered beyond recognition because of necessary, strategic, counter measures. Then, the planner does not experience the emotional satisfaction of a job well done, whereas a foreman who gets the line going again after a shutdown gets instant satisfaction, and probably praise and respect from fellow workers. The planner might get just the opposite reaction from fellow workers because he or she is not visibly contributing to production.

4. Planning is limiting. Some managers say, "If I see an opportunity to do something or to buy something not included in the budget, then I won't be able to accomplish the goal. Probably, I'll miss a lot of good opportunities with a budget hanging over my head all the time." Managers who feel this way overlook the possibility of flexible budgets that permit the operator to move quickly into areas of opportunity not anticipated by the plan, yet still keep the plans on target.

5. Planning costs too much. "People who spend their time planning are getting paid for nonproductive activities. Planning is a job to be undertaken during periods of prosperity when the company can afford to have people just sit and think and plan." Those who think planning costs too much do not feel that no planning costs anything at all. However, not planning is a symptom of poor management and one of the greatest causes of all business failures. In addition, such managers, although outwardly opposed to planning, are constantly involved in planning to get out of problem areas which might have been avoided by initial planning.

WHY PLANS FAIL

Planning is not an absolute guarantee of success. Some plans do fail. One of the reasons for this failure is that the planner does not have the necessary knowledge to formulate an accurate plan. For instance, an extremely creative advertising person might originate some appealing television commercials aimed at selling industrial machinery. But, what he or she might overlook is that machine tools are sold primarily on the basis of personal contact, and documented evidence of productivity and durability. An expensive campaign of television commercials might not produce any sales whatesoever.

A second reason for the failure of a plan is that the goals are totally unrealistic. For a buyer of high fashion, ladies apparel to buy a whole line of spring clothes because they appealed to him or her would be courting disaster if he or she did not compare personal feelings with the tastes of customers. The plan should be to buy what customers want even if the styles are ridiculous.

Third, plans fail because the planner does not project the program over a long period of time. He or she blunders through the program, going from one extreme to another, trying to adjust to every short-term variation. The manager has failed to observe the plan from an overall standpoint, allowing for minor variations from time to time.

Scapegoating is a fourth cause of failure. This occurs when a manager, sensing a discrepancy between what was anticipated and what has been produced, concentrates his or her efforts on finding a person to blame for the shortcoming. As one manager put it, "I've been able to stay in this job for eighteen years because of my ability to delegate blame." Where might he have been with a more positive attitude?

Plans fail because those persons responsible for carrying them out do not understand the plans, do not know what they are supposed to be doing. This is a result of poor communications, a topic which we will explore later, in greater depth.

A final reason for the failure of plans is that the planner has over- or underestimated the strengths and weaknesses of the company and its employees. The planner has failed to identify the company's niche—the particular position in which it can best compete and operate. This failure to estimate properly the strengths and weaknesses of a company could easily put the company in a competitive situation where it is unable to compete or omit an opportunity where it might succeed with relative ease.

Not planning is not always worse than planning if that planning is poor. In fact, there are smaller companies which have succeeded in spite of the fact that the goals and operating plans were only vague concepts in the owners' minds, never written or spoken, but somehow left to subordinates. However, it should be evident that planning is highly desirable and that a judicious and careful approach to planning will heighten the probability of favorable results.

TO WRITE OR NOT TO WRITE

Although some managers might say triumphantly that they and their companies have been successful without ever having put a plan on paper, it is preferable that plans be written. Written plans require the planner to think the plan through, stating ideas in precise language. Plans can be evaluated much better by all parties concerned when they can study the plan. An oral presentation of a plan with many "you know's" and repeated use of the same adjectives might cause the participants to initiate action in opposite directions, without any sense of priority or timing, but with the hope of accomplishing the same objectives and feeling united in their cause.

If the company is large and the plans must be transmitted to various departments, and through many layers of management and production workers, it would be nearly impossible for the lower-level managers and their subordinates to have the same interpretation of the plan given to it at its inception. If a plan is written, then somewhere in that plan is a statement of accountability. When a planner devises a plan, he makes someone responsible for carrying it out, someone responsible of the implementation of the plan. In unwritten plans, responsibility is vague at best with no one wanting to assume more responsibility than he or she is supposed to assume, and virtually no one willing to assume the blame in the event of failure.

Written plans are good reference material for those trying to implement a program. A carpenter will regularly refer to a house plan to see if progess is in keeping with what the planner has specified. Without the written plan, the understanding of the carpenter about what he must do might be quite different.

There are some disadvantages to having a written plan, but they are few. There is a possibility that a plan might be misinterpreted, but this same possibility exists if the plan is presented orally, and the probability for misintepretation is even greater. A meeting—an interchange of ideas between the planner and those responsible for its implementation—is a way by which this problem can be overcome.

Written plans are more limiting than oral plans. This might not be desirable from a management point of view. A board of directors may not want to inhibit the general manager of the company, but the board could give him or her a plan with built-in flexibility, allowing for alterations as needed.

The positive results of writing plans outweighs any disadvantages or limitations that writing might put upon the persons carrying out the plans. If the person reading the plan feels too limited by it, then he or she could ask for more authority. If granted, his or her responsibility and coverage might be broadened.

GROUP PLANNING

Until now, we have discussed planning in terms of individuals. Perhaps we should spend some time examining the advantages and disadvantages of group planning.

Everyone has been involved at one time or another in a group decision as a member of a committee, or some other type of group. You might have been asked to help prepare the budget or a part of the budget for your church, or possibly, to approve the budget once it had been prepared by others. Maybe you've been involved in a group action in your school. Let's reflect a moment on the good points of getting a committee involved in planning.

First, as in the case of the church budget, all organizations can be involved. It is necessary for the total budget to represent all the members and groups of the church,

just as it might be necessary to have the different departments of a business represented. If only one person prepares the budget, he or she might overlook many important aspects of the goals and objectives of the church. He or she might, in fact,
substitute personal objectives for those which have been adopted by the congregation. We can see that it is important to have group participation when the judgment
or the involvement of the total membership is needed. Without group participation,
facts might be overlooked, intentionally or not.

Second, if a group plans an activity, the individuals within the group are more
likely to carry out the activity because they feel they are a part of it. If the plan is
made by someone else and presented to them, those involved might reject the plan,
might not understand it, and might make a disaster of it before they are finished
working on it.

Third, group participation gives a social outlet, provides some fulfillment of
social needs of the individuals in the organization, and an opportunity to exchange
ideas and thoughts with coworkers. Even isolationists or shy people within the company, who would not on their own, initiate group action, or work with others, can
be assigned to committees with the thought that this is a social outlet as well as a
method of obtaining a group decision to be implemented by the group.

However, there are some objections to group decisions and committee work. To
begin with, committees operate rather slowly. The larger the committee, the slower
it acts. The members are not reluctant to act, but oftentimes, because of other commitments, they might not be able to meet conveniently. If the group is extremely
large, for example, a board of directors of a community-fund drive, this problem can
be overcome by appointing a smaller, executive committee of three to five members
who are authorized to make decisions and commitments on behalf of the entire committee. This can speed up the process, but nevertheless, committee action is slower
than individual action.

The second disadvantage of committees is that they are expensive. In a business
organization, each person is hired to perform certain functions, and to appoint someone to a committee, might deprive that person of the needed time to perform his or her
work. Each new person added to a committee is an added expense in that he or she is
not performing other activities. Even if we say serving on committees is part of a job,
we would still be paying each person for the committee service. Conscientious persons
might make up that time by working late, yet, others might consider committee duties
as an excuse from regular duties. Several committee assignments might result in demands for more assistants for those persons deprived of regular working hours. If ten
persons making an average of five dollars an hour are assigned to a committee, that
committee costs the company fifty dollars an hour. Add to that, the additional time
needed to complete committee assignments, the assistance given to the members by
others, the clerical and secretarial help needed to keep records and prepare exhibits,
and the work time lost because decision makers and supervisors were in a committee
meeting. It is easy to see that committees are expensive.

The third problem with committees is that there is a lack of responsibility for the
decisions made. Committee members might be inclined to make more radical deci-

sions if they feel that someone else will carry them out rather than having to do it themselves. Committees that set sales goals might be inclined to set those goals extremely high if they, themselves, do not have to make the sales. If the goals are totally unrealistic, and, if at some point in the future, it becomes apparent that the goals will not be reached, then it will be hard to blame an entire committee for not setting goals properly. Little action can be taken against a committee for poor decisions regardless of how bad those decisions were. It is certainly easier to find an individual responsible for an action and deal with him or her. The individual, by the same token, knowing that he or she alone is responsible, will be more realistic about the recommended plans knowing that he or she will be held responsible for the successful completion of that program.

We have listed four reasons for using committees and three for not using them. The manager, in trying to determine whether or not to make use of committee action, should consider these reasons and be satisfied that the use of the committee outweighs the general disadvantages of committees before turning a project over for committee action.

DISSEMINATION OF PLANS

Earlier in this chapter we said that plans ought to be written. This takes time and costs money, but ultimately, it seems to be a worthwhile endeavor. Once those plans have been written, there should be some responsibility for seeing to it that the plans are distributed to those people who have a need for those plans. To have an elaborate preparation of plans and then not to allow, or for that matter, require, everyone concerned to see them, is defeating the purpose of the plan.

Marriages fail because the partners do not communicate, because they do not understand each other, because they are tugging in opposite directions. This also applies to business associates. The business might fail because of a lack of communication of plans to the participants.

Plans should not be isolated. Any plans in a social system affect not only those toward whom the action is directed, but also affects those who are indirectly hit by the waves of that action. Generally, there is a limited supply of money, so each time plans are approved allowing one department to spend, such approval will cause money to be unavailable to another department. An addition to one department's budget will cause a deletion in another budget, or perhaps, will result in several other departmental budgets. All departments involved in any change should be made aware of what is happening so that the people can be prepared to do what is expected of them. Individuals who are not made aware of the rules in a company cannot be expected to obey those rules. The fact that he "ought to know" is not a legitimate reason for punishing a man for an infraction of a rule or policy which was never explained, never written, one which was never interpreted. Rules which have not been disseminated to those persons expected to abide by them, are not rules at all, and punishment for infractions to these unwritten rules are viewed as arbitrary actions. Arbitrary action is a problem that management must avoid at all times so that employees will not regard management as an enemy. We will not attempt to discuss the advantages and disadvantages of a union in a company at this point, but we might stress that unions (like governments, consumers, competitors, suppliers, and other forms of influence) bind managers, make them less flexible, and inhibit growth. Pressures put on management by unions are generally in response to actions taken by a management which will not regulate itself.

We will discuss communications again in a later chapter, but for now it should be stressed that management plans and related information should be distributed to all participants so that everyone concerned will be aware of what is to happen and what role he or she is to play.

FOR DISCUSSION

1. *What is meant by the "big picture?"*
2. *Describe the steps of planning.*
3. *What are the time spans of planning?*
4. *For what reasons might managers oppose planning?*
5. *Why do plans fail?*
6. *Written plans are for production workers. Managers understand what the company is trying to accomplish. Discuss these statements.*
7. *Discuss the pros and cons of committee planning.*
8. *Write a plan to accomplish one of your personal or work-related goals.*

The Disagreeable Agreement

"No way," Sally Amos told Jill Peabody, her roommate, "There's no way that I could have gotten less than an *A* in the typing course. She told us 25 words a minute for a *C*, 35 for a *B* and 45 fo ran *A*. I averaged 48 words on the last three tests and there's no way I could have gotten a *B*. This stupid *B* ruins my average and the stupid teacher gave it to me when I didn't deserve it."

"What are you going to do about it?" asked Jill.

"I'm going to see her, that's what. She can't give me a *B*. She knocked me off the Honor Roll with it. She can't do it, not after she told us how she graded. She makes me sick. This whole thing makes me sick. There must be a mistake. I've gotta go see her right now."

Sally slammed her door and started to run toward Wilton Hall, grade sheet in hand, to see her typing teacher, Miss Jessica Jones. When Sally reached Miss Jones' office, she knocked at the door and went in without waiting for a response.

"Miss Jones," Sally said as she waved her grades in the air. "This grade sheet says I got a *B* in typing and that can't be right. I was supposed to get an *A*."

"Hold on a minute, Sally," Miss Jones said. "Let me check my grade book. Let's see, 'Amos, Sally. *B*'. That's right."

"It can't be right," Sally protested. "I was averaging 48 words a minute and you said if we got 45 that would be an *A*."

"Yes," Miss Jones said with a smile, "But I didn't know so many of you would do so well. Over half the class was getting fifty words or better and I had to give them *A*s. If I had given *A*s, to the 45-to-50 wpm's, then about 80 percent of the class would have gotte*n A*s. That wouldn't have looked good at all."

"Why not?" said Sally, "You set the standard and I measured up to it. I deserve an *A*."

"Now look, Sally, that *A* would represent excellent work and I don't see how you could consider your work excellent. As a matter of fact, you were below average for the class and I'm not so sure you deserved even a *B*. After all, *C* is the grade for average."

"But you told us . . ."

"Go on now, Sally, and think about it for a while. I'm sure you'll see that I'm right," said Miss Jones.

As Sally walked away from Wilton Hall, she wondered what her next step should be.

GUIDE QUESTIONS

1. *If Miss Jones were a first level manager in a manufacturing plant and Sally and Jill were her subordinates, what kind of a reaction might follow an arbitrary action similar to the one Miss Jones took?*
2. *Should an objective of a school be for all students to make As in every subject?*
3. *Do unwritten plans help or hinder those people involved in carrying out those plans?*
4. *Do you agree with Miss Jones that about 80 percent of the class would have gotten an A and that wouldn't have looked good at all. Why?*

CASE 6–2

Rattled Mr. Randle

At one point, Mason Randle thought he was an enlightened foreman of an enlightened company, but now he felt he had reason to question his former assumptions. In fact, he questioned his attitude to the extent that he was considering turning in his notice and leaving the company.

About a year earlier, Mason's boss, Bert Palmer, the production manager, had called Mason and the other eleven foremen to his office.

"The top brass says we've got to go to a system of MBO, management by objectives, for those of you who don't know," he told the foremen. "I've never worked under the system. All I know about it right now is that we get together, me and each of you individually, and we agree on specific goals for you and on ways to measure your work. Then we meet fairly regularly during the year for progress reports and have a final annual review."

Mason liked the idea immediately. He had felt for some time that the guidelines for evaluating a foreman were too vague to be meaningful and that all attempts on Palmer's part to evaluate his subordinates had developed into personality contests with the last critical incident, good or bad, playing too great a role.

Later, at a private meeting with Palmer, Mason and Palmer had agreed that a realistic objective in Mason's department would be a 10 percent rise in production without a corresponding cost increase. (There were housekeeping, reporting, and training objectives, too, but they are not pertinent to the case).

After some thought about the matter, Mason concluded that he could reach the 10-percent increase by concentrating in the areas of production, scrap rates, and absenteeism. He could make the productivity goal if he could: (a) increase production 10 percent and maintain absenteeism and scrap rates at their current levels; or, (b) increase production 5 percent and reduce absenteeism from 10 percent to 7 percent and scrap losses from 5 percent to 3 percent. Further reductions in absenteeism and scrap losses or increases in production would result in Mason and his department exceeding the set goal.

Mason reviewed the departmental goal with each of his men and reviewed their individual production, absence, and scrap records. Each man then chose his own combination of increases and decreases to help reach the departmental goal of 10 percent increased productivity. Mason further told his men that their work would be measured against their objectives.

Those men who met their objectives would be recommended for an average raise of 5 percent; those who failed would be recommended for no raise, or a slight increase only, and, those who exceeded their goals would receive recommendations for up to a 10 percent increase.

Mason was very encouraged by the response from his men. They were excited about the new approach. Almost immediately, absenteeism and scrap losses dropped noticeably while production increased. Mason continued to be impressed as he met with his men and Palmer periodically for progress reports.

At his annual evaluation meeting with Palmer, Mason was pleased with himself and his men. Not only had they achieved the 10 percent he and Palmer had agreed upon, they had recorded an astounding 18 percent increase in production.

"Think you can do it again?" Palmer asked.

"Not unless I get the raises I promised the men," Mason said. "They know I respect them, but they want something more tangible."

Mason submitted a list of recommended increases for his men to Palmer. Recommended were two men for 1 percent, 2 for 3 percent, 6 for 5 percent, 4 for 7 percent, and 15 for 10 percent.

Two days later Palmer called Mason to his office.

"Mason, I'm afraid I'm going to have to turn you down on some of these raises."

"Why?" Mason asked.

"Too top heavy. You recommended over half of your men for the maximum raise. We can't operate like that."

"I don't know why you say that. Over half of my men did exceptional work. They were the ones who increased the productivity by 18 percent. That alone should be enough to justify the raises."

"Well, Mason, I'm just not going to be able to say yes to your recommendations. When you recommend for your men, we expect a few minimums and a few maximums, but we expect most of them to be in the middle. I can't approve more than three at the maximum level. Why don't you just pick out your three best men for the maximum raise and we'll give the others an average raise. After all, if everybody does great work, then great work is just average, isn't it?"

GUIDE QUESTIONS

1. *Define Mason Randle's problem.*
2. *What courses of action are open to him now?*
3. *How could this situation have been avoided?*
4. *How would you expect Randle to act toward MBO next year?*

At the conclusion of this chapter,
you should be able to—

- Classify various types of plans.
- Differentiate between general and competitive strategies.
- Trace the general procedure involving the use of a purchase order.
- State how rules differ from other plans.
- Explain the nature and make up of budgets.

7

Classifying Plans

Suppose our businessman read the following article in the newspaper:

Washington, D.C. "Smoking one cigarette should not be grounds for dismissal, and we're going to see to it that those guys don't get away with it." Harold E. Robinson, spokesman for the striking laundry workers at Sunbeam Dry Cleaning and Storage Company, told reporters today.

Those "guys" Robinson referred to are the officials of Sunbeam. What they are trying to get away with is firing a man for what Robinson calls a "minor infraction," a momentary act of forgetfulness."

"There's nothing at all minor about smoking in our warehouse," says company president C. George Wilson. "We pledge to our customers that we will protect their clothing from fire, theft, and insect damage. The action of this man threatened our ability to carry out the pledge. Last night when our watchman was making his rounds, he smelled smoke and immediately called the fire department. Between the time he called and the time the engines arrived, he searched for the source of the smoke. He found Robinson, a second-shift pressman, in the storage area, smoking."

Warren P. Van Dyke, the watchman, said he told Robinson to put out his cigarette and then told Robinson's supervisor about the incident. The supervisor immediately instructed Robinson to clock out, leave the company premises, and report to the personnel office the next morning. When he reported as instructed, Robinson was fired by the personnel manager, Scott A. Chambers, who said, "To have done anything less than this would have put our entire business in jeopardy. Our workers must be made to realize the seriousness of company regulations."

Robinson stood in front of the company for the rest of the morning, and then spoke with the workers as they went to lunch. More than seventy percent of the employees did not return for the afternoon shift.

GOALS AND OBJECTIVES

A businessman might have seen that there were five types of planning exhibited in this article. The first of these is one which we have discussed before—*setting goals and objectives*. In this case, the major goal of Sunbeam was to provide the customers with a secure and safe storage area for clothing. A second objective of making a profit would be realized if Sunbeam could accomplish the first goal.

OTHER TYPES OF PLANS

A second type of plan exemplified by the news story is that of *policy*. A policy is a guide which sets general boundaries within which a company will operate. It sets up a framework to which managers must refer when making decisions.

In the case of the storage company, a statement of policy might have read "the company will provide for its customers a fireproof smoking area. Employees are to smoke only in that area." The policy is specific.

The third type of plan pointed out by the story is *strategy*, the use of alternative programs (unified action plans) under various circumstances. There are two types of strategy: (1) general, or grand, strategy and, (2) competitive strategy. The general strategy spells out the normal mode of operation, the program to be followed if events happen as anticipated. The other type, competitive strategy, states what the company will do in light of what other companies are doing and how management will react to change. For instance, a major television network will run its regular programs under normal circumstances, but in cases of extraordinary news, unfavorable ratings, special events, and other happenings, regular programming will be pre-empted and competitive programming aired.

In this case, we are concerned with general strategy, the regular program to implement policy. According to the news story, the grand strategy concerning security was to hire a watchman who patrolled the warehouse. Competition, technological progress, or some other external pressure might cause changes in this strategy. Television scanning of the entire plant, operated by a single control unit might replace the watchman. Or, perhaps the use of security dogs might be considered. However, the present strategy is to use a security guard.

Detailed plans of what that security officer is to do are called *procedures*, the fourth type of planning in the story. Procedures are guides to action. They are specific items and are stated sequentially. Although it cannot be read directly from the article, we can presume that the watchman was following detailed procedures, probably according to schedule, so that he would be at a particular place at a specific time. This kind of procedure is often controlled by having the worker check in at various stations throughout the warehouse by using some sort of a mechanical time device.

The second procedure the watchman followed would come under the category of "What to do if such and such happens." In this case, the procedure might state, "If the watchman smells smoke, sees flames, or has any other evidence of a fire or smoking, the first thing he must do is call the nearest fire department. Next, he should try to locate the source of the suspected fire. Third, he should. . . ."

Another procedure that the watchman might follow could be: "If the watchman should observe someone smoking in the warehouse, he immediately should order that person to extinguish the lighted tobacco. He then should ask the smoker to leave the warehouse. If the smoker is an employee of the company, the watchman should notify the smoker's supervisor so that the supervisor might take further action. If the smoker is not an employee of the company, the watchman should try to ascertain the smoker's name, his company affiliation, and his reason for being in the warehouse. The watchman should report this information to the person in charge of the shift, or to the personnel manager, as soon as possible."

The fifth plan which can be seen in the news article is the *rule*. Rules are specific, written guides for personal behavior of employees, in our example. Normally, these rules would be accompanied by a list of punishments and reprimands for violations of these rules. Punishments usually run from an oral warning to immediate dismissal of the employee, based on the severity of the violation and the record of previous violations. Consistent infractions of the same rule, even a minor rule, without a definite change or attempt to change, might be grounds for termination.

In the case of the laundry, the rule probably said something like, "There will be absolutely no smoking in the warehouse under any circumstances because of the danger of fire. A first offense violation of this rule will bring about the immediate dismissal of the violator."

We do not know what strategy company officials will use to get the Sunbeam employees back on the job. It is evident that the general strategy has broken down, and officials will have to implement a competitive strategy (If they do that, then we'll do this), but let us move into a deeper discussion of policies, strategies, procedures and rules.

POLICY

To repeat, policy is a general guide that sets up boundaries within which a company or any other organization will operate. Suppose our pool director would go to the board of directors and propose that they build a new olympic-size pool. She might say to them, "We can estimate the cost of the pool, collect membership dues for the down payment, borrow the balance, and ask our members to pledge to repay the debt over a long period of time."

One of her board members might respond by saying, "Barbara, I'm sorry, but that's not the policy of this club. It was built on a policy of pay as we go. The original club building, pool, and all the additions were built when we had ready capital and not before. There's never been any debt against this club, and as long as our present policy is in effect, there will never be any debt against it."

Barbara might: (1) become upset with this policy and consider leaving (2) accept it without question saying only that she was unaware of it, or (3) question it to determine if the same conditions which existed when the policy was devised, continue to exist. If they don't, then she may be in a position to advocate and win approval for a policy change.

But, what are some business policies, and in what areas might policies be appropriate? Policies generally apply to the company as a whole. There are some policies which fall below company level to a regional area or even a departmental level but there are only a few of them. For instance, policies dealing with matters relating to employees would normally be company-wide. If not, those employees who feel they are being slighted would demand that they get as much or more than their coworkers.

Let's examine a few examples of corporate policy in the major functional areas:

1. Production:
    a. The company will produce hot, molded plastic products for the consumer industry.
    b. The company will have a three-shift, seven-day continuous flow operation.
    c. All machinery must have at least a two-year payback.
    d. Production supervisors will have a wide span of control.

2. Finance:
    a. Shipments will be made on a cash-in-advance or a c.o.d. basis only. No credit will be extended.
    b. Debt financing will be used to the greatest extent possible to maintain existing ownership.
    c. No dividend payments will be made in the immediate future. Internally generated cash will be used to finance expansion.
    d. All employees will be given annual financial reports so they might better understand the position of the company.

3. Sales:
    a. Sell through wholesaler vendors only.
    b. Sell only in the southeast United States.
    c. Do cooperative newspaper advertising only.
    d. Include both salary and incentive pay in salesmen compensation plans.

Although personnel is not one of the three major functions, we might want to look at some examples of the policies we could adopt with regard to the workers.

4. Personnel:
    a. All employees must have a high-school education or its equivalent.
    b. The company will pay life and health insurance for the employees only. Family coverage will be available at the employees' option and cost.
    c. Wages will be competitive with other manufacturing companies in the area.
    d. All efforts will be made to give every employee adequate training to accomplish his or her particular job.
    e. Every employee will have a job description.

These are some samples of policy we might find in any manufacturing company. These policies would have been originated by, or at least approved by, the board of directors. The policies would be guides for the managers at all levels of the company. A policy to promote from within would be as appropriate for choosing a new president as it would be for choosing a new foreman in the production area.

Policies, like other plans, should be written. The need for a policy or its justification also should be written. If a question should arise as to whether or not the policy is valid, or is no longer necessary, then a quick reference check can be made to see why the policy was adopted in the first place. If the reason for its adoption has changed, then quite probably the policy itself needs updating.

Policies are not always controlled from within, but are influenced greatly by external causes. For instance, the above-mentioned policy in personnel stated that the company would pay wages comparable to other manufacturers in the area. This policy would have been influenced by unions, by government, by supply and demand, or by competitors. Of course, many policies come from within, and any number of them reflect the thinking of a single person—the chief executive of the company.

In actual practice, the writing of a policy may come long after the policy has been put into effect.

PRECEDENCE AS POLICY

"We've always done it that way." We know from this quote that in spite of the fact that the policy was not written, or, even if it were written, regardless of how it was written, the current interpretation of the policy would be what this speaker was talking about. If management allows the members of the organization to do something contrary to the written policy, then the written policy becomes void and the action becomes policy instead. Unenforced policy yields to precedent.

Some policy is implied although it probably should be written, too. For instance, we can assume that although it was unwritten that ". . . this company shall follow the dictates of the federal, state, and local laws" the members of the company are expected to observe this implied policy.

Policies should be written in easy-to-understand terms. If the policy seems ambiguous, those who have the responsibility of carrying it out should take it upon themselves to get a concrete, specific interpretation of the policy.

Policies should undergo evaluation periodically to determine whether the current policy is facilitating the work at hand, or if by some external or internal change, the policy has become inoperative or obsolete. If it should appear to anyone that a policy has deteriorated enough to become a hindrance, the policy should be reformulated in light of the new conditions. It might also be worthwhile to evaluate the policy considering what it says should be done, versus what is actually being done. The reasoning behind such an evaluation is that the policy itself might be good, but its interpretation might be quite different from what was written.

STRATEGIES

The general strategy of a company is its program of operation that will prevail as long as operating conditions are normal. It is the game plan. Time after time, as we view the news or hear the wrap up after an athletic event, we hear the sportscaster ask, "Coach, did you follow your game plan?" If the game was won by a lopsided score, the coach will probably say "Yes. We expected them to . . . and they did exactly as we expected and fell right into our hands. We didn't deviate one bit from our plan." If the game is close, the coach might have a different answer: "We followed the game plan up until they. . . . Then we had to change our strategy to counter their moves."

Another example of this strategy can be found in a game of chess. The general, opening moves in chess are to mobilize the chess pieces as quickly as possible, in order to gain the advantage over the opponent. Any move made that would not directly mobilize the mover's pieces or actively interfere with the opponent's mobilization, would be a wasted move. Of course, it is possible to win the game by calling checkmate after a few moves, but only if the opponent is playing badly.

If you were playing chess, you would try to quickly mobilize your pieces, and your opponent should be trying to mobilize his, too. If he or she should begin an attack on your king prematurely, you should carefully evaluate your grand strategy to determine whether or not you should counter attack (a competitive strategy) or, defend your king reasonably well while you continue to mobilize your men. This defense might keep your opponent from checking your king, and give you the advantage of having your men mobile long before .

Suppose that a recently widowed mother with several children decides to supplement her income by starting a sewing business. Her policy is that she will work on clothes for individuals, doing alterations rather than make new garments. She will have to adopt a strategy for obtaining work. She might decide to go to other seamstresses in the same business and ask them to refer customers to her if they are overloaded, or suggest that they take the work and then subcontract it to her. In this way she can avoid advertising and, as a subcontractor, avoid dealing directly with customers.

She might decide, instead, that she will make an aggressive effort to attract new business by advertising in the local paper. "No one else advertises," she might say, "so I'll take a couple of ads, and develop a following from those people who have been unsuccessful in finding a seamstress. I'll have a big business before any of the other seamstresses know what's happening."

This example is an application of grand strategy. Suppose our seamstress does saturate the market for one week with ads and gets all the work that she can handle for a very long time, then her strategy will have succeeded. She will not have to change her initial strategy. But, suppose a competitor had seen her ad in the paper the first day and had countered her ad with a larger one, and then a third seamstress had countered both ads with an even larger ad, promising quicker delivery at lower prices! Our seamstress would be in a jam. Not only has she spent money for the ads, but she still doesn't have a sufficient amount of work to provide her with a livelihood. At this point, she might revert to her initial strategy, or ask her competitors for excess work. She might even develop some other competitive program.

A business strategy for a company might be that every six months the president would recommend a new product to the board for approval, but only after that product had been through an extensive twelve month research program which indicated that it is a marketable item. This would be part of the grand strategy and each six months a new product would appear before the board for approval or disapproval. If approved, the item would go into production immediately.

Suppose this is the same company which adopted the policy that it would manufacture consumer products from plastic. What might happen to the company in case of an oil shortage which would cause a shortage of raw materials? Plastics will be in short supply. The company might find itself working with another raw material, and might find that its lead time for research had been cut drastically. Instead of having twelve months to do research on another plastic product, management might find that it must find a paper, metal, or wood product within six months, or even three months. Competition for oil has caused the company to change its grand strategy. The company might also find that a competitor has developed a superior product and would find that its grand strategy would have to be switched to a competitive strategy just to stay in business. This is a reactionary strategy. If a football team finds that the pass defense of the opposition is too great to overcome, then it must change its grand strategy to a competitive strategy of going through the line on the ground, to a running game.

PROCEDURES

Procedures are plans for operations that will be repeated again and again. They are used primarily at a working level by operating personnel who are told "how to" through these procedures. Means of accomplishing tasks are not left to the operating personnel: they are required to follow procedures.

In the army, most things are done according to standard operating procedure. These procedures tell the men what they will wear, when to wear it, how they will wear their uniforms, when they must salute, how they will salute, how many paces away from the superior whom they are to salute they must be before they do salute, within what distance they must salute, how to arrange foot lockers, how to walk guard duty, and what to do if you are approached by someone while on guard. These are just a few examples of the many procedures outlined in the soldiers guide, a handbook given to new recruits.

A ritual in a church or synagogue would be a procedure. The procedure might tell the minister, rabbi, or priest conducting the service exactly when to hold his hands up, when to pray, when to ask the participants to kneel, bow their heads, or make some other gesture. The procedure would prescribe the garments to be worn, the vessels, books, and other objects to be used, the readings, songs, and prayers.

In business, there are also many procedures. One of the core documents of a business is a purchase order—an official document requesting a vendor or supplier to furnish the company with an article or service for which the company agrees to pay a stated amount. Let's look at a procedure to be followed when making a purchase:

1. The person requiring an item or service must initiate the process of purchasing

by completing a requisition in duplicate, having it authorized by the department head and distributing it as follows:

Copy 1—to purchasing department
Copy 2—to be retained by requisitioner.

2. The purchasing department, upon receipt of the requisition, shall check with the storeroom to determine if the article is in inventory. If it is, purchasing shall instruct the stockroom to deliver the item to the requisitioner, obtain a signed delivery receipt, and send copies of the delivery receipt to purchasing, accounting, retaining one for the storeroom files.

   If the article is not in stock, the purchasing department shall initiate the purchase.

3. The purchasing department will issue either: (a) a request for bid, or (b) a purchase order. The request for bid is for articles that are not normally ordered by the purchasing department. The request for bid shall be made to at least three approved vendors. The fourth copy of the bid request will be sent to a fourth vendor if deemed necessary by the purchasing department, or it will be destroyed, and the fifth copy will be kept on file by the purchasing department. At the end of the bidding time, the purchasing department will award a contract to the selected bidder, and a purchase order will be prepared. The purchase order of seven parts shall be distributed as follows:

   Copy 1 to the vendor,
   Copy 2 to the vendor (acknowledgment copy),
   Copy 3 to the accounting department,
   Copy 4 to the receiving department,
   Copy 5 to the requisitioner,
   Copy 6 to be retained in purchasing,
   Copy 7 to be retained in purchasing (for expediting).

   Any discrepancies between the description on the purchase order and the part as described by the requisitioner should be noted at this time. Expected arrival dates of items should be noted on the copies. Vendors should be instructed to send three copies of their invoices and those copies will be distributed as follows:

   Copy 1 to the purchasing office,
   Copy 2 to accounting office,
   Copy 3 to receiving department.

4. When receiving has the shipment from the vendor, receiving personnel will compare the shipment with the packing slip, the purchase order and the invoice. Receiving will prepare a receiving report in triplicate noting any over, short, or damaged items, and will send the original to the purchasing department, the second copy to the requisitioner, keeping the third copy for its files.

5. Upon receipt of the report from the receiving department, the purchasing department will: (a) issue a voucher to the accounting office certifying the invoice for payment, or (b) if the shipment is not in order, take necessary steps to verify or clarify the order so that a voucher can be prepared and sent to accounting.

In the production department, almost every part to be made or assembled will be accompanied by a procedural report or a shop traveler giving step-by-step details of how the worker is to complete the objective. His work plan might begin as follows: (a) Select stainless steel bar stock, $2'' \times 2'' \times 6''$; (b) place workpiece between centers on the engine lathe 17. Check critical areas A, F, and J with micrometers to determine conditions or tolerances; 100% inspection required.

When building, a contractor may have detailed procedures so the workmen will know exactly what they are doing, what is expected of them and what sequence they are to follow, not deviating from these plans in the least.

RULES

Rules are guides for the personal behavior of employees, members of a country club, the school, the business, or any association. There are rules for all employees from the president to the entry-level person, for the generals as well as privates, for club managers, the lifeguards, and the members. Rules tell you what you can do and what you cannot do, what you must do and what you must not do. Rules apply to dress, hairstyles, beards and mustaches, smoking, tardiness, absenteeism, methods of notification, breakage, drinking on the job, loafing, and to a multitude of behavioral activities expected of an individual.

A characteristic of a rule that is not generally found in other plans is an outline of what happens if the rule is not observed. A rule normally has a set of punishments for the offender. As people break rules, and continue to break them again and again, the punishment gets more severe with each infraction. The idea of the punishment is not to be vindictive or to cause the rulebreaker to suffer. It is to make the employee aware that he or she is not following the rules as required and to urge a change in behavior conforming to the rules.

In a plant, for instance, a man comes to work late without an acceptable excuse. Nothing is said about it. The second time he is late, he is given an oral warning by his supervisor and asked not to be late again. The third offense may call for a written reprimand by the supervisor. A fourth offense might require that the tardy employee be given a one-day suspension without pay to demonstrate the severity of the situation. A fifth offense of the same nature might bring a longer suspension. A sixth might demand that the man be fired. Punishment for breaking a rule should be outlined so employees know exactly the procedure to be followed.

At school, most students have at one time or another committed an infraction of the rules, sometimes inadvertently, sometimes on purpose. If a student is tardy one day without an excuse, he may be sent to study hall for an hour. A second unexcused tardiness might result in a three-day stint in study hall. A third offense might merit a note to the parents. A fourth could bring a one-day suspension. A fifth might require the parents to come in for a conference before the student can return to school. In some cases, the student might be expelled for a long period of time. Other, minor offenses such as smoking in rest rooms, eating, or chewing gum in class would not warrant expulsion, but could result in minor punishment. Such attendance rules apply to elementary and secondary schools, whereas colleges might have no attendance rules, trusting that the student can better judge his or her need for class attendance.

Rules in business are like all rules. They are made to further the objectives of that institution, and to keep people from taking advantage of their coworkers by infringing on their rights. Rules should be stated clearly and penalties for infractions should be made equally clear to all concerned.

SINGLE-PURPOSE PLANS

The plans we have discussed so far are standing plans, those which will continue until someone decides that they no longer fill a need. A second general type of plan is a single-purpose plan, a plan which would be used up, exhausted over the period of time for which it was intended.

A fire department may have as its goal, not only to extinguish fires as rapidly as possible, but to prevent the occurrence of fires through precautionary maintenance. A strategy for reaching this goal might be the annual observance of fire prevention week. However, to encourage the maximum participation through continual rejuvenation, the plan for the observance would be changed each year, and the fire prevention committee would announce its annual program, a single-purpose plan for that year only. Football games, annual meetings, dedications, as well as advertising plans, fringe benefit offerings, and production schedules are all single-purpose plans or programs which will not remain in force for long periods of time, but will change after each plan is exhausted.

BUDGETS

A particular type of single-purpose plan that we should become acquainted with is a budget or financial plan.

A budget is a plan (usually for one year, but sometimes for longer periods) to determine what money will be spent, how it will be spent, what revenues can be expected, and what changes will occur in assets and liabilities. There are sales budgets, purchasing budgets, capital outlay budgets, cash flow budgets, production budgets, and others.

There are some who would argue that budgets are not plans in themselves, but only quantifications of other plans. For instance, the sales department plans to increase sales. It will do this by increasing the activity, the effort in that department. This increased effort will be expressed in terms of dollars. The results of those efforts (increased sales) will also be quantified (expressed as dollars). The projections will be placed in the plan as figures. These numbers will represent action. A budget then becomes a plan representing other plans, but of itself does not constitute any action. Budgets present planners with a common denominator—dollars. Managers have to decide on one plan, and many times the quantification of these plans will help the decision maker make a better decision. Dollars and percentages, absolutes and relatives, make plans easier to compare.

When comparing figures, the person doing the comparing must make sure that the figures represent the same things in all cases. He or she must compare likes with likes. When comparing two projects, whether to repair an existing machine, or to buy a new machine, we must exercise great care in trying to equate plans in terms of cash outlay, book value, depreciation, maintenance costs, costs per year, and other considerations.

In constructing or approving budgets, we must try to ascertain whether projected budgets are truly representative of the activity to be performed. Is it really going to cost so many dollars for the project, or is the project manager trying to get more dollars than needed to protect himself in case of underestimating. Is he or she asking for twice as much as needed, hoping that he or she will get half as much and still have enough to run the project comfortably? Or, is this manager being realistic while all other managers are asking for more than enough? Will this manager, who is being realistic, be caught short if the project is evaluated on the basis of all other projects?

Budgets are usually presented in the form of balance sheets that show assets, liabilities, and owners' equity of the current year, compared with the projected year, or income statements showing sales, cost of sales, taxes, and net income. Possibly the budget will be a cash flow showing how the company plans to meet all its cash needs, daily, weekly, or monthly, over the next year. This cash flow budget is important because a company that cannot meet its financial obligations timely, cannot pay its debts, is insolvent or bankrupt. Companies cannot pay debts and meet payrolls with assets or profits. These obligations must be met with cash. A recent development in business is in this cash area where managers pay strict attention to the flow of cash knowing that this is the *must* rather than increases in assets.

We will discuss the accounting procedures and devote more time to budgets and cash flows in a later chapter, but it has been mentioned here to remind you that budgets do constitute a plan or a quantification of a plan and therefore must be regarded and observed closely. Budgets are the most common control and evaluation devices used to judge the success of a manager.

In concluding this chapter, we might refer to Figure 7.1 to visualize the relationship of plans to goals. The goal is the anticipated end result of organizational action. Objectives are subgoals. Grand strategy is the normal mode of action, but competitive strategy is used to counter competition. Procedures and methods are detailed plans, while programs and budgets are single-purpose plans. The behavior of personnel is governed and regulated by rules, and all action must take place within the confines of policy decisions made by the board of directors coupled with minimum acceptable standards of behavior and action.

FOR DISCUSSION

1. *What is policy? Who formulates it?*
2. *What are two types of strategy?*

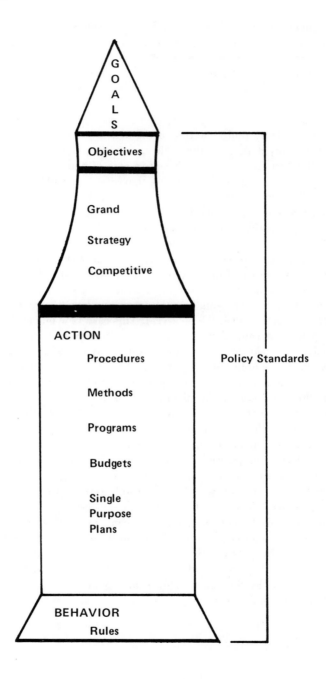

FIGURE 7.1   Relationship of plans to goals.

3. *Explain what procedures are. What procedures are you involved with in your daily life?*
4. *Define rules. Are you guided by different sets of rules depending upon the role you are playing?*
5. *What accompanies a rule that is not found with other types of plans?*
6. *Is a budget a plan? Explain.*
7. *Prepare a personal budget for yourself with both income and expenses in keeping with your choice of lifestyle.*

CASE 7–1

The Sitter Who Upset the Sittee

"I just don't think we ought to use her anymore," Marge Dixon told her husband, Ralph, as they sat at the breakfast table. "She lied to us about her experience and who knows what lies she might tell next."

"Wait a minute," Ralph said, "As I recall, we almost made her lie. We told her we could only feel confident if we had an experienced baby sitter and then said 'you do have experience, don't you?' to her. I think she said 'yes' but I can see why. If she hadn't, we wouldn't have let her sit with the children. Besides, she has plenty of experience now."

"That's not the point. The point is that this whole thing got off to a bad start because she led us to believe something that was just not true. Now that we know she lied, it seems to me that the only thing we can do is tell her we found out and not use her again. Otherwise, we'd be condoning what she's done and showing her that a few lies to the right people, at the right time, can be very helpful."

"I believe you're blowing the whole thing out of proportion," Ralph said. "It's just a baby sitter's job and she's done very well. We paid her to sit and we got a good sitter. That's as far as we ought to go. We shouldn't moralize. That's up to her parents, her school, and her church. Let's be happy with what we have and leave it alone. Besides, you're not really sure she didn't have experience. You just heard from Martha Wolfson that she didn't."

Ralph paused and then added, "And if we let her go, what are we going to do for a sitter? We were desperate when we got her."

"Okay, Ralph, maybe you're right, but I want to think about it. Let's talk about it again later."

GUIDE QUESTIONS

1. *Do you feel that the Dixons made their minimum acceptable standards clear to the sitter?*
2. *What alternatives are open to the Dixons at this point?*
3. *What would be your recommendation to the Dixons?*
4. *Is it possible that Martha Wolfson is wrong? How would this alter the case?*

110

Little Lying Laura

George McDuff, personnel manager for the Augusta Retread Company, leaned heavily on the gray, steel file cabinet which contained the records of Augusta's employees. He was greatly concerned about what he should do about Laura Edwards, a private secretary to Ernest Padgett, vice-president of marketing. George had just reviewed her records and found exactly what he had hoped he would not find. Under the heading *Name of School and Dates,* Laura had written *Jefferson Business School, 1963–65* and in the block labeled *Graduate?* she had marked *Yes.*

George had had no reason to question Laura's application until this day. When applying for a job four years ago, she had given excellent business and employment references, which he had checked and verified. In speed and accuracy tests, she had demonstrated an ability to type and take dictation far in excess of the requirements for the job. In the time since she was hired, Laura had proven herself to be a good technician, liked and respected by peers and superiors. She had risen rapidly from the typing pool to the rank of private secretary and had received superior ratings from Padgett since working for him. She had been an excellent secretary in every respect.

At lunch, George had run into a former high-school classmate, Vera Lankford, and had asked her how she was getting along and where she worked, etc. She had replied, "Jefferson Business School, admissions secretary."

When George said, "One of our girls attended your school," Vera had asked "Who?" and George said, "Laura Edwards."

"I remember her," Vera said, "She dropped out after about three months with us."

"Wrong gal," George had said, "Our Laura finished at your place. I believe it was in '65 or '66."

"Well, I was there then," Vera said, "And I do remember a Laura Edwards, the only one we ever had as far as I know. When I asked her why she was dropping out, she told me she was bored with the school work, and because she needed a full time job to support herself and her little child. I don't know if it was a boy or a girl. Anyway, I don't suppose it makes any difference. What have you been doing with yourself, George?"

George talked small talk with Vera for the next few minutes while thoughts of Laura Edwards persisted in his mind. When Vera left, he finished his lunch and quickly walked back to the office.

George was the first one to get back from lunch. He immediately pulled Laura's file himself, reviewed it, and found the previously mentioned entries on her application. George put her file back into the cabinet and sat down at his desk. He stared at a blank application in front of him. On the bottom of the second page was a phrase he had seen so often: *I certify the statements on this application are true to the best of my knowledge and understand that any misrepresentation or omission of facts is cause for separation from the company, if I am employed.*

George knew that a business school background was required by the job specifications. If Laura had not certified that she had finished Jefferson, she would not have gotten the job initially.

GUIDE QUESTIONS

1. *What is George's problem?*
2. *What alternatives are open to him?*
3. *What procedure might you recommend to George for verifying applications?*
4. *If you don't think George should try to forget the matter entirely, then who would be the next person he should contact with reference to it?*

At the conclusion of this chapter,
you should be able to—

- **Differentiate between creating and innovating.**

- **Discuss the barriers to creativity.**

- **List ways a manager can overcome barriers to creativity.**

- **Explain *changing form* and *brainstorming* ideas.**

- **List several aids to personal creativity.**

8

Creativity and Innovation

It is the responsibility of the manager to foster conditions that provide an opportunity to both create and innovate.

First we will define the two terms. To create is to cause something to come into existence, to originate, to produce, to make something where nothing has been before. This would apply to new concepts or products. To innovate, on the other hand, is to find a new application for a creation or to apply a new idea to an existing situation. Innovating is finding a practical application for a new or existing idea.

Next, we will discuss some concepts applicable to the manager and his or her subordinates in trying to unlock the doors to creativity and innovation.

WHO CAN CREATE?

Is creativity limited only to those gifted people who have the rare talent of being inventive? Is it only those few people who are inspired, or can anybody produce a new idea? We now feel that with some effort and after overcoming various blocks to creativity, practically anybody can produce good, workable, useful ideas.

The first barrier to creativity is a lack of motivation on the part of the participants which falls into two categories: (1) there is no problem to solve or situation to overcome—everything is going along very well and there seems to be no reason to change, or (2) things are not going well, it is apparent that change is needed, but the would-be creator cannot see the benefit of creating and introducing an idea.

The self-image of the rank and file employee is often quite different from that of the manager. The manager sees him- or herself as a company person, trying to overcome problems confronting the company, trying to produce at a lesser cost, and trying to increase profits. Rank and file workers might see themselves as tools of management, moved from place to place, from this machine to that, without regard to individuality. He or she might be regarded as second-class citizens, nurtured when needed, expendable in a profit squeeze. Often, the workers' attitude is, "They don't pay us to think."

If this attitude prevails in your business, you would find very few creative thoughts flowing upward to the manager. As a matter of fact, if your subordinates did have creative ideas, it might be a source of satisfaction to them not to reveal the ideas to you.

To encourage this upward flow of ideas, a boss must foster an atmosphere in which subordinates feel that they, as well as the boss, have a problem, and that a solution from anyone in the group would help the company—an atmosphere in which subordinates work along with the management for the good of the company.

Second, the boss would have to create the feeling of trust. Many employees mistrust their supervisors for fear of economic reprisals, for fear their boss will take action against them if they have better ideas, if they disagree with his or her solution to a problem. They fear that expressing true feelings to the boss about a company problem is dangerous. A manager may never completely overcome this situation. He or she can strive to be dependable and reliable and hope that doing so will earn the trust of the workers.

Subordinates also might feel that their boss is not interested in what they have to say, that even if he or she is supposedly interested, he or she doesn't act accordingly. If this sentiment is conveyed, chances are that the manager is not aware of the possible contributions to be made by subordinates.

Another problem a supervisor might have with subordinates in motivating them to be creative is that they feel they are not properly rewarded for their ideas. They feel that putting in time to find a solution to a problem is like working overtime, and they should be compensated for their efforts.

A final barrier that hinders an employee is the inaccessibility of the supervisor and an apparent lack of response to the idea or solution once it is offered. The employee who is solicited for advice, and who makes an effort to give that advice, wants to feel that the suggestion has been acted upon in some fashion and a decision has been made. If there is no feedback, he or she will assume that further suggestions will meet the same fate, and therefore, will quit making suggestions.

OVERCOMING SUBORDINATES' OBSTACLES

In addition to those methods mentioned concerning overcoming subordinates reluctance to present ideas, a supervisor can do the following things to encourage employee participation:

1. He or she can be available to subordinates, being there when they want to talk, and listen attentively to whatever they have to say.

2. He or she can reward those employees who present ideas acceptable to management. These can be financial rewards, pats on the back, or both. In any event, the rewards should be public, they should give recognition. The response from management should be one that encourages others to do similar creative work.

3. He or she must be able to accept criticism, able to view critical judgement of the present activities in a nonpersonal manner, just as a subordinate is expected to

accept criticism as constructive. If an employee is willing to go out on a limb to criticize the supervisor or the company, then, the supervisor must accept the action as a genuine gesture of concern for the good of the company.

4.   He or she can encourage subordinates to be frank, not taking punitive action against anyone who disagrees.

5.   He or she should not reject new ideas immediately. Comments such as, "That's the dumbest thing I've ever heard," or, "You must be kidding" certainly would discourage an employee from bringing any more ideas to a superior. The manager should accept or reject new ideas only after careful evaluation.

6.   He or she can process ideas promptly, evaluating them, or presenting them to others for evaluation without delay. Once a decision has been made, the originator should receive a definite response.

We can conclude that it is the manager's responsibility to create an environment in which subordinates feel comfortable in airing their ideas and innovations. This will encourage them to look for new ideas, and spend the time and effort necessary to develop the ideas into workable solutions.

OTHER CREATIVE BLOCKS

Although the supervisor has a distinct motivational advantage over subordinates, he or she must share equally with them some of the other blocks to creativity.

One of these blocks is the fear of failure or the fear people have that the idea they develop will be ridiculed, the fear that their ideas, which seem so applicable and so easy to understand, will meet complete resistance when presented to peers or supervisors. If a person has a dread of failure, he or she will play it safe by not coming up with new ideas, by being so busy doing, that there is little or no time to be creative. He or she will merely block the creative process to avoid the subsequent evaluation.

If a person never fails, never does anything wrong, it is usually because he or she is doing little which can be evaluated, or because he or she is doing very little at all. There is much to be learned even from failure. Once the person gets over the stage of self-pity, then he or she can scrutinize the failure to see what caused it, and then decide what to do to overcome the reason for failure. He or she can also gain determination to try again to succeed. Success, however, often breeds complacency, inactivity, or a feeling of infallibility.

A lack of self-confidence is another block to creativity. Many people feel that because they have less experience, less education, less innate ability, they must always take a back seat to others who possess these qualities. Creativity is not an unconscious result of education or experience, but a conscious effort to find new ideas and solutions. Many of our great inventors did not have the benefit of a formal education. They were people who saw a need, saw a problem, and found a solution to that problem. Education helps people succeed within a system, but everyone, not just the highly educated, can sense solutions to problems.

Pressure from peers makes people smother their creativity if their peers are uncreative. On the positive side, people are creative if their peers are creative. We all have a feeling of not wanting to be too different. We don't want our coworkers to accuse us of buttering up the boss, trying to get ahead. The Hawthorne studies showed that there is a pressure to curtail production to an acceptable norm for the group. The same pressure is applicable to creativity and innovation. If one member of a group is extremely creative and innovative, he or she may be pressured by the group not to bring forth new ideas.

Even in a classroom, if one person has the answers to all the questions, or has great ideas about solving case problems, or solutions to any proposition the instructor puts before the class, the other members of the class are inclined to resent that person. As a matter of fact, the teacher, just like the foreman, may try to discourage this "ratebuster." If a subordinate or a student feels such pressuures, he might want to restrict the quantity of ideas and concentrate in quality responses, giving the best answers to the most difficult situations, and not getting involved in every question and every problem.

A final block to creativity is an inability to find, or a complete refusal to occupy a setting for creativity. A person who must always be in a crowd, or feels he must, will find that he or she has little time to think about a problem. Sometimes this person becomes nervous when in a position to think, and will set up some artificial condition to distract him- or herself from seeking a solution to a problem or creating a new idea. This block might stem from any of the other conditions such as lack of motivation, lack of self-confidence, peer pressure, or fear of failure. To be creative, a person must be immersed in an environment which permits the thinking process can take place.

THE CREATIVE PROCESS

To be creative, we must go through a logical process, just as when solving a problem. The first step in this process is to become thoroughly familiar with the situation. This is sometimes called saturation. It is at this point that we must be sure we understand the whole problem, not just part of it, and see how this problem relates to all parts of the total system. The person who has a problem may find at this stage that he or she is unable to view the problem objectively. For example, if an employee is doing something wrong consistently, the supervisor may find it extremely difficult, if not impossible, to see this as anything other than a problem related directly to that person's lack of ability, not because he or she has poor guidance, poor instruction, or poor training. The supervisor can only see that the worker is incapable or unable to do the job.

Once a person has become thoroughly familiar with the problem, then he or she might find that it is beneficial to mull over the problem, to sleep on it, to think about it for a period of time, to challenge the existing way, to create many logical or even illogical answers. This step compared to the decision-making process would be that step of originating alternative solutions. Then, or she could have a problem with three, six, or ten possible solutions. He or she can proceed to the third step of compar-ing alternatives, or stop and let his or her subconscious work. Again, that person might want to sleep on the problem. Strangely enough, many people who do sleep on problems, often awake with answers. It might be an alternative proposed origi-nally, or it might be a combination of some of these alternatives, emerging as a com-pletely new idea, the one, best idea.

If this illumination does not occur after the person has slept on the problem, he or she at least will have an opportunity to analyze the alternatives from a fresh point of view. Some of the ones he or she might have thought worthwhile, may, in the light of a new day, appear to be silly. Some of those that were silly yesterday, may, with some polish, turn into the one, best solution.

When you have made a selection, when you have made that one, best choice, then, you must convert your ideas into concrete plans for further action. This action might be to present your plan to a boss or some group responsible for evaluation. You might present it to your peers or subordinates, or you might go ahead and put the idea into effect if you have the power and authority. You might want to test the idea in a labora-tory, or under controlled conditions, to see if the idea is really as good as you thought. Why test it? So that you will not expend money, manpower, materials, and efforts before knowing whether the idea will be a workable one or not.

ALTERING FORMS

Alex F. Osborn brought forth many ideas in creativity, two of which we might note here: the first is experimenting with changing the form of the existing product, idea or solution, and the second is a system of creating new ideas through brainstorming.[1]

By changing the existing form, we can look at a product or a situation and say such things as: Can we put this to other uses? If we have a cigarette-making machine, can we make it into a cigar-making machine by using different raw materials and by changing our concept of what is a cigarette and what is a cigar?

Can we adapt this product or this idea to something else? What else do we have that is like this? What does the form of this idea suggest to us? Can the decision-making process be used to find solutions in one industry as well as another? Can the basic ingredients be used to make a similar product?

Can we modify what we have now? Can we change the color of it? Can we change the odor, the taste, the form, the shape? Can we change our current product or concept to be more acceptable to our customers, to our subordinates, to our superiors?

Can we magnify what we have? Can we make it larger, can we make it stronger? Can we change this little model car which thrills the small boy into a larger model which would make his father happy?

Can we reduce what we have? Since the Winnebago motor home is satisfying to the whole family, can we make the little girl happy by presenting it to her as a scale model? Can we make anything into a pleasing scale model?

Can we rearrange what we have? If we have an unacceptable golf course because it has three 500-yard holes in a row, can we rearrange the layout to alternate distances. If the nine-o'clock coffee break is too close to breakfast, and the eleven-o'clock break is too close to lunch, can we make them acceptable to everybody? Can we place a usually hot machine in a cold area so that the temperature will be balanced, rather than placing a hot machine in a hot area which would make working on that machine unbearable?

Can we reverse what we are doing? Can we run it upside down, backward, turn it inside out? Can we line this green skirt with red in a way that the red can be worn outside? Can we build a locomotive or an automobile that has a front on both ends so that it can be going forward in either direction?

What can we substitute for the product which we are using now? Can we anticipate two distinct sources of power so that if one runs short, we can change to the other without suffering heavy losses of time and money? Can we substitute raw materials so that either will give us a final product of comparable quality? Can we replace our men with women, or high school students or machines? Can we have police people instead of policemen, or fire fighters instead of firemen?

BRAINSTORMING

The second idea that Osborn had was brainstorming which is a group endeavor to be more creative. If we have a problem that we are unable to solve, one which calls for creativeness, then we might call together a group of subordinates or peers, or any kind of a group, and present the problem. The idea of brainstorming is that the group will generate a number of solutions in which they change, build upon, or modify the suggestions of others as well as create their own solutions.

There are certain rules to follow according to Osborn. First, we should forbid criticism of the ideas, we should not judge the merit of any of the ideas until the brainstorming session is over. Second, we should encourage any kind of ideas that might possibly contribute to the solution of the problem. The third thing we should be looking for would be quantities of ideas without demanding quality. The fourth rule we should follow would be to allow all participants to alter, modify, and improve the suggestions of others.

A session of brainstorming of an hour or less might produce twenty, forty, even a hundred ideas. Later, after the brainstorming session, these ideas woulld have to be evaluated to determine if they have any merit. Probably most of them would not be any good, but some worthwhile ideas would emerge from the session.

PERSONAL OBJECTIVE AIDS

There are certain things that the creative person might do to enhance creativity and to retain original ideas. Some of them are as follows:

Use recording devices. Although a pencil and a pad of paper may not appear to be very sophisticated in this world of electronic gadgetry, it is important that the creative person has, at his or her immediate disposal a pad on which to record ideas, structure a solution to a problem, do calculations, draw figures, or anything else that might be forgotten easily.

In recent years, much use has been made of the tape recorder. Miniature recorders are carried in pockets, on wrists, in cars, and travel with the person making the record. Such recorders need not be of the finest quality. They only have to be of a quality which can be replayed and the material transcribed. The idea of using the recorder is to capture the thought at the time of creation. Later, the idea can be evaluated, discussed, streamlined or expanded. But, at that moment, the idea is captured and does not elude the creator.

Another recording device that can be used is the camera. There are cameras available now which are quite small and can be carried easily in a pocket. These cameras require no flash attachments, and, as the tape recorder, can capture the moment, can record the impressions of the viewer. If, on an inspection tour, a person finds something wrong or finds something that can be improved, it would be helpful to express his or her feelings on tape, and take a picture of the scene, so that back at the office, when he or she begins to contemplate what was seen, a visual reproduction of the actual condition is at hand. It might also be of value to have a camera that produces instant, self-developing pictures. This would prevent the problem of going back to the office and having the pictures developed (which may take several days) only to find that the picture which was to show something specific was the one which didn't come out as expected.

Be observant. As you look around, try to envision the relevance of situations. How does this affect that? How does an increase in an employee's pay increase productivity? Or does it? How does the new see-through package make the customer more likely to buy? Ask why. Ask it of your subordinates, your peers, your superiors. If a relationship has a reason for being, then you should be able to discover that reason. If that relationship has outgrown its usefulness, then you should be able to detect this. You should ask yourself why. Why do I do things this way? Why not do them another way?

Organize think time. Everyone has the same amount of time available each day. Some seem to be able to do more with their time than others, because they are more organized. To a person who wants to concentrate on an idea, it is quite beneficial to group time periods so that he or she can have longer periods of time to contemplate an idea. One hour is much more beneficial in terms of meditating about a problem than are six ten-minute periods. In a ten-minute period it is almost impossible to get yourself in a proper frame of mind to even think about the problem, much less come up with solutions or analyze relationships.

First-level supervisors have a harder time organizing their personal time than do higher-level managers. Some supervisors have more than a thousand activity changes in one day, and it is difficult for them to arrange think time. Industry leaders have many fewer meetings of long duration and can find more time to think. Many managers find it to their advantage to come to work earlier than required, stay late, or even take an extended break during the day, so that they can give themselves time to concentrate on various problems.

Structure your thinking. Once you get into this quiet time in which you can concentrate on a problem, state the problem or opportunity in specific terms, so that you can concentrate your thinking toward finding a solution with that specific objective in mind. Unstructured thinking can lead you all over the place and might wind up as a daydreaming exercise rather than one of creative endeavor. If you have a problem employee, consider the alternative actions you might take to keep from disrupting the activities of the company. If you have a windfall gain, reflect on the alternative opportunities for spending the money to its best advantage. If you have an entirely new product, think of the applications it might have in the commercial world, then, consider which of these might be best suited to your company.

Conclude your thoughts. When you are considering the alternatives in step four, analyze them to find which might be best suited to the situation. Often, we find ourselves confronted with a problem and maybe we even consider the alternatives, and we consider them and consider them and consider them. And then we reconsider them, finally forgetting some of the ones we have considered because we fail to arrive at a definite conclusion about the situation. We do not carry this process through to the stage where the best alternative can be chosen. The choice need not be rash, and it might take more than one sitting to consider this choice. But, to refuse to make the decision, stops the creative process. Creativity is hard work. It seldom comes in a flash. Those people who always seem to come up with the best ideas, the best creations, the best innovations, are those people who work the hardest at making ideas pay off.

Reverse viewpoints. Once you have made a decision solving the problem confronting you, look at your decision from the point of view of those people who will be affected by the decision. If you envision a new product, look at it from the customers' viewpoint, from the viewpoint of the production supervisor who must be responsible for making the thing, from the design engineer's viewpoint, from the viewpoint of the stockholder who is looking for a return on an investment. Try to determine if this idea, which seems good to you, will seem equally as good to all others involved.

You might also view problems from the viewpoint of others. You might say, "If I were the customer of this company, what would I want from it?" "If I were buying this from my company, how would I think the company might improve?" "If I were one of my subordinates, how would I look at me?" "What actions might I take to improve myself as a manager?" "What do I look for in a superior, so that I might make myself that kind of a superior?"

Listen. When you are in a position to listen, to look, to see, and to read—do it. Try not to be preoccupied with something at all times. When a subordinate is dissatisfied, listen. When a customer has an idea for a better product, listen. If you can adopt the idea to your process, then you have an innovation. When a newscaster says there is going to be an energy crisis, listen. How is it going to affect you and your company? How can you relate what is happening in the world today with your job, with your future?

Broaden your interests. Don't allow yourself to become so lost in your job to the extent that you are unaware of what is happening around you. It is up to you to enlarge your interests and be receptive to all those ideas which will flow in as a result of outside contacts.

We have talked about ideas, how to get them, how to help others get them, how to encourage others to pass them on to you. A manager must sift through ideas, his or her ideas and those which come from others, and adopt those he or she feels will be beneficial to the company. Good ideas are like race horses which must be freed of their restraints before they can run to their fullest potential. In the next chapter, we will deal with getting others—superiors, peers, and subordinates—to accept our ideas and give them life.

FOR DISCUSSION

1. *Creativity is limited to gifted people. Discuss this statement.*
2. *Production workers and supervisors always view creativity in the same way. Discuss this statement.*
3. *How can a manager overcome subordinates' blocks to creativity?*
4. *Describe the creative process.*
5. *What is brainstorming?*
6. *What aids might you use to enhance your creative abilities?*
7. *Do you think that five people in thirty minutes could generate as many ideas as thirty people in five minutes?*

ENDNOTE

1. Alex F. Osborn, *Applied Imagination: Principles and Procedures of Creative Thinking*, rev. ed. (New York: Charles Scribner's Sons, 1957), p. 87.

Getting Stuck with the Sticks

Frankie Brubaker walked into the Evans Pharmacy and took a seat at the counter. He caught the eye of the fellow behind the counter, his best buddy, Ricky Mines, who came over to wait on him.

"Boy, you sure are filthy. What have you been doing?" Ricky asked.

"Give me a large Coke and I'll tell you," Frankie replied. After a pause he said, "Cleaning out my Grandfather's garage."

"For what?" Ricky asked, "I though he was in the hospital. If it was dirty when he was out, why do you need to clean it now?"

"The problem is that when he was at home, he parked the car in front of the house. Now, Grandma says she doesn't like to come in from the hospital and park out there. She wants to pull the car into the garage. So, Mama told me to get over there and clean it out."

"Find anything interesting?" Ricky asked.

"As a matter of fact, I did," Frankie said. "Would you believe ten thousand sticks?"

"What do you mean, ten thousand sticks? What kind of sticks? Popcicle?"

"No, they're kinda like handles. Handles for brooms or rakes or something. They're all the same. They're about five feet long, round, and a little more than an inch in diameter. They're in bundles of a hundred. I figure there are about a hundred bundles—so, ten thousand altogether."

"Where did they come from?"

"Grandma said Granddaddy brought them home from work several years ago. You know, he worked on the railroad, in the freight house. Somebody shipped these things here and nobody ever claimed them. He let them lay there about a year, then he bought them for almost nothing and brought them home, a couple of bunches a day, everyday, until he got them all home."

"What did he want them for?"

"Who knows?" Frankie said. "Grandma said one time he brought home three hundred baby chickens, and not a sign of a chicken house. He left them out in the yard in a great big box. Rained like crazy one day and they all drowned. I think Grandma was really relieved. And, speaking of Grandma, she said we could have all the sticks."

"Great," said Ricky. "But, I've got two questions. Who is 'we' and, if I'm part of 'we', what are 'we' going to do with ten thousand sticks?"

"I was thinking that we might be the school band, so you are included, but the 'what' is something else. Every year we have to do something to make money, right? Sell candy, lightbulbs, or something. Just think, if we could sell these sticks for a dollar apiece, we'd make ten times as much as we ever made!"

"You must be crazy. Who's going to pay a dollar for a stick?"

"Nobody. That's why we've got to turn those sticks into something else, something we can sell," Frankie said. "The Green Bay–Chicago football game starts tomorrow at one. We can't do anything during the game, but about four we could have a meeting. Let's each of us invite about ten guys or girls from the band over to my house to see the game and meet afterward. We should be able to come up with a bunch of good ideas.

GUIDE QUESTIONS

1. *In this situation, what are some of the advantages to brainstorming?*
2. *What is the objective of this session? Could a different objective, such as wide community participation, bring about different alternatives?*

The F.I.N.K. Bank Think Tank

"Some ideas are born, grow slowly, ripen to maturity, decline and die," president W. B. Fox told the employees of the First Industrial National Bank of Kanawa City. "But, unlike people, most ideas fail to achieve the total life cycle. In fact, they experience great trouble getting born.

"When a young girl gets pregnant, she knows it," he said forcefully, and was embarrassed when the audience laughed. "What I mean is she has physical manifestations of her change in condition. People pregnant with ideas often don't know it. When it is time for the baby to be born, nature provides a great deal of assistance. Ideas come too soon, too late or never. Only occasionally do they arrive on time.

"Even when they are on time and we put the ideas to work, the result will not last long in this business. Everything that was in this bank twenty-five years ago has changed. The teller's cages have been replaced by counters. Checks are free. We have drive-ins, TV tellers, and twenty-four hour banking by computer. When I started here, the only advertising we did was to give away a calendar at Christmas, one to each customer. Now look at us. Radios, TVs, newspapers, and novelties. We support little league teams; providing outdoor signs and scoreboards. You name it, and it has a F.I.N.K. sign on it.

"Yes, we've changed, but we must continue to change, continue to be out in front with new services and products for our customers. That's why I've asked you to attend this meeting today. I want to announce a new idea: The executive committee wants to start a program to help ideas reach evaluation. This means that an idea must take on some concrete form. It must be plucked from someone's mind and be set down on paper.

"To stimulate such action, we want to set up some sort of financial rewards. For instance, we might pay a hundred dollars minimum for any usable idea and up to five hundred for the best. We'll settle on the amounts later, but for now, this project needs a name.

"I suggested 'Smash Through.' Harvey wanted 'Born Again.' But, we decided to let you choose an appropriate name.

"To show you we mean business, we are going to hire one of you for five hundred dollars an hour. (That's a little more than I make.) Who are we going to hire? I'll tell you. Over the next thirty minutes, one-half hour, I want you to brainstorm. Come up with as many names as possible. Build on each other's ideas. Let yourselves go. At the end of that time, the entire group will vote on the name. Whoever submitted that idea will get a check for $250. Two fifty for a half hour is five hundred dollars an hour. Right? One of you will leave the bank today with two hundred and fifty dollars extra, and it will all be legal. Now, if there are no questions, we'll begin."

GUIDE QUESTIONS

1. *What are some names you might propose for the project?*
2. *Would picking a name and telling the bank employees about it be just as effective as brainstorming?*

At the conclusion of this chapter,
you should be able to—

- Determine what is likely to happen in cases of premature criticism or idea presentation.

- Give reasons why inferior ideas are adopted.

- Describe the steps in making a presentation.

- Qualify an audience.

- Understand how anticipating objections can greatly improve your chance of selling your idea.

9

Selling Ideas

In the previous chapter, developing ideas was discussed. Now we will turn our attention to having our ideas accepted by others, whether they be superiors, subordinates, or peers.

The phrase *go or no go* is a cliche, but it achieved special meaning through the space program. We have heard missile control say, "All systems are go and we are counting," meaning every detail of the whole missile system has been checked through computers and is set to go. You've also heard, "We have a hold," meaning something may be a possible malfunction and the mission will be stopped until the problem is cleared. If the problem is cleared, then the countdown is resumed. If not, the entire mission will be delayed or even scrapped.

However, if the evaluation was go, if everything was acceptable to the computers and the men who monitor them, then the missile will blast off. So accurate and detailed are these checks, that no astronauts have been lost from blast off to pick up, through and including the Space Lab series. Certainly a remarkable feat and a credit to the concepts of planning and preparedness.

IDEA EVALUATION

What proportion of ideas, do you think, reach the "launch pad" with such thoroughness, and how many of them are held, stopped, delayed, or thrown out because of the lack of preparedness on the part of the originator? How many plans have not been incorporated because "they didn't listen?" How many reasonably good ideas have been stymied because the presenter was unable to answer audience questions?

Almost every student has been in at least one class that he or she did not like. Although the dislike probably was not vocalized to the instructor, his or her classmates most likely were made aware of it. Suppose the instructor gets the message that some students are talking about the class, saying that they would do things differently. Let us also suppose that at the next class, either out of genuine concern or vindictiveness, the instructor says to the students, "I understand that you have been critical of this class and that you have a certain number of recommendations about changing it. I wish you would make a presentation to the class, indicating those changes. The class and I will then critique the recommendations to see if they have any merit."

Do you suppose that the students would be in a position to make the presentation as requested? Probably not. Instead of being heroes, they become scapegoats. The teacher, even if one of the worst in the business, would have succeeded in putting down his or her main critics.

This example shows three things: (1) If a person is critical of an existing program, he or she should think of changes in positive terms. For example, "This would be a better program if participants were discouraged from using more than three minutes during each one-hour class period." In saying this, the speaker has been specific, and is able to think the recommendations through to a logical conclusion and evalaute it. He or she can also anticipate questions and objections to the idea he would be putting forth. (2) When placing oneself in a position of being called upon to speak or make a presentation, a person should be prepared to do so. If he or she is not completely ready, he or she should defer the presentation, if possible. If the presentation cannot be delayed, he or she should say as little as possible about the matter at hand. Making a poor presentation could jeopardize that person's job and future, as well as kill a good idea. (3) Ideas which are presented prematurely may never get a second hearing. In the example cited, do you think the instructor will come back each week and ask for criticism from the class, or give the students a second chance if they ask? Even if given a second chance to make a presentation, who will listen?

Many good ideas are lost because of poor presentations, and poor ideas are incorporated into the plans of an organization because of a slick presentation, or because, of the two or three presentations made in support of various alternatives, the one chosen was presented best.

Looking into history, hundreds or thousands of years ago, or just last year, we wonder why a plan was followed when it seems to us that this plan, without question, must have been the worst plan available. If we had been there, or could remember the circumstances under which that plan was chosen, we would probably find that among all the alternatives this was the one which appeared to be the best.

How can we best present our ideas? We can do this by planning for the presentation, being completely aware of what we are doing and why we are doing it, from the beginning of the presentation to the end. There are six steps involved in making a presentation, whether to one's subordinates, peers, or superiors. They are as follows: (1) familiarizing oneself with the idea, (2) qualifying the audience, (3) holding the attention of the audience, (4) presenting the main idea, (5) asking for action, and (6) overcoming objections from the audience. We will discuss each of these.

FAMILIARIZING ONESELF WITH THE IDEA

If you are going to sell an idea to an audience, whether that audience be one or one thousand, you are the first person who must be convinced of the idea's value. You have to sell yourself first. You have to sell yourself on the idea that the plan you are about to present is the best idea available. Once you believe that it is the best, once you believe in your own idea, selling it becomes much easier. Getting a positive nod from your audience happens more often because of your conviction. Because of conviction, an audience, unless it is definitely against an idea, will vote in favor of it. What we are saying is that if there are some people who have not made up their minds one way or the other, they might be swayed by the conviction of the presenter.

This is a results world. Salesman are paid commissions on what they sell, not on the things they almost sold. Production workers are deemed successes or failures based upon what they produce, not on what they planned to produce, their goals, or their ambitions, but only on the final products. It is up to the presenter to get results. He or she must secure an affirmative vote on the project or it will be lost. This concept of results applies in the same way to the minister asking the congregation to work for the church. It applies to the superintendent of schools when asking the school committee for more money to build a new school, or to provide higher salaries to attract talented teachers, or to appropriate money for band uniforms for the high school band so it can compete in a state contest. It applies to the businessman, as well, as he tries to convince his board of directors, or his customers, or his subordinates, his suppliers, or anyone else. It also applies to you whether you are talking to your boss, to your parents, your spouse, or your children. If the audience does not buy the idea you are presenting, you have not sold it.

As a manager, what kind of ideas might you be trying to sell? In a supervisory position, you might be trying to convince your boss or the personnel manager that another production worker is needed in your department. You might be trying to convince them that the company would be better off if a new, more efficient machine were purchased instead of maintaining the present machine. You may be trying to convince your audience or your boss, that you are the best person for a future opening, that you deserve a chance for promotion. You might be trying to convince your peers, your fellow supervisors, that being kind, polite, and understanding toward the worker will get more production results than will a tough policy. You might be trying to convince your subordinates that it is to their advantage to get to work on time, have fewer absences, and maintain projected quotas in production. You might tell them that it is to their benefit to observe the posted safety regulations, to report violations of these rules, and to suggest improvements which would result in fewer injuries.

Generally speaking, what you are telling your audience, regardless of who makes up that audiene, is that if the members of the audience adopt the program you propose, they will benefit in some way. If your superior promotes you, or your coworker changes his method of supervision, or if your subordinate improves his production, both they and the company will be helped.

People do not change for the sake of changing. They change because they feel that change will be beneficial. If you are driving a car which operates smoothly, gives you little trouble, requires no maintenance, and gets good gas mileage, and if you have need of such a car, then you will continue to drive that same car *until* you become dissatisfied. This would not necessarily have to be a physical barrier. It could be a psychological one. If you received a promotion and then began to feel that the car, which had been satisfactory up to that point, would no longer be enough car for a man of your status, or if you felt that you should change your image or lifestyle and the car you were driving did not project the image you want, then you might consider changing cars. A television ad showing a person about your age with about your self-image, slowly moving through a drive-in restaurant lot, the subject of admiring and envious looks from the other patrons (those types which you might want to impress) because she is driving a cute little Flash, might encourage you to trade your car in for a Flash, too. Then again, the reason for the dissatisfaction could be physical. You might take the car for an inspection and find that it will cost several hundred dollars to put it in good shape. When the car itself, even with the repairs, will be worth slightly more, or even less, than the cost of the repairs, you might consider a change.

Change only occurs when there is some dissatisfaction on the part of the change maker. Often it is up to the seller (the presenter) to promote this dissatisfaction. There is no implication here that this dissatisfaction promotion is, or will be, illegal, immoral, or conniving. The seller has to show that his is the better way.

The first thing, then, is for the presenter to sell himself. To do this, he must know the idea thoroughly. He must learn the basic characteristics of the idea and how the idea affects everybody connected with it, directly or indirectly. In a company, all persons who are selling ideas are in competition with each other, trying to get attention, trying to get additional employees, or additional money to promote their own ideas. Money and manpower are limited commodities in any company. There is a great demand for both. Therefore, the presenter must know that when he gets the extra man, the extra dollars, someone else might have to do without. He has got to be able to compare his project with projects he is competing with, compare the machine he wants with the machine someone else is trying to obtain. He's got to know all the consequences of his idea.

What will happen to the company if we take on this new product? How much money will be necessary to buy the machinery? How many new men must we employ? How many old men must we let go or retrain? What kind of sales can we reasonably expect from it? How much money must we invest before we begin to see a profit? Is the market large enough to support this product we are planning to make? What about our competitors? Will the government allow us to make this thing and distribute it? How will we advertise it? What channels of distribution are we going to use? Literally hundreds of questions must be asked and answered before any idea such as a new product could be presented to an audience with any hope of acceptance. Any presentation, before these answers could be ascertained, would be premature and might jeopardize the whole project. As we stated earlier, in the decision-making section, the presenter must carry his analysis of the alternatives through to a logical conclusion. If he does not, he is in for an abrupt awakening from his audience. If he does not know the answers to the audience's questions, his project is doomed.

QUALIFYING THE AUDIENCE

The presenter must qualify his audience as a salesman must qualify his customer. Qualifying is determining in advance whether or not that audience or that member of the audience is able to consider your presentation and take action as a result of it. Qualified prospects need not be only those whom we expect to take affirmative action, but they must be people who can make a decision, one way or the other.

Suppose you are married and the only time you would consider buying life insurance is after both you and your spouse have listened to the presentation by the insurance salesman. If the salesman should catch you at a meeting, a baseball game, or someplace where you are without your wife, then you would not be qualified to hear his presentation because you would be unable to consider his presentation and take definite action. For the insurance man to qualify you, he must make an appointment with you and your spouse, thereby eliminating the barrier which would keep you from purchasing the policy (taking action).

To qualify an audience, you will have to ask three questions: (1) Do they have a need for, or can they benefit from this proposal. Some of the benefits they might receive from the proposition might be to save money, improve profits, satisfy the employees, get a better grade of raw material, get faster and quicker shipments and service, increase production, and maybe make them look good in the eyes of others. Any benefit, whether material or psychological, will make the listener alert to the presenter's message.

(2) Can they make a decision concerning the proposal? If we study the situation, we can see that telling the secretary, talking with our peers during the coffee break, or presenting an idea to our subordinates will do very little good if they are unable to take any definite action to facilitate the plan. The only way to turn our plan into action is to talk to those people who can make binding decisions. It can be helpful to discuss an idea with others before that idea is presented to the decision-making group, so that the presenter might get reactions and determine if he has covered all issues, but excessive talk to nondecision-makers will not help the presenter. A person might have his ego boosted by having a fellow worker tell him that he has a great idea, and that might be satisfactory for a while, but the real test of an idea is whether or not someone or some group is willing to finance it or to adopt it. Regardless of what is in effect at the moment, the decision makers prefer your idea and they are willing to implement that decision. Even a pat on the back from a fellow worker may be only a halfhearted approval. Not that he is not sincere, but he probably has not studied the plan with as critical an eye as one would if he were being asked to back an idea with money or authority.

(3) Can they put the idea into effect? If the idea calls for an allocation of money, can they authorize it? If the idea calls for more people, can they hire them? If it is an entirely new process, can they obtain the money, machinery, and everything else that goes with the process?

The qualified decision maker must be able to use, approve, and back the proposal with money, men, machinery, and materials. If he or she can do these things, he or she is well "qualified."

GETTING THE ATTENTION OF THE AUDIENCE

Suppose that person who you have qualified as being able to act upon your plan is the vice-president of production. How could you get to see him? Or, do you need to see him? If you are a rank and file employee or a first-level manager, you would probably go through the chain of command. Now, how could you get your immediate boss to let you go see the vice-president? You likely would use the same technique on him that you would use with the vice-president. You would show him how he might benefit from letting you go. You might allow him to "discover" you and your idea. You could, at this point, let him take your idea to his manager, and have his manager's manager carry it on up until it reaches the decision maker. But, if you want your plan to remain intact, you would do better to get permission and go to the decision maker yourself. An informed supervisor would much prefer that his subordinate go through him to a top manager, rather than have that subordinate go around him.

Once you have an appointment with the vice-president, you then must carefully prepare your presentation. The vice-president is busy, his time for your project is limited. He can only spend a few minutes with you, and unless you can impress him, he will spend those few minutes thinking about more pressing problems. Your presentation will have to be brief, concise, and to the point.

First, you must get his attention. Getting his attention is not merely getting him to look at you, or invite you into his office, or provide time for your presentation. Getting his attention is getting him involved, getting to think how your plan is going to be helpful to him and the company. Once he can see there is a potential benefit, then he becomes a captive audience. He is doing his job. He is finding things which will benefit the company—cultivating ideas, innovating for the good of the company.

Some basic approaches are as follows:

Curiosity. "Mr. Brown, I've come up with a method of turning that scrap metal 'in the production department into a saleable item. Would you like to hear about it?" He would like to hear about it and you should have all the information from the process to the customer. Be sure of your facts and figures before you go to see him.

Benefit. "Mr. Smith, I have a way in which we can increase our production twenty percent without increasing our raw material consumption at all." Mr. Smith will want to hear more, and again, the presenter should be sure of himself before he proposes the benefit.

Problem-Solving. "Mr. Jones, I'm sure the increased costs in our raw materials are giving our profits a fit. I have a substitute product which will solve that problem." And you'd better have that product.

Factual. "Mr. Green, I compared our annual report with industry averages and found that we are ten percent below average in profits. We have a much higher raw materials costs than other companies, and I feel I can offer a purchasing plan which will bring our costs more in line."

News. "Mrs. White, I've read a number of articles recently about tape-controlled machines and I have discovered a spot in our department where one could be used profitably."

There are other types of approaches such as praise—"You've done so well here there seems to be little room for improvement, but. . . ." Or, an opinion approach— "Why do you think we are outselling our competitors and still not being as profitable as they are? I think I have the answer." Or, the shock approach—"Did you know that half of the men in the production department are now looking for other jobs? I'll tell you why they are, and how I think we can remedy the situation."

One thing that you are doing for the vice-president is something that few other of his associates are doing—you are coming to him with *solutions*. Maybe solutions to problems he was unaware of, but you are giving him answers rather than asking questions; you are proposing solutions rather than presenting problems. He will be glad to see you if you can deliver the goods you say you can from the approach.

Remember, he is looking for profit, safety, ease, and convenience, for personal pride and prestige, for answers. If you can appeal to any of these motives, you will hold his attention.

PRESENTING THE MAIN IDEA

Now that you have your vice-president or your audience listening to you and looking for that benefit you promised, you have to hold that interest and create a desire for action.

The first fact to consider about your presentation is that it must be complete, it must tell the whole story. It does not have to be in minute detail, but it must cover all the important facets of the plan. This includes the scope of the work, costs, projected savings or earnings, the effects on existing personnel and on new personnel, new machinery, on implications of this proposal with the government, with unions, competitors, customers, and other relationships which might be involved.

Next, the presenter must show why this project, above all others, should be adopted. Here again, it might be a matter of conviction on the part of the presenter which would sell the project. Ofter the presenter does not know against whom he is competing. All he knows is that his project can offer benefits to the adopters and he can detail these benefits along with the investments required to realize them. Many plans are adopted, not because they are the best, but because they are presented in the best fashion, because they appear to be the best of those presented. There is certainly no doubt that the person who thinks his project is the best and prepares in advance, will make a far better impression on the audience—the decision makers—than those who appear before them in a haphazard fashion. We might mention here, too, that to make derogatory remarks about other known projects or those persons who are presenting the projects, will usually backfire. He should eliminate his competition, not by condemning it, but by building up his own project.

Build the presentation based on questions which you would ask if you were the decision maker, and those which you think might be asked of you. Some of those questions are going to be: How much will it cost? How much can we save? How much profit will we make? How long will the payback period be? How many men or man hours will it save us? What will be the life of the project?

There is no way or reason to avoid these questions and the presenter must be prepared to meet them head on. Vice-presidents, boards of directors, and supervisors are not interested in committing undetermined amounts of money to undefined projects for nebulous profits. Decision makers must have facts. If the facts are not built into the presentation, the members of the audience will confront the presenter with the questions.

You cannot avoid the question of costs. Therefore, any plan which has financial implications such as additional capital outlays, more raw materials, projected payback periods, profitability, or return on investment, should have these figures spelled out and should be projected on the basis of reasonable economic forecasts. *Reasonable* is a vague term. It might mean something different to your audience than it does to you. Nevertheless, it must be dealt with, and *reasonable* in this sense would be an acceptable, logical, step-by-step change in the economic fortunes as a result of this new plan. Quadrupling sales in three months is not reasonable. Immediate results from new machines are not reasonable. Machines, like people, have to be brought into the organization slowly. Continued growth on a straight-line basis is reasonable, and additional growth with additional inputs is also reasonable. Again, meet the financial question directly with reasonable assumptions concerning the anticipated results.

Your presentation should be clear enough for your audience to understand it. If you have a number of illustrations, charts, or financial projections, make sure you have a blackboard handy or copies for handouts so that the audience can see exactly what you are talking about. Other visual aids, such as slides, charts, models, and so on, can be used for the presentation. Again, the presentation must be clear enough so that the audience understands it.

Look at your audience. The eyes of the individuals will indicate if they have an understanding of the presentation. If the audience is small, involve them in the presentation, asking as you go along, "Do you understand?" Often this does not satisfy the problem of reaching an audience because the people often do not understand enough to ask questions. Occasionally, audiences are such that that question might be avoided and members of the audience might be asked to repeat something, or in some way demonstrate that they have understood what has been presented. The presenter should summarize frequently so that the audience can keep up with him. Speech instructors tell students that they should tell the audience what it is going to be told, tell it, and finally tell the audience what it has been told, so that the audience is never in doubt as to what is happening.

ASKING FOR ACTION

Inform your audience, or the vice-president, in this case, how he will benefit from what you are going to tell him. You've told him your plan, eliminated competition, and showed him facts and figures about how he can put this plan in action and begin to get the benefits. Now you have reached the point of asking him to take action. Again, drawing on the sales techniques, we might use one of the following closings:

Assumptive. "It looks like a good program, doesn't it, Mr. Green?"
"Yes, it does."
"Then if you'll just sign this purchase order, I'll go ahead and order the machine right away."
You have gotten him to say yes to the proposal without exactly saying yes. You got his name on the purchase order and that is what you were trying to accomplish. Maybe if board action is required, you might tell him: "I'll just ask your secretary to help us get a time on the next board agenda." This is being very assumptive, though, and you'd better be careful that you don't alienate the vice-president and lose the opportunity you have so carefully cultivated.

Ask for the Action. "If you agree that this is a good proposal, Mr. Green, then we'll put it into effect immediately. What do you think?" Now it is up to him to say yes or no, to agree or disagree. This closing is different from the assumptive in that the decision maker has got to object. In the direct approach he must give an answer.

Narrowing the Choice. "If we continue to use the present method, we'll fall even further behind our competitors. If we adopt the Henley proposal, we'll have only a partial solution. And so, we would be far ahead of our competitors if we adopt the proposal I have made." You might say the Cadillac is too large, the Volkswagon is not prestigious enough, so we will have to use the Mercedes. This is not always logical, but it makes the point.

T-Account or Balance. "And so, Mr. White, with only two points against the proposal and seven in its favor, we would have to conclude that this is the logical course to follow." This is making use of a scale or a T-account, with the assets on one side and the liabilities on the other.
We may use other calls for action such as "Our competitor is getting the jump on us because they have adopted a similar method." (Fear) Or, "We would be leading our competitors if we adopted this new plan." (Pride) Or, "Everybody else is doing it." (Bandwagon) Or, "If we don't act now, we might go under." (Combination of Shock and Last Chance)

OVERCOMING OBJECTIONS
FROM THE AUDIENCE

You have asked for the action from your audience, the vice-president. If he agrees to adopt the plan, then you have succeeded in accomplishing what you set out to do. If he objects to your program, then you have to overcome his objections and, hopefully, get him to say yes. If he says no, ask why. The most common reason for a negative response will be that there is not enough money available or the project costs too much. You should have covered this in your presentation, but he apparently did not understand how his benefits were going to exceed his costs. You might agree with him and repeat the benefits he will receive. Or, you might say, "Look at the money we will save." Or, "Look at the profits we will make." If he says we cannot afford to do it, you might use the technique of saying "We can't afford not to do it, and still maintain our position."

The decision maker might say he does not want to make a decision at this time. "On what date can I expect a decision?" you might ask. Or, "Will you have a decision by next Thursday?" Or, "Is there any point I might clarify to aid you in making a decision?" You might even ask him for a specific appointment at a later date to hear the final decision.

The vice-president might tell you that the idea is too new or too different. You could tell him, "This is an opportunity for our company to become a leader in the industry, rather than a follower." If he says he has to discuss it with someone else, ask if you can be included in the discussion to help clear up any points which might arise.

Quite often, the know how of financing is not within your scope, but in a small company, your advice on financing the project might be taken, or at least the fact that you had looked into the financial aspects could be a point in your favor. If you are able to tell the audience that General Electric Credit Corporation will finance the new machine at seven percent, add-on, for forty-eight months, the decision maker will know that you have done your homework even if he does not take your advice.

So, you have done it. You had a good idea, thought about it, carried it through to a logical conclusion, analyzed it from every point of view, and decided to make a presentation to a decision maker. You have qualified him as one who could benefit, make a decision, and enforce it. You have attracted his attention by showing him how he and the company could benefit from adopting the program. You have presented it with all the facts, asked for action, and fought off the objections. Now, hopefully, your idea is a part of the company program, and you have succeeded in bringing your idea to life.

FOR DISCUSSION

1. *Why do you need to concentrate on idea acceptance?*
2. *Describe the six steps in making a presentation.*
3. *"Good ideas sell themselves." Discuss this statement.*

4. *What must you do to qualify your audience?*
5. *What are some basic attention-getting approaches?*
6. *"You can build your idea by knocking down others." Discuss this statement.*
7. *What are some ways you can ask your audience to take action?*
8. *Devise a program for a class period and sell your instructor and the rest of the class on adopting it.*
9. *Should you present your conclusions at the beginning of your presentation or at the end? Discuss each approach.*

CASE 9–1

Plugging Up the Holes in the Doughnut Plan

"Girls, we've got to do better this year than we did last time," Donna Wil-
helm, head cheerleader for Hamilton Junior College, told the other cheerleaders. "According to our records, last year, on Doughnut Saturday, we
ordered five hundred boxes of doughnuts and there were ten of us to sell
them—fifty boxes apiece. We were to start selling at ten o'clock and hoped
to be finished by noon, considering family sales and multiple box sales.
Those of you who were here then know that by noon we had really just gotten started and at two o'clock we still had a hundred and sixty boxes left.
We cut that down to a hundred by four o'clock and luckily, the doughnut
man took those back without any cost to us. Otherwise, we wouldn't have
made enough money to carry on our activities all year."

"Hey, Donna, how much did we make last year?" asked Marie Spencer,
a recently elected freshman.

"Let's see, we bought them for seventy-five cents and sold them for a
dollar. Twenty-five cents a box times four hundred is one hundred dollars
profit. If we had had to pay seventy-five cents each for the hundred boxes
we didn't sell, that would have cut us to twenty-five dollars."

"Didn't we decide we'd have to have a hundred and fifty dollars this
year?" asked Lila Jones. "If we couldn't sell but four hundred boxes last
year, how can we sell, let's see . . . uh . . . six hundred boxes this year?"

"Yea," said Ruth Miller, "Maybe we'd better do something else."

"I guess we could do something else," said Donna, "But I believe we
would do a better job of selling doughnuts. You remember Shirley Crockett,
don't you? Well, according to our records, she by far outsold everybody
else last year. I called her at home last night to see if she could remember
why . . . if she did anything special to make her sell so many. She said that
the night before Doughnut Saturday, she and her father, who is a real estate
salesman, sat down and figured out some of the objections she would run
into when she tried to sell the doughnuts, and then they tried to figure out
ways to overcome the objections. For instance, when she knocked on a
door and some guy came out and said 'Sure, I'd like to have a box, but I
don't have any money.' She'd say, 'I'll take a check.' If he said, 'I don't
have a blank check,' she'd say, 'I'll bill you for it,'" and would immediately
begin to write the guy's address on a blank sheet and say 'What name
should I put this in?' Usually, by this time, she told me, he'd say 'Wait a

140

minute,' and he'd go find a dollar. I think if we do what Shirley did, we could sell the six hundred boxes without any problem."

"I agree with Donna," Marlene Wise said. "We could do a better job. Last year when somebody told me they'd like to have the doughnuts, but they didn't have the money, I'd just smile and say 'Well, thank you anyway' and go on. I think we ought to go over some of the problems right now and figure out a way to make Doughnut Saturday a success and not string this money-making business over the whole year."

GUIDE QUESTIONS

1. *What are some of the approaches the girls might use in selling the doughnuts?*
2. *If the problem is how to raise one hundred fifty dollars to support the year's program, what are some of the alternatives you might suggest?*
3. *How does this episode compare with other business ventures?*

CASE 9–2

The Young Presenters

Gerald Faulkner was competing with Mike Montgomery and both of them knew it. They were assistant production supervisors and were the youngest men, in age and management seniority, to be invited to the weekly staff meeting on Monday morning.

"We've got to do something in the production department," the Old Man had said. He had looked first at Gerald, then at Mike and finally at Roy Cummins, their supervisor. "We're straining our facilities now and Harry Houchens, manager of Northeast Aircraft, called me at home over the weekend and said he wants to increase his orders by sixty percent. Northeast is our biggest customer now and a sixty percent increase in their work would be an overall company increase of about twenty-five percent. The work will start arriving in about six weeks and last for at least six months. He can't guarantee anything after that, but there might be more. Anyway, he's got to know by next week if we can handle it. I told him I was sure we could do it, but I'd have to get the production department to tell me how."

A short while after the general staff meeting, Gerald, Mike, and Roy met to discuss the proposed increase in production. At the conclusion of a two-hour meeting, Roy summed it up:

"As I see it," he said, "We have four reasonable courses of action:

(1) Tell Northeast we can't accept the increase.

(2) Expand our production area about twenty-five percent and buy about thirty new machines. Hire another thirty men to run them.

(3) Go on a sixty-hour optional work week and hope to average fifty hours of overtime, or go on a compulsory fifty-hour work week.

(4) Expand to a two-shift operation with a 10% shift premium.

Number one may appear reasonable to us, but I'm afraid the Old Man won't buy it. I'll study number two and report back by Friday. Gerald, you take number three—overtime—and Mike, you study the shift situation. We'll pick out the one we can live with best, and whoever makes the study will present it to the Old Man at next Monday's meeting."

Neither Gerald nor Mike had presented anything to the staff before. They had just sat and nodded their heads one way or another in support of Roy's positions up to now. This would be a tremendous chance for recognition. To get it, Gerald would have to convince Roy first and the others later.

"This is really strange," Gerald thought. "To get ahead, I've got to hitch my wagon to a position I was assigned. I didn't even get to pick it. Oh well, whether I picked it or not, I've got to find some strong evidence to support it."

In devising his plan, Gerald reviewed some of the facts about the production department. It was composed of about a hundred skilled and semi-skilled machine operators. For each ten operators, there was a leadman, a working machine operator who also was a work assigner. Leadmen were not supervisors, they could not give orders to their fellow workers nor discipline them—they simply assigned work to be done. Leadmen were paid a premium of 25¢ an hour and could be counted on to be productive about seventy percent of the time. Through the use of leadmen, supervision was held to a minimum, Roy, Gerald, and Mike running the whole show. Roy did most of the office work—planning, scheduling, interviewing, reviewing, coordinating—while Gerald and Mike stayed out on the floor.

Roy made $375 a week, while Gerald and Mike each made $300. None of them were eligible for overtime pay. Top operators were paid $5.00 per hour. Entry level was $2.25 per hour. Pay for the one hundred operators was as follows: ten at $2.25, twelve at $2.40, fifteen at $3.00, twenty at $3.60, fourteen at $4.25, nineteen at $4.60, and ten at $5.00.

The sixty-hour work week would be: Monday to Thursday—12 hours, Friday—8 hours, and Saturday—4 hours. The fifty-hour compulsory work week would be ten hours a day, Monday through Friday.

An average machine occupied approximately 250 square feet including aisle space. Local construction costs were approximately $15.00 a square foot for industrial buildings such as the company presently occupied. Production machines cost the company between $3,000 and $10,000 with the average slightly more than $6,000. The company was producing precision parts for an auxiliary gear system used on a jet manufactured by Northeast under a government contract.

GUIDE QUESTIONS

1. *Should Gerald try to determine what kind of plans his coworkers will present? Why?*
2. *What are some of the non-figure aspects Faulkner will have to consider?*
3. *If his plan is adopted, will that be the end of Faulkner's troubles? Why?*

part 3

_____

organizing

At the conclusion of this chapter,
you should be able to—

- Differentiate between line and staff positions.

- Explain the principle of unity of command.

- Define and give uses of the various forms of organization.

- Recognize some of the problems of staff personnel.

- Identify formal and informal groups and relationships.

10

Organizational Structure

In Chapter one, we briefly mentioned organization as one of the four major functions of management. Organizing is the task of establishing a structure and dividing the work, and establishing formal relationships between and among the jobs and job holders.

In addition to formal relationships, all companies and organizations have informal organizations which managers do not establish, but should be aware of and possibly use to the advantage of the company. These informal relationships sometimes become as strong, or stronger, than the formal relationships established by management.

Let us envisage the process of organization as a businessperson opens and expands a new company. In the beginning, there is only one person. He or she has to do everything: planning, organizing, activating, and controlling. Suppose our one-person business decides to incorporate. Most states require that corporations be run by a board of directors with the minimum number of directors being three. Even if it continues to be a one-person-business, he or she must have two more directors to meet the legal requirements.

How does he go about selecting these other two? Once this business grows from one person to more than one, relationships between and among those parties must be established. What will the relationships of our businessperson be to these new parties? If Directors A and B are asked to become directors only to fulfill a legal requirement, then our businessperson will probably dominate them. They will have little or no say in the operation of the business. Often businesspeople choose such directors from among relatives or others who know, or care to know, little about the business.

If, on the other hand, our businessperson asks two people to become board members because he or she wants their help in making decisions, then he or she might decide that the relationship should be a one-person, one-vote relationship so that even the owner will not be able to adopt major policy decisions without the concurrence of at least one of the other directors. This can help make better decisions and keep him or her from making mistakes which are obvious to those people who are not emotionally involved in the decision.

Let us explore three concepts to consider among these three people: (1) unity of command, (2) line and staff, and (3) the scaler principle or chain of command. Of the three listed, two of them, unity of command and chain of command, were first set forth by Henri Fayol.

UNITY OF COMMAND

Unity of command means oneness of command. It means that each employee should have only one direct supervisor. No employee, including managers, should report to more than one supervisor for any one function. Let's look at an example. Suppose Supervisor A is the immediate superior of Employee 1, and Supervisor B is the immediate superior of Employee 2:

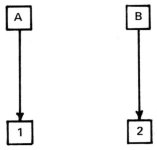

Supervisor A tells Employee 1 what he wants him to do. A is responsible for Employee 1 doing the job and he has the authority to require Employee 1 to do it. Supervisor B has the same relationship with Employee 2.

Suppose Employee 1 reported to both Supervisors A and B, that he is a janitor with the responsibility of cleaning the departments of A and B. The relationship would be shown:

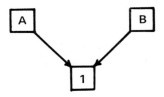

Now, who becomes the decision maker? A, B, or 1? In such a case, Employee 1, the subordinate, begins to make the decisions, and this is just the opposite of what we were trying to accomplish by having supervisors. Employee 1 can now do whatever he wants. He can do as supervisor A tells him, or as B tells him, or he can make up his own plan using parts of instructions from A and B and possibly C, D, E, and everybody else. He can even make up his own plan without using any inputs from supervisors. In spite of the fact that the offices might not be cleaned, it would be hard to place the blame on Employee 1.

To overcome a situation like this, Employee 1 should report only to A or to B. If 1 reported to A, and B wanted some work done, then B would request A to instruct Employee 1 to do that work. If A would not instruct Employee 1 to do as B wanted, then B could go to a higher-level manager for a settlement. In any event, Supervisor A would have charge of the activities of Employee 1 at all times.

Suppose Employee 1 reported to a third party, Supervisor C, who had charge of janitorial and maintenance services. Now, both A and B would request C to send Employee 1 over at a certain time to do a particular job. Supervisor C would now have direct authority over Employee 1 and should arrange Employee 1's schedule so that it would include the work desired by A, B, and all other supervisors.

The same unity of command should be displayed throughout the organization. The president should not report to two persons on the board of directors. He or she should not report to each director, but to the board as a single unit. He or she should respond to the board relative to activities stemming from board action which would result from a majority decision. By responding this way, the president is not subjected to the opinions, whims, or arbitrary decrees of each member.

When unity of command is established, each employee knows that person to whom he or she reports. They also know those persons over whom they have direct authority.

LINE AND STAFF

Before we can talk about organizational structures—line, functional, or line and staff—we must first determine what "line" is and what "staff" means. When we hear these words, our first reaction is to think of the military. If we have been in the armed forces, we have heard these words. We are familiar with such expressions as the "general and his staff" or "injured in the line of duty" or a "line officer." These words have a specific meaning in the armed forces, but that meaning does not carry over into the business world. Only a person who has worked in or around business would know what they mean in a business context.

In the military we think of those people who aid the general, as his staff members. If you are asked the question, "Is the vice-president of production a staff member who helps the president?", you would probably answer yes. You would be wrong. In business, an employee is a line or staff person depending upon his relationship with others and the relationship of his department to the final product or service output. The company president is always line because he is in a position of authority and directs others to take the action necessary to accomplish the goals of the company. The vice-president of production would also be a line person because he or she, too, can accomplish goals through direct commands and control of people. The vice-president of personnel, however, may not be able to command except in a limited fashion. His or her relationship with the vice-president of production and the vice-president of sales would be an advisory relationship. He or she must try to persuade them to take an action, to hire a particular person, but cannot command them to do so. He or she would therefore be a staff person.

Suppose the vice-president of sales would find a need for an additional salesperson. The need would be made known to the personnel department. Personnel would recruit, screen and choose a candidate for the job and then recommend that the vice-president accept the applicant. The relationship is an advisory one, personnel being unable to take direct action, only to assist. The vice-president of sales can make the decision to hire, authorize expenses, and take direct action to sell the product. He or she is a line person.

Personnel is always considered a staff function, yet there are people working in the personnel department who regard the personnel manager as a line person because he or she has direct authority over them. This is a proper assumption because they have a line relationship with their manager. Generally speaking, however, a department head who acts in an advisory capacity to all departments is a staff man. But, because he or she has a line relationship with subordinates, he or she is both line and staff. (See Figure 10.4.)

If the person is doing a job directly related to making a product, marketing that product, or obtaining funds to finance the company, he or she is regarded as a line man. Production personnel, salespeople, assemblers, foremen, sales managers, and financial vice-presidents are examples of line people. Engineers, marketing-research personnel, purchasing agents, safety, security, and maintenance men, janitors, accountants, quality-control managers are common examples of staff positions. Accountants do not make money, they count it and account for it. Quality control personnel do not make products, they check to see if those products are being made according to specifications. Market researchers try to determine what people want or what they think of particular products. These researchers then recommend products or changes, but they do not adopt new programs or do away with old ones. A staff person does not issue any orders or commands except to direct subordinates. Instead, he or she advises others, serves as a consultant to the line people, recommends and tries to accomplish through persuasion and suggestion.

Line people are not superior to staff people, they simply have a different relationship with them than they do with other line people. A line person accomplishes things by exercising direct authority over others. He or she can, and has the right, to command subordinates to do what is necessary to accomplish a job, so long as his commands do not violate company policy.

CHAIN OF COMMAND

Within each organization there is a hierarchy of power that can be viewed as a pyramid with the smallest group, top management, being the most powerful, and so on down the pyramid to its base where we find the majority of workers who have the least amount of power. (See Figure 10.1.) This same relationship applies to all organizations wherein the control rests with the few at the top.

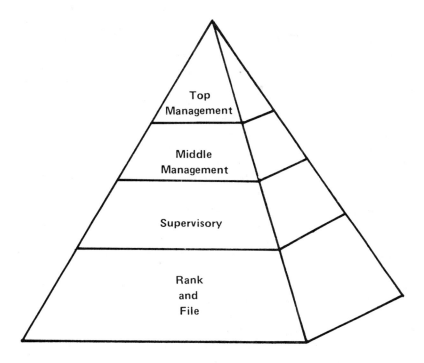

FIGURE 10.1   The organization pyramid of power.

The chain of command, or scalar principle, refers to the direct-authority relationships of the top-management personnel to subordinates, these subordinates to their subordinates, and so on down the line to the worker lowest on the pyramid. The organization might be flat, having only a few levels from the lowest to the highest positions, or it might be tall, having as many as fifteen to twenty levels. But, regardless of the number of levels, it is imperative that the members of the organization realize the relationships between the levels, and know how they, as individuals, fit into the hierarchy.

In the U.S. Army, the new recruit, or private, reports to the squad leader, who reports to the platoon leader, who reports to the company commander, to the battalion commander, to the regimental commander, to the division commander, to the corps commander, to the Army commander, to the Chief of Staff, to the Secretary of the Army, to the Secretary of Defense, and finally, to the President of the United States. This is the chain of command in the Army.

In a corporation, we might find a chain of command which would have the new inductee, a machine operator, for example, reporting to a foreman, who reports to the machine shop supervisor, who reports to the manufacturing superintendent, to the vice-president of manufacturing, who reports to the company president.

When people are made aware of the chain of command in their particular situation, they can see how they relate to those above, below, and around them, who their superiors are, and who are their subordinates and their peers. The chain of command does not normally apply through rank. That is, persons who have a higher rank, but are not in the direct chain of command, do not have authority over those who are subordinate in rank. The superintendent of production cannot tell an accounting clerk what to do. He or she must work through the accounting clerk's chain of command, usually by making a request of a peer (in this case, the supervisor of accounting) for the desired activity. If the peer agrees, then the peer would pass the instruction down to the accounting clerk. If he or she does not agree, then a refusal is in order, and the production superintendent would have to give up or go to a higher power within the chain of command to try and get a more favorable decision.

Generally speaking, departures from the chain of command will undermine the organizational structure and its members. If the production superintendent had ordered the accounting clerk to do something, and the clerk had done it, then the clerk would be acknowledging two supervisors, violating the unit-of-command concept. On the other hand, if that clerk had gone to the vice-president to complain about the production superintendent rather than going to the immediate supervisor, he would be violating the chain of command and undermining his boss, giving the outward appearance that his boss could do nothing to countermand the action. The vice-president would bring the situation back to the accounting supervisor for an explanation, and all this would lead to a bad relationship which would otherwise be prevented by observance of the chain-of-command principle.

Most companies have policies that allow a person who is dissatisfied with the actions or decisions of immediate supervisors to go one step beyond the supervisors, but only after the entire situation has been discussed at the lower level and permission has been sought for a higher-level interview. Employees are directed to work through the chain of command so long as their needs are met.

The open-door policy, where top management people invite lower level personnel to come in and discuss problems, is an effort to keep the line of communications open from bottom to top, but it can also succeed in weakening the authority of the intermediate levels of supervision, unless top management requires notification to the members of the chain. Adoption of the open door policy should be entered into with an objective of having problems solved at the lowest, practical, management level, and not let it degenerate to a point of bypassing supervision for every item of disagreement.

FORMS OF ORGANIZATION

Our businessperson might propose to his or her two directors that they establish a one-person, one-vote board consisting of three equal members, none having authority over the others, and each having one vote in policy matters with a majority controlling company activities.

One of the first matters the three directors would have to face might be to determine what form of organization they want. There are three from which they might choose: (1) the line organization, (2) the functional organization, and (3) the line-staff organization.

In the line organization (Figure 10.2), the president confers authority to each functional head who passes authority down the line. Each function is self-contained. It has no need to seek advice from, or be controlled by anyone other than the president. Functional heads share equal rank with none having authority over the others. This type of organization would have its greatest usefulness and would most likely be found in a small organization that had not grown to such an extent that staff people would be necessary to carry out the company objectives. As the company became larger, the form of organization would probably be changed to the line-staff form.

The second type of organization, the functional organization, is almost extinct (Figure 10.3). All workers in this type of an organization are subjected to a great many bosses and a multiplicity of supervision. Each boss is a specialist with authority over all subordinates who work within the general scope covered by the specialist. For instance, a truck mechanic might roll out from under a truck and find that he reports to the following bosses: the chief mechanic, the driver of the truck, the dispatcher who controls the truck's routing, the accountant who needed to keep records on the repairs, the safety inspector, and the parts manager, and so on. It should be apparent why this form is almost extinct. Subordinates find themselves with so many superiors they do not know what to do first, particularly when conflicting instructions from each of them are received. The result of all this is a frustrated worker, inadequate control, and a race to see whether the employee will quit first or be fired for not being able to do the job.

The most common form of organization is the line-staff plan (Figure 10.4). Such a plan has the benefits of the line organization with the added plus of staff specialists who can assist line managers. The line supervisor needs the staff people to help with specific problems which are outside of the line person's competence. Generally, the line supervisor is not compelled to follow the advice of the staff person, under the theory that the line person maintains full responsibility and, therefore, must have the authority to make his or her own decisions. Most often, however, the supervisor accepts the help and advice of the staff people because they are experts.

There are occasions when staff personnel do have functional authority over line officers in spite of the abovementioned theory. For example, the chief accountant can require a supervisor to provide financial information, cost sheets, time cards, work-in-process reports and other items. In such cases, the line supervisor will have little choice in the matter. He or he must obey the request or try to have it changed. It cannot be disregarded.

TYPES OF ASSISTANTS

There is a difference between an assistant manager and an assistant *to* the manager, a very discernible difference that should be recognized when a person considers estab-

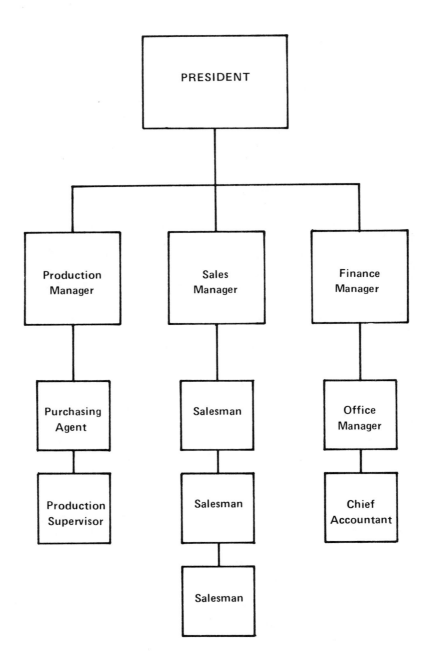

FIGURE 10.2   The Line Organization

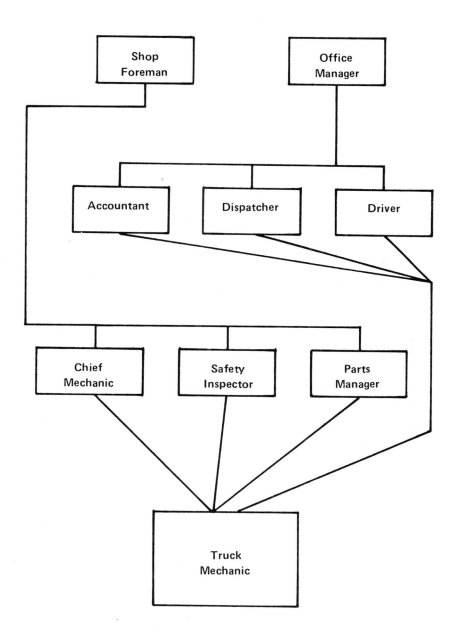

FIGURE 10.3   The Functional Organization

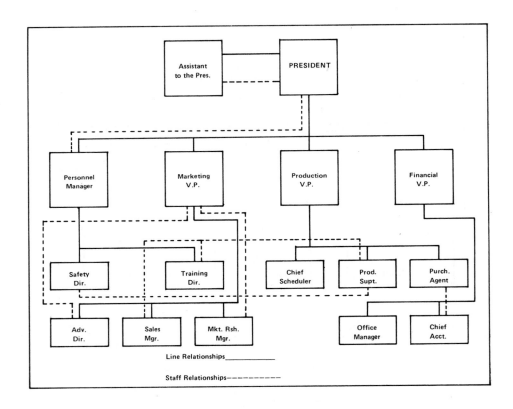

FIGURE 10.4   The Line-Staff Organization

lishing or accepting either of these jobs. An assistant can take charge, take over when the superior is absent. He or she has line authority while the manager is on the job. The assistant is in the chain of command: subordinates report to him or her who must, in turn, report to a superior.

The assistant-to is in a much different position. He or she is a staff person reporting to the manager. His or her duties consist of whatever the boss assigns. When the superior is absent, he or she cannot take the place of a superior. In fact, the assistant's-to position is usually weakened when his or her superior is not there, and a question arises as to whether or not the assistant-to is acting for the superior. In the superior's absence, those decisions which have to be made will be made either by a lower or higher ranking manager, but not by the assistant-to, although he or she might be able to advise on those decisions. The assistant-to sometimes exercises functional authority in areas where he or she is particularly knowledgeable or experienced. But often, in a showdown, his or her boss will not uphold this functional authority, but will, instead, ask the assistant-to to work through him and observe the existing line authority. Robert Townsend, former chief executive of Avis says, "The only people who thoroughly enjoy being assistants to are vampires." He adds that, "In my book anyone who has an assistant-to should be fined a hundred dollars a day until he eliminates the position."[1]

On the positive side, the assistant-to position, although a difficult one, can bring immediate top-level experience to a young person, a recent college graduate, who would not be active at this level for many years if he or she had to reach it through line promotions.

PROBLEMS OF STAFF PERSONNEL

There are a number of situations that cause problems with regard to the use of staff personnel. The first of these is a vague definition of the staff person's duties, and a failure to clarify these duties to the line people who will be concerned with the staff person. Let's look at some examples. In Company A, the new foreman does not know the policy, but assumes that when a worker is sent to him by the personnel department, in response to a request for an additional worker, the foreman is required to take that man whether he likes him or not. He feels that the personnel people, with their special abilities, are better equipped to predict the probability of this man's success than is the foreman. He therefore reacts to the staff advice as if it were a line command and he accepts it that way. He might feel his responsibility is lessened because his authority is limited, that he cannot control his factors of production.

In Company B, under similar circumstances, the supervisor may feel that the personnel department screens candidates for the job, and it is up to him, the supervisor, to make the final decision on candidates, based on his estimate of whether or not they can succeed.

The supervisor of Company C might feel that the people in the personnel department do not know nearly as much about his department as he does, and he will go out looking for candidates himself, enticing them to leave other jobs, offering them whatever they "have to have" to come to work for the company.

It would be up to the organizers of these companies, or this company, to establish a relationship between the personnel department and the line supervisors delineating the responsibilities of each. Once this relationship is established, it should then be enforced.

The second problem with staff is that staff people often violate the nature of their positions by giving direct orders or commanding by implication. For instance, a staff man, wanting to put an idea into effect might confer with the president of the organization and then tell the production superintendent, "I have conferred with the president about this plan and he feels that you should put it into effect immediately." The directive for the implementation of the plan should come from the president, the line authority, rather than from the staff man, but the production man would find himself in a dilemma knowing he should not be commanded by a staff man, but realizing that that staff man probably has the backing of the boss. Should he wait until a direct order is issued by the president? Yes, he should, unless the plan is in response to an emergency situation, in which case the production man should view what the staff man has told him as advice, and decide accordingly.

A third problem with the use of staff is the disregard of staff and staff principles by the top executive. Suppose the personnel department is charged with securing candidates for all jobs in the company, and, after screening and testing the applicants, personnel makes its recommendations to those department heads who must approve them. Then, the boss meets an old friend at a convention or is placed in contact with a bright, young man, hires that person, and then tells personnel to process the new hire. The boss himself has disobeyed company policy with regard to staff assistance and set a precedent for other, subordinate, line personnel. If he does not rely on the staff with confidence, as being experts in the field, then why should other, line subordinates? In this case, the proper thing for the manager to do would be to suggest that a would-be employee stop by and see the personnel manager, and then inform the personnel manager that the candidate is coming. While the personnel manager might feel some pressure from a superior, he or she would at least be able to make an objective decision as to whether or not the candidate might succeed in the job, and he could make a recommendation accordingly.

FORMAL AND INFORMAL ORGANIZATION

We might stop here for a moment to discuss the formal organization as envisioned by the organizers and the informal one which exists despite the formal one. The formal organization is the one outlined on the organization chart showing the relationships of the members of the company with each other. Straight lines on the chart between one position and another indicate a direct line authority, as shown.

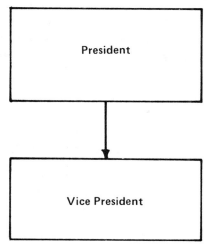

A dotted line shows an advisory relationship, such as a staff man to a line man where the line man would listen to the recommendations of the staff man, but make a decision on his own.

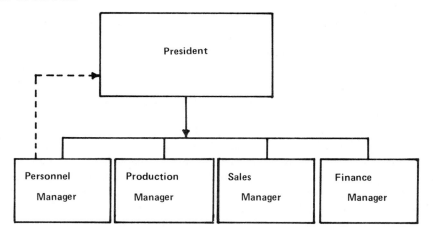

These formal relationships are not the extent of relationships between people in a company. There are the informal relationships between people—such relationships do not appear on the organization chart.

What kinds of relationships might these be? These are relationships which come into being because of the mutual interests of the participants, regardless of the formal setting. For instance, the secretary of the vice-president of production and the secretary of the assistant personnel manager go to lunch together. Their bosses are on different levels, but these girls enjoy each other's company. They may never see each other away from the job, but they get this "social pay" while on the job. That is, they find a human side of the work which might help them enjoy the work more.

To an extent, everyone works for money, because this pay represents to that person his or her worth to the company. And it also represents buying power. The employee feels that the more the company recognizes his or her contributions, the more he or she will be paid, thus increasing a feeling of being needed. Certainly, money is not the only compensation for working. People need a feeling of belonging, a feeling of satisfaction on the job. Often, such feelings of satisfaction will not come from the work itself because the work is dull and drab. But, a chance to meet with people, to become friends, to find someone to talk to, to listen to, and to enjoy being with fulfills the social needs of members of the organization. Workers as well as managers become members of informal groups.

Managers do not consciously create informal groups. They are formed by the members of the organization, at all levels including management, to satisfy human needs. Even in a prisoner-of-war camp informal groups exist. People form informal groups because of common interests, because of their similar backgrounds, even because they have been subjected to the same treatment. One of the first things a manager ought to recognize about informal groups is that they are not necessarily bad. In fact, it may be good. If an informal group accepts, adopts, and approves of a management practice, then this informal group can put pressure on its members to go along with the action.

An informal group could be bad. When the informal groups put pressure on their members to restrict output, or do no work at all, or cases where existing groups reject new employees, or, if informal groups sanction activities which management views as detrimental to the best interests of the company, management must take steps to counteract the informal group. For instance, if the group adopted an attitude that pilfering is a fringe benefit, management would have to take a hard stand against this practice, severely enforcing regulations against stealing.

Informal groups and relationships might form when the formal structures do not accomplish the desired or expected goals. If the manager of a department is lazy or hard to get along with, the assistant manager or even the assistant-to might become the informal leader because the subordinates will go to him or her rather than the nominal boss, the one recognized on the organization chart. If a staff person, who is supposed to be acting in an advisory capacity, is more knowledgeable of a particular situation than the line boss, subordinates might go to this staff man, bypassing their line boss, so that they can get immediate answers to their problems.

A particular kind of informal group is a clique—a group of people who band together to support a common cause. A clique's members might not have anything else in common other than this cause. Its members could come from all socio-economic strata to support a cause or combat a problem, ranging from electing a person to a legislative position, to rallying forces to eliminate a disease. In a company, if management recognizes that a clique exists, it should first determine the cause the clique supports. If the cause is one with which management agrees or simply does not oppose, it should allow the clique to continue to exist and even support it, if it appears deserving. Management might even have a goal it would like to encourage, and would look for support from a clique or could make an effort to find individuals who would agree with this cause and, in effect, establish a clique.

DEPARTMENTATION

Our businessman must expand the number of employees in his business because he can no longer do all the work himself. He must divide his work, both managerial and operational, with these new employees. He already has the two new board members to help him in corporate planning and policy making, but, now he needs help in his daily activities, he needs full-time employees. When he goes about dividing the work, he will have to find a basis for the division of labor, a reason for the allocation of certain activities to certain individuals or groups.

When a businessman divides workers into groups, he must establish relationships between and among the groups and individuals, as well as devise methods of coordinating the activities of these groups. He must establish these relationships so that the work of each group will contribute to the accomplishment of the total objectives of the company. There are many bases for dividing work or departmentation. We will examine some of them:

Function

The most common method by which work is broken down is according to function. These are such breakdowns as the three basic functional areas of work: finance, production, and sales. The secondary functional areas are personnel, purchasing, research, engineering, accounting, traffic management, and others. This functional system is easily understood and can be implemented by the smallest organization or the largest. As soon as there is one man doing a production job, you can have a production department. As soon as there is one salesman you can have a sales department. Any new employees can be readily classified as production, sales, or according to some other function.

When a company is broken down into functional departments, the manager of each department can direct his or her total efforts toward accomplishing the objectives within that function. When a person is involved in several functional areas, it becomes difficult to divide his or her time between these functions, allocating the proper energies to each. When workers and managers become specialists in a field, they can make that field more productive.

Letters and Numbers

As a company continues to grow, functions are broken down even further into letters and numbers. For instance, you might have in the production area Department A,

A Function	Manager	Personnel Production Sales
B Letters & Numbers	Manager	Department A Department B Department C
C Time	Manager	First Shift Second Shift Third Shift
D Products	Manager	Textbooks Fiction Children
E Customers	Manager	Retail Wholesale O. E. M.
F Geography	Manager	Northeast Mid-Atlantic Southeast
G Job	Manager	Civic Center Job Rock Creek Job Warehouse Job
H Machinery	Manager	Grinding Room Lathe Department Assembly Room

FIGURE 10.5 *Departmentalization by various classifications.*

Department B, Department 127, and so on. This system is not used as widely as it once was because of the human relations aspect which makes it difficult for people to identify with a number or letter. However, in most labor unions, the local units are known by number, and great group spirit is exemplified by those persons who take pride in being members of Local 675.

Time

Those people who are working for a company on the Number 5 paper machine in Board Mill Number 3 might also be further divided into the first, second, third, or swing shifts. Or, they may be members of the day or night shifts. Such time divisions are almost always involved with production workers and departments, rather than administrative departments, or sales departments, which seldom work at any time other than normal business hours.

Products

As a company grows and begins to diversify, offering different products or services, departmentation can be made according to product. Examples might be the toy department, the children's book department, the piece-goods department, the upholstered-furniture department, or any department specified by the product or service. Examples of service units might be the window-washing department, the customer-auditing department, the new-car sales department, or the lubrication department. As the production of these goods and services increases, further breakdowns might occur according to time, number, letter, or function.

Customers

Products are sold to different types of customers through different channels of distribution. Examples of customer breakdowns are the original-equipment-manufacturers department, the wholesale and retail departments, the service-station department, the catalogue department, the men's, women's and children's departments, or any other departments specified as such because of the customers served.

Geography

Geographical departmentation generally is reserved for those large companies with national or regional manufacturing and or selling facilities. As the name implies, this is a departmentation of areas such as the northern division, the southeastern division, the east and west divisions, the North Atlantic states, Virginia and West Virginia, southern Mississippi, the Phoenix division, or the south Houston division. Geographical departmentation lends itself to decentralization, allowing divisions to make decisions based on the individual requirements of the people in the area.

Job

In an organization, groups are formed to do particular jobs. The department may assume the name of the job it performs. It might be a job with a customer's name such as the DuPont job. It could be job #5481, or, it might have a code number or name, possibly a crew number or name. In World War II, a group of people worked in Oak Ridge, Tennessee, on the secret "Manhattan Project," which was later identified as the project developing the atomic bomb.

Machinery

Companies might be departmentalized by the tools that are used in the department such as the lathe room, the grinding room, the boiler room, or the precision-instrument room. The department may also have the name of the skilled persons involved in running these machines such as the machinist's department, the patternmaker's loft, the grinder's department, the crane-operator's perch, or the wine-tester's department.

Once our businessman divides his company into departments, his work is not ended because, as the company grows, the need for new divisions occurs. Departmentation is not a static process. It is dynamic, always changing and adjusting to meet the needs of the organization. In large companies, major organizational changes take place about every two years. Minor changes occur at more frequent intervals. When a change in organization takes place, the relationships between groups and individuals must be redefined, organizational charts must be redrawn, and job descriptions reworked.

FOR DISCUSSION

1. *What is unity of command?*
2. *In business, what is line and what is staff?*
3. *Discuss the chain of command.*
4. *What do you think of the open-door policy?*
5. *What are the three forms of organization?*
6. *What is the difference between an assistant manager and an assistant to the manager?*
7. *What are some problems of staff?*
8. *What is a clique?*
9. *In what ways might a company be organized according to department?*

ENDNOTE

1. Robert Townsend, *Up the Organization* (New York: Alfred A. Knopf, Inc., 1970), pp. 22–24.

Righting the Wrong Boss

"Mr. Parker, I've got a problem that you might be able to help me with," Lynn Ripley told her senior advisor. "This old guy down at work is driving me crazy."

"How's he doing that?" Parker asked.

"He keeps giving me work to do and he's not supposed to. He's not my boss."

"I don't understand what you are saying. If he's not your boss, why do you take the work?"

"That's part of the problem now. Yesterday, I decided I wasn't going to do the work and I told him so. He has a secretary. Let her do it, I told him."

"What did he say?"

"He cussed me out. Then he went back into his office and slammed the door," Lynn said.

"Well, who is your boss?"

"Mr. Donaldson."

"What does he say about it?"

" 'Just go ahead and do it,' " he says. " 'Don't rock the boat.' " He's afraid of old Simpson. He doesn't want to cross him. So he doesn't care how much work I have to do, so long as I keep quiet."

"Are you working more than your regular hours?"

"Sometimes. If I can't finish my regular work and Simpson's work by quitting time, they ask me to stay late. Of course, I get paid for the extra time but that's not the point. I resent having to do his work while his girl sits around doing nothing. I don't know whether I told you or not, but I think that, although he's about seventy, he's got a crush on his secretary. Loves her but could care less about me. He thinks I'm some kind of robot."

"Well, Lynn, is there anybody else, your boss's boss or somebody, you could go to?"

"I went to my boss's boss once, but he sided with Donaldson and Simpson. It wasn't about work, though, it was about an insurance claim. They were going to fire me over that until I signed a release. Worst company I've ever seen."

"Hmmm," Parker said. "Lynn, how about giving me a chance to think about the situation. Why don't you stop in here tomorrow. Maybe I'll have an idea about what you ought to do."

"Okay," Mr. Parker," Lynn said. "I'm going to be thinking about it, too. That old devil had better leave me alone today, or we won't have anything to talk about tomorrow. I'm going to knock him on the head."

She and Parker both laughed as Lynn walked down the hall to her last class.

GUIDE QUESTIONS

1. *Who has the problem?*
2. *Who can take action to solve the problem?*
3. *What alternatives are open to Lynn?*
4. *How do you predict the case will be resolved?*

The Cascade of Confidential Claims

"Molly, I told you when I left here Thursday afternoon that I wanted this quotation typed up and sent in on Friday and it's still on your desk."

"Okay, Mr. Goodman," Molly said, "I'm sorry. I'll get on it right away."

"Right away! For what? Time ran out on this request Friday at midnight—no postmark, no bid. There's no way we can get in on it now. This kind of stuff really burns me up, Molly. I purposely waited until the last day so I could make certain of some raw-material prices. I'm almost sure we'd have gotten the job. And we needed it to keep the grinding room busy for the last two weeks of next month."

"I'm sorry, Mr. Goodman, I just got busy. . . ."

"Busy," he interrupted, "with what? This is the only thing I left you to do."

"Yes, but Mr. Hipperd came in with some financial reports for his files. Mr. Pardue came in and had to have some expediting sheets made right then. Mr. McCleary wanted the income statement and balance sheet for last month done so he could get those in the mail. I worked an hour late just to get them done."

"When I give you work to do, Molly, I expect you to do it, Molly. You are not to do their work until you've finished mine. You work for me, not them."

"Yes, but I have to do their confidential work, and they said they couldn't let a clerk spread everything around. And, all of them were in a hurry. I don't know what you expect from me. I try my best. People are after me all the time."

With that Molly got up from her desk and ran down the hall. Goodman was sorry that he had upset her, but he was still quite disturbed at having lost the bid. He looked at the organization chart and wondered how to prevent the same situation from occurring again.

GUIDE QUESTIONS

1. *Was the lost job Molly's fault?*
2. *What can be done to keep this from happening again?*
3. *Discuss what can be done about the lost bid.*

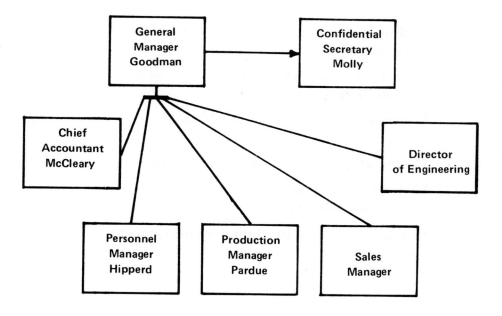

At the conclusion of this chapter,
you should be able to—

- **Define a job and those concepts relating to designing a job.**

- **Contrast and compare the two sources of a manager's authority.**

- **Determine whether or not an obligation can be delegated.**

- **Decide when a manager needs to delegate.**

- **Understand why some managers have a difficult time delegating.**

- **List those factors which influence the span of control.**

11

Organization Concepts

In the last chapter, we said that organizing is a dynamic process, one which must be updated constantly in accordance with corporate changes in personnel, technology, emphasis, and markets. We also said that positions must be redefined and relationships reestablished as a result of these organizational changes.

A JOB

A group of tasks assigned to one person is a job. When a job is created, a description of the job seldom exists because the designer, the person making up the job, is not quite sure what he will require of the worker who will hold the job. Therefore, in small or newly formed companies, one will seldom find job descriptions for all of the employees, just as one will seldom find written policy or stated objectives. The philosophy of the company is expressed or implied by the general manager, the president, the leader, and he or she simply directs all the subordinates to do what must be done. Communications are face to face and messages do not get lost in transmission devices. However, as the company grows, the need for job descriptions and written policies also grows. This becomes obvious when things happen, such as leaving critical work undone because no one knows who is supposed to do it, subordinates are unable to decide to whom they should report, employees duplicate jobs, or find their responsibilities greatly overlapping because they have to assume too much.

Before we can write a job description or set forth minimum job specifications, we must do a job analysis which consists of collecting and studying data related to a specific job, including the work itself, the responsibility involved, and the relationships of that job to others. The person making the job analysis (usually is attached to the personnel department) gets his information from three sources: (1) questioning the worker, (2) questioning superiors, and (3) observing the worker. To get the best results, the analyst should be introduced to the worker and state why the job is being analyzed. Once a job analysis is completed, a job description can be written.

A job description is a written document which identifies a job, summarizes it, then states in detail the duties of the job—what is to be done, why it is to be done, and how it should be done. The duties might be broken down into percentages such as: operates engine lathe, 75%; operates multi-spindle drill press, 15%; gauges and measures, 10%.

The job description should stipulate the working conditions. It should state the number and classification of people who report to the job holder, and that person to whom the job holder would report. If there are any staff functions or advisory relationships involved, these, too, should be specified. An example of a job description is shown in Figure 11.1.

In addition to a job description, the analysis should provide a basis for preparing job specifications—the minimum human characteristics required of the job applicant before he or she can be considered seriously for a job. The specs should include educational requirements and skills acquired through education and experience, or a combination of both. They might also include personality evaluations such as capacity for leadership.

Generally speaking, the advertisements listed in help wanted sections of the newspaper contain job specifications, and each day, hundreds of them are listed. Below are some samples taken from one edition of a metropolitan daily paper: self starter, full-time, preferably retired military, over 30 years of age, must be mechanically inclined, RN, journeyman, no experience needed, BS, experienced, experienced in SEC reporting, minimum 2 years experience, at least 21, over 16, some insurance knowledge helpful, typing, must have tools and transportation, references required, able-bodied, A.D.A. registered, college background, drive, flair for leadership, ability to read construction plans, must have following, college student, take charge, mature, shorthand, drivers permit, high school graduate.

AUTHORITY

Within the job description, we find a section which says something like "Supervises ———," and "Reports to ———." These are inserted into the description to define the relationship this person has to other job holders within the company. It would appear that this is where authority originates in any job.

What is authority? We can define authority as the right to make decisions within the scope and limitations imposed by the granting superior, and the right to carry out these decisions by giving orders and commands to subordinates and requiring compliance from them.

We normally think of authority as being granted to a subordinate by a superior, such as a board of directors being granted authority by the owners or the stockholders, to act within certain limits, or the president being given authority by the board, or a production man being given some decision-making authority by his foreman. This is called the downward source of authority, the granting of authority by a superior to a subordinate. This authority is an extension of the right to own property and the freedom to exercise control over that property as granted by the United States Constitution. There is a second theory concerning the granting of authority—the upward source, or the subordinate-acceptance theory.

JOB DESCRIPTION

Job Title: Billing Clerk, Level 1.

Department: Billing.

Division: Miami.

Job Summary: Under the supervision of billing department manager, with no subordinates, responsible for collecting documents and calculating customer invoices, distributing and filing invoice copies.

Work Content:
1. Fifteen percent: Go into plant, collect loading receipts, weight tickets, bills of lading, and other special documents.
2. Five percent: Match collected documents with customer orders according to assigned job numbers.
3. Fifty percent: Calculate invoice work sheets using customer order and related shipping documents.
4. Fifteen percent: Type customer invoices.
5. Ten percent: Disassemble invoices. Mail copies to customers. Route intracompany copies.
6. Five percent: File documents in accordance with general filing system.

Working Conditions:

1. Walking, 20 percent; standing, 20 percent; sitting, 60 percent.
2. Billing office, 75 percent; plant, 20 percent; mailroom, 5 percent.
3. Regular office hours, overtime upon request.

FIGURE 11.1   *Sample of a job description.*

The subordinate-acceptance theory says that a superior has only as much authority as his subordinates are willing to give him. If they refuse to be led by the leader, then he has no authority. If they agree to accept him and his authority as granted by a higher level, then he has full authority. Normally, the subordinate-acceptance theory is most applicable in group situations. That is to say that if only one person out of twenty subordinates refuses to accept the authority of his boss, then the boss will take action against the non-accepting subordinate, possibly to the extent of firing him to preserve the rights of the manager. If, however, none of the twenty accept the authority of the boss, then his authority does not exist. He will not be able to get respect or compliance from his subordinates, and he will probably have to modify his position or perhaps, even leave his job. There are certain economic conditions when this theory of subordinate-acceptance is not applicable. When jobs are scarce, when there is no substitute for the current job, subordinates are compelled, even as a group, to accept the authority of the boss, particularly if the jobs are lower level ones, are quickly and easily learned, require no prior training or credentials, and there is a large number of candidates eager to get jobs.

Even if the subordinate-acceptance theory is not widely held or discussed, most managers realize that it does exist to an extent, and it is this knowledge that keeps managers from acting as dictators, having no regard for the feelings of the subordinates.

There are many cases where subordinates outwardly accept the authority of their superior, but do negative things to erode his authority and his ability to get things done. They might slow the normal work rate, restrict output to a certain number of units, or do work of marginal quality which would cause the boss to get into trouble, but would not be bad enough to get the whole group fired.

Limits of Authority

Can a manager command his subordinates to do anything and everything? No, he can not. He must stay within certain limits. First, he must stay within the boundaries of the authority delegated to him by his superiors. This could limit his decisions or limit what he requires others to do. He can only order his men to do those things which appear to be reasonable and necessary for the accomplishment of company objectives. He cannot order his people to do things which are illegal, exceed the abilities of the workers, are dangerous beyond that which the worker feels necessary in his line of duty, or those things which have not been sanctioned by the workers' representatives such as the union.

This brings up a second limitation of authority—overlapping authority. Although no worker should have two bosses, most workers have several authorities from which they choose priorities. The church, government, the worker's spouse, his or her personal philosophy, the union, and other organizations limit a manager's authority over subordinates.

There is a question of ethics which will be taken up in a later chapter, but we might mention ethics here in connection with the third limiting factor—subordinate acceptance. The subordinate might feel that he or she is ethically unable to accept a superior's command, that he or she cannot do certain things that the superior feels are ethical, but the subordinate feels are not. Moreover, the subordinate might feel that certain things are personal rights in which the company should not interfere. For instance, a boss might order all his men to contribute a certain amount of money or a percentage of their pay to a cause. The employee feels that his contribution is a personal affair in which the company should have no say. The subordinate might appeal these matters of ethics and personal rights to a higher level for resolution of the matter.

REPONSIBILITY

When a person in an organization has the authority to give orders and commands and expects compliance with them, or the authority to make decisions within specific limitations, then he or she must bear the responsibility of these decisions and orders. If he or she commands subordinates to do a certain unit of work, then he or she must be responsible to see that those subordinates complete the work and that the work is, in fact, relative to the overall objectives of the company. If the subordinates do not complete the work, or if the work itself is not germane to the total effort of the company, then the efforts of the employees and the money expended in these efforts are wasted, and the responsibility for this waste must fall upon the shoulders of that person who had the authority to bring the desired results into being.

Let us define responsibility as the obligation of completing a job to the best of a worker's ability. In the case of a production worker, a clerical person, or anyone without managerial assignments, then the assigned job might be to run a machine, to bag groceries, to cut meat, to type reports, to file, or to do some other specific job. In the case of a manager, from first-level supervisory positions right up to the president of the company, there exists the responsibility for achieving results, for getting jobs done by working through others, and making meaningful decisions. The board of directors makes decisions and issues orders which affect the efforts and direction of the whole company. Therefore, the board is ultimately responsible for all the results of the organization. These board members, acting as a group, give the president authority to make decisions and require subordinates to carry out these decisions and, in turn, the board holds him responsible for accomplishing acceptable results. For example, the president does not normally make policy. Policy making is left up to the board of directors. However, the president is given the authority to and the responsibility for carrying out the policies adopted by the board. The president gives his subordinates certain responsibilities and authority to carry them out, and so on, down through the various levels of the organization.

There is a generally accepted rule of responsibility: that no one can be held responsible for accomplishing a goal if he or she does not have authority commensurate with or equal to that responsibility. That is, he or she must have the authority to direct the activities if held responsible for the results of those activities. A doctor tells his patient, "I cannot be responsible for your well being unless you give me the authority to act as I see fit."

Responsibility and authority should go hand in hand, giving workers enough authority to carry out their responsibilities, and only as much responsibility as can be met with the given amount of authority.

In the case of line personnel, where managers have direct authority over others within their chain of command, then they must also bear direct responsibility for those subordinates and their actions. Staff personnel, on the other hand, do not have direct authority over line personnel and therefore, regardless of whether the line personnel accept or reject the suggestions and recommendations of the staff people, the staff people are not held responsible for the actions of the line men. Only those persons who have the authority and capability of making commands and decisions can be held responsible.

OBLIGATIONS

There is another proposition we should look into in the context of authority and responsibility—that responsibility is an obligation, and can never be delegated. At face value, this would appear to be false. If you give a person a job to do and he does not do it, then he has failed in his responsibility. Yes, he has failed, but so has the person who gave him the responsibility.

As we look into the rationale of delegation, we can see that the board of directors can delegate authority and responsibility to the president, but if the president fails to accomplish his goals, then the board has also failed to accomplish its goals, and must, ultimately bear the total responsibility and the obligation for the failure (or success) of the company. The president gives the vice-president of production certain authority and responsibility to produce goods, but if the vice-president fails, if costs are too high, turnover too great, quality too poor, then the president has also failed to accomplish his obligation. Everyone in the chain of command, from the top to the level where the failure takes place, must share the responsibility for the failure.

The matter of who gets reprimanded for misdeeds or praised for success does not necessarily follow lines of authority and responsibility. Often we see instances where presidents get praised for work subordinates do in spite of the president, and where subordinates are fired regardless of the fact that they are following instructions exactly as ordered. Those discharged become scapegoats sacrificed for the good of the company. One television character boasted that he had been able to maintain his position in his business because he had been able to delegate blame for misdeeds to others in the company. These incidents touch on the larger question of ethics which we will consider later.

In making a plan, in shaping up an organization, it is extremely important to assign the responsibility of completing a task to the personnel involved, or to fix this responsibility to certain positions so that persons occupying those positions will be totally aware of the goals they are to accomplish. It is also just as important to give these job holders enough authority to accomplish the goals which they have been assigned. When people have been made aware of their responsibility and have accepted it, then they can proceed knowing what they are to accomplish, what they are being held responsible for, and knowing that they will be evaluated on the manner in which they achieve the results for which they are accountable.

DELEGATION AND DECENTRALIZATION

We have discussed authority, responsibility, and giving subordinates more responsibility and therefore more authority, and this, in itself, is the act of delegating. We call this delegation of authority, not delegation of responsibility, although it is implied that the two go together. Normally, delegation of authority is the delegation of decision making to a lower level of the organizational structure. For instance, in Hopeful College, if the department chairman is in a direct line relationship over Miss Linda Fairweather, the accounting instructor, he might elect to retain the authority to choose the textbook for the class or he might delegate this authority to Miss Fairweather. If he delegates the authority, then she is responsible for the decision she makes in choosing the text, as well as for imparting this material to the students. However, if the department chairman retains the authority to make the decision regarding the text, then Miss Fairweather is responsible only for delivering the message and not the message itself. She cannot be held responsible for something she has no authority to change.

The degree to which delegation of decision-making authority is granted is referred to as the degree of decentralization. Centralization, on the other hand, refers to the tendency toward making decisions at the highest levels, at the top of the pyramid of authority. A decentralized organization is one in which decisions are made at all levels of the organization depending upon the nature and importance of the decision.

Why would a manager want to delegate authority when he knows that he must still be responsible for all his subordinates' actions and decisions? There are several reasons. Let us examine some of them:

1. The job gets so big that the top man doesn't have time to do everything that must be done.
2. The manager finds himself taking home work every night and week-end.
3. Vital projects are being delayed until he has time to get to them.
4. Men are standing idle waiting for the manager to make decisions.
5. Morale is deteriorating because subordinates don't have the authority to go ahead with their work.

With such reasons confronting him, it would seem that the manager should welcome a chance to delegate authority, to give his subordinates opportunities to make decisions and be responsible for various projects within the manager's scope. We find, however, that very often managers have an extremely hard time delegating work to subordinates in spite of the obvious need for this action. Some reasons advanced for the inability of managers to delegate are:

1. Subordinates are not properly trained for the work.
2. Superiors lack confidence in their subordinates.
3. Superiors are afraid their subordinates will do the job better than the superior.
4. Superiors want to appear indispensable.
5. Superiors like the jobs too much to give them up.
6. It is easier to do the job than to show someone else how to do it.
7. Objectives and procedures are so vague the manager would find it all but impossible to convey expectations to the subordinate.

So there are many reasons for not delegating, but there are better reasons for allowing subordinates to share the responsibility of the manager. Delegation should work for the manager. It should make his work easier and attainable, where formerly it might have been impossible. Delegation makes good sense under most circumstances.

First, if a manager is to be promoted to a higher level, if he is to take on more responsibility in the organization, he must have someone who can replace him in his present position without upsetting the group. Delegation is a way of grooming a subordinate to take his manager's place. There are cases where a manager feels that to delegate to a subordinate is to show that the superior is not indispensable. Such a manager is insecure and lacks confidence in himself. He will probably accomplish what he has set out to do—prove that he is indispensable—and will at the same time lock himself into a lower-level position for lack of a competent replacement.

Second, part of any manager's job is to develop other managers for the good of the organization. Delegation of authority and responsibility is one of the best methods available for management training. Being thrown into the water and told to sink or swim, being required to depend upon his own abilities under real conditions, has been the most valuable training for many top-management candidates.

Third, a manager's job is to get things done through others and the more he delegates, the more he can get done and the wider he can expand his activities. The more he delegates, the more he can enlarge his span of control.

SPAN OF CONTROL

All organizations can be characterized as being flat, figure 11.2, or tall, figure 11.3, in their organizational structure. Flat organizations are those which have few oganizational levels in the chain of command from the bottom to the top, with many people in each level. Tall organizations are those with many levels but fewer people in each level. What determines, to a great extent, the "tallness" or "flatness" of an organization is the span of control of the managers in that organization.

Span of control is the number of subordinates a manager has reporting to him

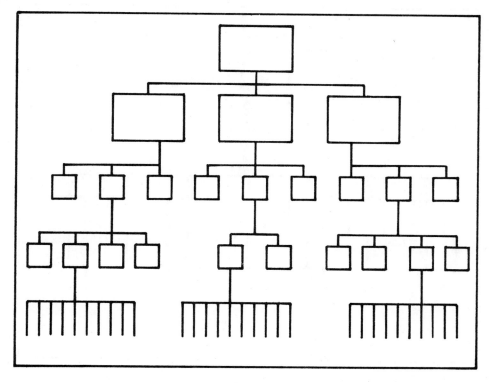

FIGURE 11.2   A Tall Organizational Structure.

and effective span of control would refer to the number of subordinates a manager can effectively control. In flat organizations, managers have a large number of subordinates reporting to them and in tall organizations, only a few subordinates report to each manager.

We might emphasize in the beginning of our discussion of span of control that there is no definite figure, no magic number of subordinates that a manager can effectively supervise. There are many factors and variables involved in how many subordinates one manager can supervise although some management writers such as L. F. Urwick who feel that five or possibly six is the most one might control, particularly if their work interlocks. This figure has been quoted widely and often relied upon as *the* number. However, this number is refuted in actual practice. The President of the United States personally supervises many more than the suggested five or six. Line foremen often supervise twenty, thirty, or even forty subordinates. Department chairmen in colleges and universities have five or ten times Urwick's number reporting to them. The American Management Association surveys show a higher number of subordinates (seven to nine) reporting to chief executives of the larger companies in this country. Whether or not these managers could be more effective by having fewer subordinates reporting to them is debatable, but, we do know that

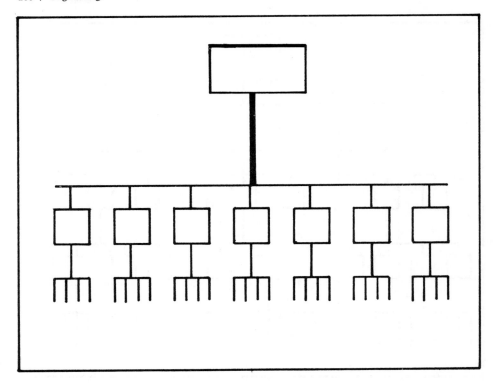

FIGURE 11.3   A Flat Organizational Structure.

these conditions exist in the business world and organizations do succeed in accomplishing their purposes.

Now let's look at span of control and examine some of the factors which might determine how many a single manager can or should attempt to control:

Similarity of Functions.   If all subordinates do approximately the same thing, then the supervisor can manage a large number, but if each subordinate does something different, the span must be contracted. For instance, a foreman might be able to supervise twenty-five machine operators if all the operators do the same job on identical machines. The president of the same company who would be supervising the vice-presidents of finance, sales, and production, in addition to a personnel manager, a chief engineer, a secretary, and an attorney, might find he has his hands full.

Complexity of the Job.   Again, the president might find that the complexity of the jobs of his subordinates is great compared with the jobs of the machine operators, and the president ideally can supervise fewer people.

Training of Subordinates.   If the training of the subordinates has been in-depth and extensive, then the subordinates should be less dependent on the manager. The president's vice-president of sales might have a master's degree in sales management as well as many years experience, and will be in a position to act with minimal supervision. A person filling an entry-level job probably has had little training and experience and will require much initial attention.

Supervision Required. This aspect would follow the same reasoning as number three, except that some people will require more or less supervision regardless of the amount of their training and experience. The importance of the job to the company might be an influence.

Geographical Considerations. The location of subordinates will increase or diminish the number of workers a supervisor can control. If all the subordinates are in one room, as in the case of the machine operators, the supervisor can manage large numbers. If the sales manager has salesmen scattered all over the East Coast, he might have trouble effectively supervising and working with his subordinates simply because of the logistics of the activity. The sales manager will have to limit the number of salesmen reporting to him if he has to spend much time in training and accompanying his men on calls.

Available Staff Assistance. Staff personnel who can assist the manager in getting his work accomplished can extend the number the manager can directly control. For instance, if the foreman of the machine operators has lead men—working assistants with no line authority, who assign jobs, help set up work, and train operators— then he can supervise a large number of subordinates. If the foreman has to do all the assigning, all the setups, and all the training, he will find himself very limited in the number he can effectively control.

Interrelationships of Subordinates The need for subordinates to interrelate with each other, with members of other departments, and with outside people (customers, suppliers, competitors, government officials) will affect the manager's ability to supervise a large number of subordinates. If the subordinate's coordination with others is extensive, complex and nonrecurring, the manager's span of control will be limited. If interrelationships are held to a minimum then he can supervise more people.

One final observation we can make in reference to span of control is that generally, the higher the level of the manager, the fewer subordinates he has reporting to him, while lower-level managers, foremen, and supervisors have many more subordinates under their direct control. There is no magic number of subordinates a manager can control.

DYNAMIC ORGANIZATION

At the beginning of this chapter we said that a business organization is dynamic, not something which having been established, remains the same forever. Organizations must be updated and reorganized to meet ever changing needs and demands.

What are some of the needs which demand change? Probably the one change which causes the most alterations in a company is that of growth. Even without changing philosophies, directions, products, or any other feature, growth demands change. Managers reach their limits of control. Communications within an organization deteriorate. Workloads become excessive. Morale falls. Confusion develops. These things point to change—a new way, a better way.

Product or service expansion and contraction will necessitate change. A new product demands exposure, promotion, advertising. After the product has been accepted, the emphasis changes. Production costs must be controlled. Competition must be met. A new product or service might call for new customers, new channels of distribution, new methods—all calling for a new organization.

Minor changes occur daily in an organization, major shakeups every few years, all in an effort to make that organization more effective, more able to serve, to compete, and to be profitable.

FOR DISCUSSION

1. *What is a job? a job analysis? a job description? job specifications?*
2. *What do classified ads describe?*
3. *What are the two theories of authority?*
4. *Can you delegate an obligation?*
5. *What is centralization? decentralization?*
6. *Why might managers be unable to delegate?*
7. *What is the difference between a flat structure and a tall structure?*
8. *What is span of control? What is the best number of subordinates?*

The Quarterback Quota

"I think you've made your share of touchdowns for the season," Sam Miller, right tackle for the Greenbrier Gobblers, told his quarterback, Earl Davidson, as they stood in a loose huddle.

"What do you mean?" laughed Davidson, "I believe I can score fifteen more this year, if I get half a chance."

"What I mean," said Miller without a smile, "is that we think you should give some of the other guys a chance to score. They get their heads beat in getting the ball close to the goal, then you call an option play and take the ball for a score without even looking for receivers. They do the work and you get the glory."

"Now wait a minute!" Davidson said. "When I score a touchdown, it's for Greenbrier, not for me. And the Gobblers get the points, not Davidson. Anyway, what difference does it make who scores as long as we win?"

"If it doesn't make any difference who scores, then I'm sure you wouldn't mind giving somebody else a chance," Sam said.

"Okay," Davidson said sarcastically, "the next time I'll call 'right tackle eligible' or 'right tackle around' so you can score. We want everybody to get a shot at the goal line."

Just then, the whistle blew calling the Gobblers to a first-and-goal huddle.

"He's got some nerve, that guy," Davidson said to himself, "I've scored over half the touchdowns myself and thrown for another twenty-five percent of them. I'm responsible for three-fourths of the scoring, and he tells me to lay off. Lay off! That's what he's doing. He stands up there and leans against somebody while I run all over the place and get smeared."

"Quarterback option on three," Davidson said in the huddle and glared directly at Miller.

"Ready?" Davidson said as he began to call signals, "Down! One! Two! Three!"

On three the ball was snapped and immediately four opposing linemen fell on top of Davidson.

"Why didn't you guys block?" he asked as they got back in the huddle. "Let's try that same play again on four."

At the count of four, the ball was centered to Davidson. Again, the sky seemed to open and drop linemen on him.

Davidson slowly rose to his feet and looked toward the bench where Coach Hayslett was frantically signaling for a time out.

Davidson called time and went over to him.

"What's the matter with the option?" Hayslett asked.

"The team won't block," Davidson told him matter-of-factly.

"Why?" asked the coach.

"They don't want me to score."

"How do you know?"

"Miller told me."

"Get in there for Miller," Coach Hayslett told a substitute.

When Miller got to the sideline, the coach was steaming. "Why aren't you guys blocking on the option?" he demanded.

"We are," Miller said.

"Davidson says you're setting him up."

"No, we're not," Miller said, "He's mad because he can't score every-time he gets his hands on the ball. Wants to put all the blame on us."

Miller glared at Davidson defiantly.

"Both of you get back in there and play to win," Hayslett said. "I don't want heroes or excuses; I want touchdowns!"

As he jogged back onto the field toward the huddle, Davidson wondered if he should call the option play again.

GUIDE QUESTIONS

1. *Could you write a job description and job specifications for Sam Miller's job?*
2. *What alternatives does Earl Davidson have now?*
3. *If the Greenbrier Gobblers win, who should get the praise? If they lose, who should be blamed?*
4. *The coach delegated authority to Earl Davidson to direct the team. Is this the only authority Earl needs?*
5. *A coach must delegate authority and responsibility to his players. Does this rid him of his obligation? Are there any rules which compel managers to delegate?*

The Busted Ratebuster

"I just wanted to be a good secretary," sobbed Mary Alice English to Anita Doss, typing pool supervisor. "Now look what they've done."

Anita did look. Ink eradicator had been poured on the work Mary Alice had done that morning. Banana peelings were smashed on the keys of her typewriter. The ribbon was pulled out. Glue was smeared on the earpiece of her telephone. The usually neat desk was a mess.

"Who do you think did this?" Anita asked.

"They did. The other girls."

"I don't know why they would, or why you would even think they would do a thing like this."

"They hate me."

"Mary Alice, you can't believe that."

"They do. They hate me. They resent the work I do. They're always after me to take it easy. 'Don't do too much work, Mary Alice.' 'Don't hurry back from breaks, Mary Alice.' 'Don't ask for work, Mary Alice.' 'Relax,' they say. Well, I don't want to relax. I want to work. I want to get ahead. I want to show you I can do anything you tell me to do, faster and better than anyone you have ever had working here. Miss Doss, I have two children to support. We need the money now. We can't wait ten years for a promotion. That's why I work hard. I want to get ahead."

"And you will, Mary Alice," said Anita, "I assure you of that."

"But when?" Mary Alice asked.

"I don't know," Anita said. "You've only been here six months. Some of these girls have been in the pool for more than three years."

"But I'm better than they are. I've proven it," Mary Alice said. Then she added savagely, "You're just like they are. You don't care how hard I work or how much I do. You're going to promote your pets anyway."

"Now, Mary Alice, you're saying things you don't mean," Anita told her. "Go on down to the lounge and try to get hold of yourself."

Mary Alice rushed from the office, tears streaming down her face.

"At least nobody else was here and heard that," thought Anita. "I don't have to worry about losing face, but I'd better get this mess straightened out."

About that time, the rest of the girls in the secretarial pool came into the office in a single group. Each of them looked at Mary Alice's desk and then at Anita. None asked any questions, offered to help clean the mess, or made any comments. They went quietly and mechanically to their desks and began the afternoon's work.

GUIDE QUESTIONS

1. *Who has the problem?*
2. *What are some alternative solutions to the problem?*
3. *Is strict adherence to a job description all that is required of an employee?*
4. *Anita has the authority to command someone to clean up the typewriter and desk. Will that solve the problem?*
5. *Is there more to being a manager than just giving orders?*
6. *How do you think this case will end?*

part 4

---

activating

At the conclusion of this chapter,
you should be able to—

- Determine who is responsible for recruiting in a company.

- State, in line with the concept of authority and responsibility, who has the final decision on hiring an applicant.

- Know where and how to seek recruits.

- Outline the procedure for conducting an interview.

- Explain the importance of proper induction.

12

Staffing the Organization

An author writes a play and divides its plot into roles that are independent yet inter-dependent. Then, he must activate his drama, put it into motion. He must secure finances, hire actors, sell tickets. It is here that we find the business manager. He has plotted his course of action—planned it. He has separated the roles—organized it. Now it is time for him to activate his business. He must get money, buy machines and materials, hire operators to run the machines, motivate and direct these people, and do all the things which are involved in activating. We could call this managerial step *actuating*, putting things into action.

In this first phase of the activating process, we will be concerned primarily with the staffing of the company, moving from that position of only planners working in the company to a point of full employment. Let us start by examining a term familiar to all of us.

RECRUITING

We were all exposed to recruiting in high school. Probably the most familiar of all the recruiters was the military recruiter. He was the sergeant or chief who came to your school and tried to get the graduates, both boys and girls, to join the armed service, to become a member of Uncle Sam's team. Speaking of joining teams, you may have been exposed to a second type of recruiter, the athletic recruiter, someone who tried to get the best school athletes to join college or professional teams. These recruiters offered scholarships, bonuses, or other types of rewards to those who would agee to become members of the team.

A third type of recruiter you are likely to have encountered was a school re-cruiter, someone from the local business school, the community college, or from four year institutions from around your state or other nearby states who might have come in on "college night" to display their "wares" to the graduating students and to en-courage them to enroll. Yet another type of recruiter you might have seen was the business recruiter, the personnel man from a nearby company who came to the high school to try to get the graduates to take jobs in the industry or business he represented.

From our observations of the recruiters, we can see that recruiting is common to all types of group endeavor. All organizations must have some means of supplying themselves with manpower to carry on the functions of those organizations. This process is recruiting.

Who Recruits?

Recruiting is carried on in many ways by different companies. Some companies use a variety of methods at the same time while others stick to just one. Some companies are forced to use every conceivable method to attract manpower, while other companies, through their good reputations, high wages, an abundant supply of labor, or for other reasons, have an ample number of applicants without making a conscious effort to attract them. However, before we get too deeply into the how of getting manpower, let's first talk about who is responsible for recruiting.

If our businessman is going to operate a one-man company, then he already has his manpower. He will do all the work that is to be done. But, as his business expands, he will need others to help manage and do the productive work necessary to achieve the objectives of his company. He will be the "who." He will be the recruiter for his company. He will hire most, if not all, of the employees necessary for his company until the company reaches a size and complexity which will require him to delegate this responsibility and devote his time to other problems. The greatest number of companies are small companies, and so it follows that in most companies, the owner, the entrepreneur, the manager will do the recruiting.

But we cannot stop here in our discussion of who recruits. As the company grows, the recruiting responsibility is delegated to a personnel manager or a personnel department, if the company is large enough to require one. In fact, we probably have spent many hours sitting in personnel offices searching for jobs.

Does the personnel manager actually hire people? We have heard friends talk of, or maybe we have been called by a man from personnel who told us to report to work on Monday. We may have felt that after he evaluated us and others, he chose us. If we have been turned down for a job, we felt that the personnel manager rejected us. However, if we look back on our discussion on line and staff relationships, we find that the personnel department is a staff department, one which accomplishes its objectives by convincing, advising, or assisting others. We should remember also from previous discussions that for someone to be held responsible for accomplishing a job, he must be given the authority to make decisions and issue commands to successfully complete that job. Therefore, when we put these concepts together, it seems that in a company where a personnel department exists, that department screens applicants and recommends candidates to line managers. The line managers make the final decision, or do, in fact, hire the worker. This is true for most organizations. By hiring in this manner, the staff relationship is maintained by personnel, and the line relationship, with its authority and responsibility concept, is maintained by the line manager.

There is an exception to this procedure in some companies. The exception is that the personnel manager actually hires entry-level people into the organization when a position is open, and tells those already hired people to report to their supervisors for assignments. When this happens, the staff people have assumed line authority to make decisions and command that the foremen accept subordinates that staff men have chosen. In these cases, the line men, the foremen, have the responsibility but not the commensurate authority to reject employees who have been chosen by someone else. When situations such as this are coupled with similar situations such as appraisals and evaluations by the personnel department, raises given by the personnel department, and workers fired by personnel, a strained relationship exists between the workers and their immediate supervisors, since it appears to the workers that the personnel department is the superior and not the line foreman or manager. This is normally a disruptive practice, and if the workers are represented by a collective-bargaining unit, it is exceedingly disruptive because the supervisor has a compounded problem of commanding no respect from his subordinates. When the personnel department has this authority, it is called functional authority.

Good management principles indicate that weakening of the manager's position should be overcome by proper line and staff relationships, and most companies do not follow this functional approach to hiring. Withholding of the right of line managers to hire could occur in an organization which is just beginning or expanding and the line managers are inexperienced in their jobs and need to be relieved of the burden of interviewing candidates. On the other hand, it could happen that management simply has failed to delegate the authority along with the responsibility it has given its line managers.

Our original question was who recruits and we can summarize the answer by saying that most of the recruiting in small companies is done by the manager. In larger companies, it is done by the personnel department. There are some variations when the manager appoints someone other than personnel to recruit, or when a line manager might be asked to look around for workers for his department, but again, it is usually the function of the general manager or a personnel department.

Means of Recruiting

In a small company, sending people out of the plant to search for candidates and urging them to apply for positions would be difficult. Small companies therefore rely on methods by which the message is communicated to the candidates and they come to the plant to be interviewed. Larger companies use this same method, too, but they also have the means to send recruiters out to review prospective candidates at times and places most convenient to the candidates rather than at the company's convenience.

In recruiting, we are trying to increase the number of applicants for the jobs so that we have more to pick from. In hiring, we eliminate most candidates and wind up with what we feel are the very best. Now let us look at some of the means by which we would attract persons to our company:

Advertising. Probably the most widely used form of recruiting is that of advertising in the local newspapers. Magazine, television, and radio advertising are also used in recruiting, but not nearly to the extent that newspaper ads are used. In the preceeding chapter, we noted some job specifications which were listed in a local newspaper. Most ads are constructed so that they mention the qualities which the applicant must have before he or she can be considered for the job, as well as the salary offered. A help wanted ad in a local paper might look like those shown in Figure 12.1.

FIGURE 12.1   *Examples of help-wanted advertisements.*

Ads similar to these might appear in trade magazines and newsletters, but the timing of a magazine makes it difficult for a manager to contend with unless he has a long lead time before filling a vacancy. The reason for this is that he may have to submit his ad five or six weeks before the magazine appears on the newsstand, and so he could not hope for any response until six or more weeks after placement of the ad. On the other hand, newspaper response can be, and often is, immediate. Most recruiting is done for entry level people who are needed to fill immediate vacancies and who live commuting distance. Newspapers, therefore, are the logical medium for spreading the message.

Employment Agencies. Employers are not the only ones who place help-wanted ads in the papers. Many of these ads, perhaps the majority of them in some locations, are placed by public and private employment agencies. The difference between the two is that the public agency is a branch of the government such as the Virginia Employment Commission and the private agency is a private, profit-oriented business which provides a service to other businesses and individuals for a fee. These private agencies can be local, national, or franchised organizations with nationwide representation. Normally, the typical fee charged by a private agency is about eight to fifteen percent of the annual salary of the person for whom the job was obtained. The fee would be paid by the jobholder, his company, or split in some fashion according to an agreement between the jobholder and the company.

Public agencies do not charge any fees. While these agencies have as their major duty the finding of jobs for the unemployed, they will work with applicants who want to upgrade themselves. A private agency is normally involved with higher level positions and will seek people who are already employed to get them to bid on these jobs while negotiating from the stronger, employed posture. Unemployed persons can also make use of the services of the private agency. Both of these kinds of agencies are necessary in the total recruiting strategy and they, as well as the employers, use the papers, radio, and television in advertising for applicants.

Casuals. A person who walks in off the street and applies for a job without being prompted in any way is called a casual. A person who writes to a company after seeing the name of that company in some directory or other publication unrelated to recruiting is also considered a casual. Casuals increase and decrease as the economy rises and falls, or as the reputation of the company grows or declines. There are many companies with good, solid reputations whose sole method of recruiting is through casuals. They have an abundant supply of applicants who come to the company unsolicited and supply the recruiting needs of that company.

Employee Recommendations. Management can encourage its existing employees to recommend to their friends and acquaintances that they apply for jobs with the company. If the employees like their situations, they will recommend the company to their friends enthusiastically. If they do not like the company, they will tell their friends to stay away. The management of a company which finds itself in a position of having many employee-recommended applicants will know that the employees like the company, although management might not know why. A drawback to this method of recruiting is that if many of the people recommended by employees are not hired, this might create a morale problem within the company. A second disadvantage could be that if too many friends get together in the company, production functions might become secondary to the socialization of the workers. This last problem could be overcome by effective management, however. Recruiting by employees is closely associated with nepotism.

Nepotism. Nepotism is favoritism in hiring relatives or close friends of employees. Many large companies have found this to be an excellent source of personnel and encourage it by giving preferential treatment to those relatives. Other companies discourage nepotism to the extent that they will not hire anyone who has a relative working with the company. In some companies, if two employees marry, then one is asked to resign.[1] The use of this method as a means of recruiting is governed exclusively by the policy of that company and would not be open to all companies.

Labor Unions. Some companies under contract with unions look to the union to supply most of its manpower because of the complications and restrictions involved when other than union employees are hired. Examples are companies which use only Teamster truck drivers, International-Longshoremen's-Association (ILA) cargo handlers, or American-Federation-of-Musicians (AFM) piano players. According to whatever agreement existed between the company and the union, the company would probably use one of the following: (a) hire its own men who join the union after a specified number of working days; (b) hire men who are already union members; or (c) have the union recommend for a specific job.

Visitations. All the means of recruiting mentioned above can be handled from the office of the employing company. The other method used, primarily by larger companies, is to go out into the field to recruit through visitation. This entails making campus visits to the colleges, going to the local high schools in areas near the plants, meeting people at prearranged times in distant cities, and, as some personnel management teams are now doing, running a mobile employment office on a pre-arranged schedule in communities hundreds of miles from the plant. In colleges and universities, with well-known and respected curriculums, major employers will have recruiting specialists who interview graduates. Those who pass the initial screening are asked to make plant visits for further interviews and more evaluation, as well as to give the prospects the chance to get an impression of the company which might make them an offer. Normally the college recruiting program is for higher level technical or management positions.

Temporaries. There is another method of recruiting: renting workers from agencies for short periods of time. This usually occurs when there is a special job to be done which is not in the normal line of duty of the company, or an unusual circumstance which will last only for a short period. This could range from unloading trucks every Monday night to typing an annual catalogue mailing list. The workers are rented from temporary-employment agencies such as Manpower, Kelly Services, Western Girl, or some other company whose function is to hire people for companies requiring temporary workers. This is a good situation for the employing company because it can hire people for short periods without providing them with fringe benefits or becoming liable for their unemployment compensation.

SCREENING

Once an applicant becomes interested in an organization, through ads or personal contact, he is invited to come to that company for an initial screening interview during which company officials eliminate those people who do not meet minimum qualifications. Applicants also have the chance to weed out companies which fall short of their expectations. When the applicant comes to the company, he first completes an application form, and is then initially screened by the personnel people. Applications are fairly standardized in their content. (See Figure 12.2.) They ask for personal information about the applicant and deal primarily in the areas of former employment, education, and references, quite often, from former teachers and supervisors, as well as from personal acquaintances and creditors. The reason for all this background information is to help the interviewers determine the likelihood that the candidate will be able to perform the duties assigned and to minimize the risk failure in the job.

Some applicants may be eliminated from further consideration as a result of having completed the application blank. If they fail to meet the job specifications, the education, or experience requirements, or some other basic requirements, they might be rejected at this point. However, if the applications indicate that they still warrant consideration for the job, they would be interviewed.

THE INTERVIEW

Besides the hiring interview, there are many kinds of interviews which take place between the prospective employee and employers. Some of them are concerned with evaluating the worker, praising when necessary and pointing out deficiencies and methods of correcting them, or interviews when he or she is to be disciplined or fired, when he or she might be in line for a promotion or transfer, when the employee needs or wants personal counseling, or even when the worker leaves the company and has an exit interview.

We will now speak specifically of the employment interview when the applicant talks with the personnel manager or the line manager who would be trying to determine the applicant's capacity for success on the job. The employment interview follows the same basic requirements of other interviews. The first requirement is that the interviewer determine in advance what type of interview (directive or nondirective) the interview is to be. The directive interview is one in which the interviewer himself knows exactly what information he wants from the applicant, asking specific questions and expecting direct answers.

The nondirective interview is one in which the interviewer wants to allow the applicant as much latitude as possible while still continuing to dscuss the predetermined reason for the interview. The nondirective interview does not restrict the person being interviewed to a specific answer. It allows him more freedom in his discussion. However, the nondirective interview is not one which rambles on and on without

PLEASE FURNISH COMPLETE ANSWERS TO ALL THE QUESTIONS. WRITE IN INK (OR USE TYPEWRITER)

Date_____ Social Security No. _____

NAME _____
      Last   First   Middle   Maiden Name

HOME ADDRESS _____ Tel. No. _____
         Street   City   State   Zip Code

Do you live at home?_____ Rent? _____ Own Home? _____   U.S. Citizen: Yes _____   No _____

Are you single?_____ Engaged? _____ Married? _____ Separated? _____ Widowed? _____ Divorced? _____

Number of dependent children _____ Other dependents _____

Height _____ Weight _____ Present condition of health _____ Are you willing to have a physical examination by our doctor? _____

Number of days ill during last two years and types of illness _____

Have you ever applied for a position with ███████ before? _____ When? _____ Where? _____

Have you any friends or relatives with ███████? _____ Who? _____ Relationship _____

Draft Classification _____ Member of Reserves? _____ Active? _____ Inactive? _____ Date Active Reserve Duty completed: _____

List all military, business and social organizations to which you belong EXCEPT organizations of a religious or racial character or that indicate national

origin of its members: _____

In order to have a complete overview of your qualifications, please complete the following sections in conjunction with your employment history.

Education	Name of School	Where Located	FROM Mo. Yr.	TO Mo. Yr.	Course of Study	Graduate?	Degree
Elementary							
Prep or High							
College							
Other Education							

College major:_____ Minor: _____ Special Studies: _____

What was your standing and average in H.S.? _____ In College? _____

Extra curricular activities in high school or college? _____

Are you studying now? _____ What and where? _____

What further courses do you expect to take? _____ When? _____

Position applied for _____ Referred to ███████, Inc. by _____

Salary desired _____ Current Salary _____ When can you start work? _____

Toward what type position do you want to work? _____

Do you operate a typewriter? _____ Words per minute? _____ What other office machines can you operate? _____

FIGURE 12.2   *A sample of a short application blank.*

any purpose. It should be controlled by a check sheet in which the interviewer makes certain that those points which he wants to discuss have been brought out, and at the conclusion of the interview, all pertinent matters concerning the applicant have been included. The interviewer must be careful in his use of the nondirective interview because it can easily lead to a discussion of fishing, politics, religion, or life in general, without revealing any specific information about the applicant.

The physical setting for the interview should be one of privacy. It is difficult for an applicant, often already tense, to concentrate on the questions of the interviewer if people are constantly moving in and out of the room, or if they are bombarding the interviewer with questions regarding operations, or if the telephone is ringing constantly. The setting also should be, as much as possible, a place of comfort. It need not be luxurious, but it should at least be a place where the applicant will not be ill at ease.

The atmosphere of the interview should be informal, but the conversation should always lead back to the check sheet so that the interviewer elicits all the necessary information from the applicant.

Though the interviewer knows the general nature of the job to be filled, the person being interviewed does not know anything about it. Often, if the interviewer likes the applicant, he or she may oversell the job, promising things the company might not be able to deliver, glossing over the negative aspects of the job, trying to make everything seem attractive to the applicant, so that he or she will accept the job. The interviewer should guard against overselling the job because the more the job is oversold, the more the applicant will be upset when he or she finds that the job is not exactly what was presented. If the policy of the company prohibits a new employee from getting a raise before working for at least three months, the applicant should not be told he or she will get a raise as soon as the job is learned because that may happen in two weeks.

If the applicant is to be reviewed in three months after accepting the job and begins working, the manager should make certain that he notes this and follows up on it as promised, otherwise, the employee will become disenchanted. The manager should not promise any more in an interview than can be delivered. When a person gets a job, he or she tells lots of other people about it—parents, children, spouse, and friends. He or she also tells them about the promises made. "A review after three months." If the employee is not reviewed after three months, he or she will be upset, but might not say anything to the manager and suffer in silence. With anxiety and the possible pressure from a spouse, the employee could easily become an extremely poor worker until such time as the review takes place. He or she might even leave the company if that review does not take place shortly after the time promised. And he or she may do this with no notice or without telling anyone his reason for seeking other employment.

The manager in an interview should be straightforward and not try to lure the person being interviewed, nor should he, unless he has had special training, attempt to use psychological techniques for interviewing. He also should avoid, in his evaluation of the applicant, the tendency to use pseudosciences such as phrenology (analyzing a person's character by studying the shape of his head) or graphology (determining personality by studying handwriting).

EVALUATING THE APPLICANTS

Once all the applicants have been interviewed, the manager must make a choice from among them. He must compare them to get the best possible candidate for the job. To do this, he should compare the information provided on the application forms to determine which applicants most nearly meet the specifications of the job. He should compare the recommendations given by former teachers, employers, and other personal references. We might note here that references *should* be checked. A person who is in a position to be denied a job because of one or more past experiences, will have a tendency to change that experience to one more suitable.

Again, all candidate references, particularly work references, should be checked. The best method of checking these references is in person or by telephone. People often will respond more candidly to an oral question rather than a written question because a written question requires a written answer, and many former employers would not care to write the answers they have concerning the work habits and other activities of a former employee. This is not to imply that what they have to say would be inaccurate, but that they would not want a written record of their honest judgement about an employee to be open for indiscriminate viewing. For instance, if that employee had been fired for incompetence, the former employer might be called upon to prove the charge, an action that could consume much time and effort. To avoid this, former employers often make a practice of saying either good things or nothing.

A question a potential employer might ask a former employer, which could have a great bearing on the applicant being considered, is, "Would you rehire this person?" If the answer is no, the interviewer might want to dig deeper.

Test results might also be used as a comparative item. Although the use of tests has been questioned in recent years (because some tests were proven to be discriminatory), many tests are still used today. Intelligence tests were given by potential employers for years until it was determined that these tests were biased toward white, middle-class workers, discriminating against minority groups and those persons from impoverished backgrounds. In addition, it was difficult for an employer to prove that he would have to have someone with that particular intelligence level before the candidate would be qualified to do the job at hand. Today, the basis for the use of tests in industry is that the tests must be impartial, reliable, valid, and necessary. Reliability refers to the degree of consistency of the test. Validity relates to the test's ability to measure that quality which is under consideration. Personality tests are used now, as well as tests for aptitude, interests, and achievement tests such as those that measure typing or shorthand skills. Again, we might emphasize that testing should be used if that test can be proven helpful in evaluating potential for success of the candidate.

SELECTING

The larger the number of candidates or applicants for a job, the greater the number from which the manager might select. The function of the personnel department is to screen the applicants so that the line supervisor can select the best of the candidates recommended by personnel.

In addition to satisfying the authority-responsibility principle mentioned earlier, the line supervisor should be given an opportunity to interview the applicant to judge him on things other than those which would show up on tests. Some of these might be his initial evaluation of the man, how he feels they might work together, whether he thinks the man has leadership potential, and whether he thinks he will fit in with the other members of the group. This is not a process of discrimination against a candidate, but the assignment by the supervisor of the candidate's likelihood for success.

When the line supervisor makes his choice for the job, the personnel manager will so inform all the candidates, the successful as well as the unsuccessful ones. To the unsuccessful ones, being told still has great meaning. It means that they can begin immediately to look for other opportunities and not cling to false expectations for another couple of weeks, hoping that this particular job will come through. It is an obligation of the personnel manager to inform the persons not chosen.

For the successful candidate, the personnel manager will go into more detail about the need for a physical examination to ascertain the capabilities of the applicant and to protect the company against injury claims and the other employees against diseases. Other things the employee needs to know such as work hours, overtime policies, and so on.

INDUCTION

Just as the military comes to mind when we think of recruiting, it again comes to mind when we consider induction. We think of civilians being inducted into the service. The same process applies to men and women going into business and industry; they are inducted.

Induction is extremely important. Many of you have worked in organizations where a new hire was brought into the company in the morning, went to lunch, and never came back. This probably resulted from the treatment they were given during the first few hours on the job. If a person feels wanted, needed, and appreciated, he is likely to stay. If he feels unwanted, as if he is intruding in someone else's domain, that he can never replace the person he has been hired to replace, then he will want to leave as soon as he can.

The induction should be a planned process so that every aspect of the company and its activities can be covered by the personnel department and the line supervisor. The induction should include a statement of the hours of work, the function and the use of the time card (what to do if he's late, makes a mistake, etc.), frequency of pay, the rules and regulations of the company, general policies which would apply to the new hire, the locations of washrooms, locker rooms, rest rooms, and lunch area. It should include an explanation of the fringe benefits and his eligibility, what they mean to him, how much they cost, and items pertaining to the job. Larger companies prepare employee handbooks so that new employees, as well as some of the older ones, will have a written document to which they might refer if they forget some of the answers to questions covered on the first day.

Once the personnel department has finished its orientation, the new employee is taken to his line supervisor. The supervisor will go over the work plan with him, explaining the peculiarities of the department in which he will work. Then the supervisor will take the new hire around and have him meet coworkers. It would be a good idea for the supervisor to assign the new man to a special person who is sympathetic to the problems of a new person, who will be enthusiastic about helping new people, and will work to help the new person become adjusted.

If the induction is handled well, it will go a long way toward keeping the employee over the initial three- to six-month period when most voluntary quits occur.

TRAINING

As the new employee is inducted into the company, he will begin some type of training. Even though the person has had experience in the kind of work he will be doing, there are some specifics in every job which must be learned. If the new hire is an entry level person, it might take some while to teach him the policies and rules of the company and the methods and procedures of operating the machinery, tools and instruments when necessary.

In training, a form of communication in which the trainer is endeavoring to teach the trainee to perform in a specified manner, the trainer (usually the supervisor) should be aware of exactly what he is trying to accomplish and what his goals are in the program. If he does the training well, he will reap many benefits. He will have a subordinate who can work by himself with little or no supervision, a subordinate who will be pleased with himself and his ability to do the job. There are few things more frustrating, more anxiety-producing, than being unable to do the job one is being paid to do.

The trainer should begin the training process by creating an atmosphere in which the worker wants to learn. The worker is expecting to be required to do something, so he is somewhat eager to learn at this point, probably as anxious as he will ever be during his entire tenure on that job. The trainer should realize this and make an extra effort to present the job sequence in a complete and enthusiastic manner.

The trainer will tell the trainee how the job he is doing adds to the total sequence and how the worker fits into the "big picture." The worker should know how his work, the work of his department, and the work of his plant or store fit into the overall accomplishments of his company.

Then the trainer will tell the trainee how he is to do his job, will show him once or twice, how the job is to be done. For example, if the job necessitates operating a machine, the instructor will run the machine through the total operation, explaining what he is doing and why he is doing it. It is important that the trainer continues to emphasize the *why* of the job and not expect a you-do-it-because-I-say-do-it attitude to satisfy the trainee.

Once the trainer has shown the trainee how to do the job, then he should let the trainee begin to do it himself, a little bit at first, gradually increasing until he is doing the total job. The instructor, who did the total job for the first couple of times, does less and less until he is doing no technical work and resumes his position as the manager, leading, evaluating, and controlling the trainee.

If the job is complicated, requiring many training sessions, the instructor should divide the total job into parts, with a check sheet of the requirements and objectives, along with the time limitations for control purposes. The trainer should set norms or estimates based on his previous experience so that he will be able to evaluate the progress of his student. He might write, "Learning the filing system: one day. Typing the monthly income statement: three days. Learning standard company format for letters: one-half day." Using this method, both the trainer and the trainee know what is to be accomplished and what is being accomplished, and they can both strive to meet the goals.

In addition to this minimal statement of norms and objectives, it may be possible to have a training manual to accompany every job. In small companies this would be prohibitive, but it could be a valuable tool in larger companies when training numbers of people who hold essentially the same jobs. Often, even in smaller companies, job descriptions are available and these descriptions can be given to the new employee so that he knows what is being expected of him.

There are many methods of instruction including movies, textbooks, overhead projections, slide presentations, flannel-board displays, teaching machines, programmed instruction, role playing, simulation, and lectures, which could be used in a series of training sessions.

COMPENSATION

When staffing, the line supervisor is not normally involved in setting up a pay schedule, but he may be involved in selecting a level on a schedule where the new person should be placed. If he has had little or no training or experience, the line manager would recommend that he be placed at the entry pay level. If the new worker's background is extensive, then the supervisor might recommend that he be placed in an upper level, if that agrees with company policy. The recommendation for the pay level is normally the responsibility of the line manager because it is the line manager who can best evaluate the man's ability to meet the objectives of the job which he will hold and to fit in with the rest of the men to accomplish overall unit goals.

Personnel managers must construct a salary or wage schedule which will depend on internal and external factors, and which should be reviewed annually. Some of those factors will include the overall wage structure of the community, the going wage for the skill the employee possesses, the necessity of the skill that person has, the availability of people in that skill and wage category, working conditions, background in education and or experience, responsibility, and the amount of effort expended by the worker.

Compensation will be discussed again in the chapter on motivation as it applies to rewarding workers for good performances.

The staffing of a company, whether it is the initial staffing or replacing or adding employees, is the first step in the activating phase of a manager's job—getting people into jobs which must be done to achieve the goals of the company. In our next chapter, we will turn our attention to how we can encourage those people to do the work we want them to do.

FOR DISCUSSION

1. *What are several types of recruiting with which you are familiar?*

2. *Who does the recruiting for most companies?*

3. *When a personnel manager actually hires people for work in the plant or store, he violates a management principle. What is the principle and how does he violate it?*

4. *Name and discuss four or more methods used by recruiters to get more job applicants.*

5. *Screening can be done outside of the hiring company. How would this be accomplished?*

6. *The interviewer should guard against casual promises and overselling. Discuss this statement.*

7. *Why is it important to check references? How should this be done?*

8. *Discuss what you would include in an induction program.*

9. *What is meant by a pay schedule with "internal and external" consistency?*

ENDNOTE

1. David Ogilvy, *Confessions of an Advertising Man* (New York: Atheneum, 1966), p. 914.

The Unstaffed Staff

In early September, Carol Mitchell, editor-in-chief of the *Northland News,* the student newspaper of Northside Community College, found that one of the first duties of her office would be to get some help in gathering, writing, and editing the news, as well as laying out the paper.

She decided to organize her reporters along functional lines to cover all school activities, leaning toward the more experienced, more mature students. She also felt she should concentrate on those students who were competent in English and who had a working knowledge of typing, so that delays in getting stories typed might be avoided.

A heavy emphasis on grammar would be in keeping with what she felt was the most necessary requirement for the editing staff members, those people who check stories for accuracy and clarity, for grammar and punctuation, and then write headlines for the stories. These people would have to read and interpret a style book so that the style of all stories published would be consistent.

Although the style would be consistent, Carol hoped for just the opposite in layouts. She wanted long and short pages, large and long headlines, a wild, unconventional paper which would still be attractive and readable. Carol, herself, would manage the staff and write the editorial page.

As she sat down to write help-wanted ads for the positions, Carol was aware that she needed the very best help she could get, but that she could not offer any pay to the job applicants, only non-financial incentives such as recognition and prestige through titles and by-lines.

GUIDE QUESTIONS

1. *What kind of an ad would you recommend to attract reporters?*
2. *Would all layout people perform the same job in the same manner?*
3. *Where and how should Carol seek recruits?*

The Growing Concern for the Growing Concern (B)

Once Roy Martin, president of Prepared Paper Products, Inc., had decided to go big, he knew he would have to come to grips with a troublesome situation which had existed in his company for several years. This was the problem of salary for his chief lieutenants, a problem which he had avoided until he was faced with other, related personnel matters.

What Martin had done with regard to salary was to pay every man the same, raising each man, each year, and starting new men at whatever rate he currently was paying his existing personnel. At the time of consideration, he had an assistant to the president, a personnel manager, a controller, a production manager, and a sales manager all making $16,000 a year. Martin knew he could not continue this stopgap measure indefinitely and with a new position of executive vice-president being created, he would have to take steps to set up a permanent salary schedule.

He, himself, was being paid $40,000 a year. He anticipated that the executive vice-president, who would have virtually all the responsibility for Paper Products, would be paid approximately $25,000 a year. He also felt that he must structure the salary scale more in accordance with the contribution to the company made by the position rather than by the men who filled those positions.

The assistant to the president, whose position would become the assistant to the executive vice-president, had helped build the company from a public relations standpoint and had created a very favorable company image which was quite helpful in acquiring a following for the first public issue of stock. He continued to build and maintain the image of the company. Any successor would also be charged with this responsibility.

The personnel man had devised, recommended, and established a personnel policy in accordance with national norms and existing industry practices. He had a flair for determining which men and women might be trustworthy and loyal to the company. His intuition and testing methods had proven to be so effective that there was little turnover in Paper Products. He, or his successor (in the event that he would be promoted), would continue to do this and would be responsible for directing an assistant and a secretary, and possibly other assistants if the company continued to grow.

The controller and chief accountant was responsible for the accuracy and timeliness of all financial figures in the company. He was the top finan-

cial man who determined such things as how capital items should be fi-
nanced, when and at what price to sell stock, where and at what rate to get
loans when those loans were necessary. He had secured an extremely favorable line of credit from a local bank and had established great rapport
with the members of the financial community. His successor would continue to work in these same areas where he supervised an accountant and
two bookkeepers as well as one secretary.

The sales manager used a management-by-objectives approach with
his eleven sales personnel. He would work with them to establish quotas
for themselves and allow them to determine how they would meet these
quotas. He knew that other sales managers hammered away at their men,
threatening, promising, or rewarding them as the case might be, constantly
after them to produce more. The sales manager, if he would continue in the
same position, would continue to use the same philosophy. A replacement
might try a different approach to sales and get different results.

The production manager, along with his superintendents and foremen,
had the responsibility for the greatest number of men in the company.
There were approximately one hundred fifty members of the production
department including the staff engineers and the production control people, all of whom were under the leadership of the production manager. The
production manager believed it necessary to compete with all subordinates in the production department because he felt he must be able to do
everything better than all his men. A new production manager might view
management in an entirely different way, but this man had succeeded in
getting production when production was needed and had maintained
steady growth in output, as sales for the company increased.

Martin had to decide who should be getting what, and whether to provide big increases for some and decreases for others, or just how he
should settle the problem.

GUIDE QUESTIONS

1. *What do you think of Martin's present policy of
   paying all his chief personnel the same salary?*
2. *What are some of the factors you would consider
   in establishing a salary scale?*
3. *How would you recommend that Martin solve his
   dilemma?*

At the conclusion of this chapter,
you should be able to—

- Define motivation and tell what part a manager plays in it.

- Give examples of both positive and negative incentives.

- Identify, discuss, and give examples of Maslow's hierarchy of needs.

- Equate Herzberg's motivators and satisfiers with Maslow's hierarchy.

- Discuss Theory X and Theory Y people.

- Discuss morale and its implications.

13

Motivation and Morale

If you should stop on your way out of a marketing class and say to the professor, "Dr. Bryant, that was a good lecture today," he might reply, "Thank you very much. I put all I had into that one," and we might wonder why he worked so hard on that particular lecture, and if he worked harder on it than on previous lectures, or if he works hard on all of them. When does he reach a point when he stops working and what does he work for? These are some of the questions to which we will address ourselves in the first part of this chapter.

MOTIVATION

If a person is *motivated* then we assume that he will work hard to achieve whatever it is that he is motivated to do, to accomplish that goal which he seeks, to reach that position he desires, to make that sum of money which he feels is necessary. We could say that motivation is the measure of effort a person will exert to satisfy his own needs. The more intense his need is, the harder he will drive himself.

A person has need for shelter. What he does with regard to providing himself with shelter would be an index of his motivation to satisfy that need. He may find a cave and move in and set up housekeeping. This would indicate that he had a relatively easily satisfied need for shelter. His motivation for providing himself with some sort of super shelter would be nonexistent. On the other hand, he might have an overwhelming need for a shelter which not only protects him from the elements, but also keeps him safe from his fellow man, boosts his ego, causes him to be held in high esteem by his peers, or even a home which would enable him to fulfill himself, one in which he could use his total energies and imagination in building, in which he could get total satisfaction by completing and occupying.

Motivation is not an easy thing to determine, particularly when we are dealing with many people with diverse personalities, all of whom might have different motivations at different times. Again, motivation is the drive a person has to satisfy his needs.

If motivation is something a person does to satisfy his own needs, then what can a manager do to motivate a subordinate? Or, can he, in fact, motivate a subordinate?

The only true motivation is self motivation and in this sense a manager cannot motivate a subordinate, but a manager can provide opportunities for subordinates to do things or provide incentives which would lead to the satisfying of a subordinate's need. Managers, in motivating people, are providing chances for their subordinates to fulfill their needs. The manager can also provide a negative incentive when he threatens to withhold opportunities and rewards from subordinates when they do not do what he wants them to do. This negative motivation is a punishment of sorts, a deprivation of rewards. Normally, negative incentives do not make subordinates go about their work with enthusiasm or determination. When motivated with a negative stimulus, subordinates work hard enough to accomplish the very minimum, the least amount necessary to keep them from being deprived of their normal rewards, but they do not seek to be outstanding in their accomplishments. Some negative motivators include the threat of being fired, not receiving a bonus, a possible demotion, public humiliation, a poor evaluation, no raise, no promotion, and a temporary layoff.

THE HISTORY OF MOTIVATION

In Chapter 3, we mentioned the studies conducted by Mayo, Roethlisberger, and Dickson at the Hawthorne Western Electric plant. As we stated in that chapter, prior to these studies, it was thought that most people worked harder when they were promised more money and slacked off when deprived of the monetary rewards. The results of these investigations showed that people had many other needs which were not influenced by money. There were needs influenced by group pressures, by feelings of importance, by feelings of what had to be done. The results of that study showed us that the attitude of the worker with regard to his work, what he got out of doing the work to satisfy his needs, was as important, or even more important than the scientific approach which showed him what he should or should not be doing to save time. This was the beginning of the human relations approach to management, and it marked the need for a manager to analyze his subordinates to clarify their individual needs, so that he might present opportunities to them to achieve their goals, both for the company and for themselves.

The primary source of satisfaction of needs away from the company is money. Money itself is worthless as a motivator unless it can buy what is necessary to fulfill the needs of the possessor of that money. If, for example, a person is hungry and there is food available for a certain price. Then the acquisition of money to buy that food is a great motivator. The person would work to earn money to buy food. Why not steal the money or the food? The negative motivator of being deprived of freedom or possibly religious convictions would keep the person from becoming a thief. If the amount of food available is rationed through a quota system controlled by food stamps, then the payment of money to the worker would not satisfy his food need. He would have to be paid in stamps if we expect him to be motivated to work to get the reward. Money can be used to buy or achieve nonmaterial goods, too. For instance, if a person has a need to be associated with a certain group of people, and that group of people belong to a certain country club, then money could be used to pay the dues of that club, and therefore achieve the social need to be associated with a select group.

WHAT ARE MAN'S NEEDS?

In all of history and even to this day, in this world, the majority of people spend most of their time and effort trying to achieve the basic goals of providing themselves and their families with an ample supply of food and drink and with shelter from the elements. The majority of people in this world are not concerned with paid vacations, or medical coverage for catastrophies, or double-time-and-a-half for Sunday work, or sabbatical leaves, or the many things for which the workers of this country expend their efforts. No, most of the people of this world are concerned with trying to satisfy their physiological needs.

However, we in the developed countries do not have to expend all our energies trying to fulfill physical needs. We spend much of our time in an attempt to satisfy other needs. What are these needs? Why do we have to do things? Behavioral scientists say that if we did not have needs, we would do nothing. We'd just sit around until we died. Probably the most widely discussed theory of needs was presented by behavioral psychologist Abraham H. Maslow.[1] Maslow believed that man has a hierarchy of needs, which stem from the very basic physiological needs to what he considered the highest, the need for self-actualization—the need for a man to reach his full potential. Maslow said that these needs are arranged in a hierarchy because a person would not move to a second or higher set of needs until he had accomplished a reasonable amount of satisfaction of those needs in the first set. At least this is what a typical person would do. There would be people who would jump around in the hierarchy of needs because of some individual personality traits. Figure 13.1 shows the needs as Maslow presented them.

The first step in the hierarchy of needs is the physiological step. This includes such needs for physical things such as air, water, food, rest, shelter, leisure activities, and other bodily needs. In thinking of these physiological needs, you might ask yourself, "What would I need before I needed anything more?" In response you might check how quickly you would react under different sorts of deprivation. For instance, what if you lost your vacation? What would you do? Probably nothing. If you were evicted from your house, what would you do? You would have to act rather quickly, but you might go several days without having a home, if you possessed a car or had access to a motel, hotel or some other form of accommodation.

If you were deprived of food you would have to move even more quickly because a person can only go without food for a limited period of time. Remember, too, that coupled with an individual's personal physiological needs are the needs of his family. A hungry family or a thirsty family can provide as much or more motivation for a person as the drive to satisfy his own hunger or thirst.

And, speaking of thirst, water is a basic need which would be felt more quickly than the need for food. But to find the most basic need of all, consider what a child

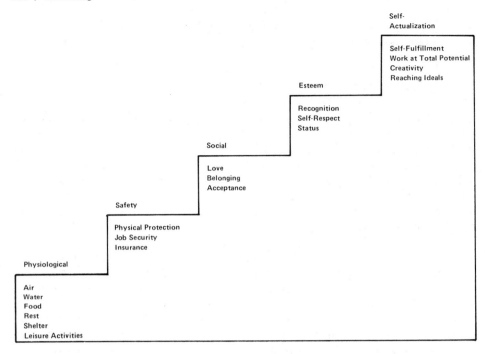

FIGURE 13.1   Abraham Maslow's Hierarchy of Needs.

must have first when he is born—air. The child has got to begin breathing within seconds after he is born and continue that breathing until he dies. If he is deprived of air for just a few minutes, his body begins to deteriorate, his brain becomes damaged. If you would like to check this physiological need, put your hand over the mouth and nose of the most sophisticated person you know and see how quickly he changes from his level of sophistication to a fighting, flailing, terrified person. In seconds, how quickly he is reduced to a struggle to obtain the most basic of all physiological needs.

Earlier, we said that most people are still trying to provide themselves with physical items, but there are many who have partially satisfied this stage in the hierarchy and are reaching for the second level—safety. Being safe is synonymous with being secure, being able to "hold what you've got." In early days, man hid in caves to protect his health, to protect his possessions against all dangers, the elements, animals, and even his fellow man. Then man progressed to houses and fortresses, and he gathered with other people to make towns and cities in an effort to protect himself against others.

We are living in a modern world where we need different types of protection. We want job security and we try to get it through unions, employment contracts, in not telling anyone our whole job so that we will be indispensable, through education, or by doing a better job than anyone else. The fear of arbitrary action by superiors often causes subordinates to resort to a negative action to maintain job security. This fear is possibly the chief cause of unionization and the most difficult for management to overcome.

There are other forms of safety, such as insurance for accidents, for sickness, insurance against natural disasters such as tornadoes, fires, floods, automobile wrecks, insurance against robberies, against being laid off and being denied the earnings one normally would have, insurance against job elimination through technological innovations or work simplification. There are all sorts of insurance to secure us, to provide for our needs of safety. Some people pay as much as twenty per cent of their salaries to protect themselves against every possibility of losing what they have, against having to give up the material possessions which they have accumulated. Some men never progress beyond this need for safety. The chance to satisfy a higher need is abandoned in favor of the lower need of security. For instance, a man is asked to take a job in supervision which would take him out of the union ranks and make him an entry level manager. Many men will not give up the security of the union to take this new position, preferring to stay with something with which they have enjoyed success rather than risk a chance of failing and losing what they have garnered thus far. This is not the only reason people refuse to take supervisory or higher level jobs, but it can be, and often is, the reason someone would keep the same job and not go to the unknown where the potential is much greater than in the present position the person is holding.

The next need according to Maslow is the social need, the need for man to belong or to find acceptance, to find love, to be wanted by his fellow man. This need has many implications for the work setting. There are people who come to work to satisfy this social need, and managers who offer rewards or incentives which do not meet this need but meet physical and safety needs will find that they are not providing the necessary motivation. For example, suppose a worker is deprived of social contact with her fellow workers because of some isolation factor such as the shift or the work place. This employee might quit her job and go with a company which would offer less security and money, but greater chance to satisfy this need for belonging. The fulfillment of this social need of the job is sometimes called job enjoyment. It is the ability of a person to enjoy his work because of the people he works with, even if his job is monotonous and wearying. Many companies recognize this need and support group endeavors which give the employees chances for group participation and social activity. Among these activities are political clubs, sports teams, family picnics and dances, special activities groups such as rock collecting, ceramics, cooking and gourmet clubs, square dancing, and many other pursuits within the company to provide this social outlet.

In many companies, employees are paid extra for "social isolation" because the company officials realize that depriving the workers of their social fulfillment has to be compensated by more chances for off-the-job satisfaction which would come from additional pay. The most common example of this is the shift differential pay.

The fourth level of the hierarchy of needs is that of esteem, both esteem from others and self-esteem. This esteem comes to man in the form of recognition, high regard, and rewards. Companies, again in trying to meet employee needs, recognize their successful people in many ways. Pay is an indication of the company's recognition of a man's efforts and achievements. The higher he goes in a company, the more he is paid, the greater his pay, the more chance he has for off the job satisfaction through a bigger car, a house in an exclusive suburb, children in private schools, and extended vacations. So, pay gives a person esteem. It is an external characteristic, a sign which indicates to all that this man has apparently succeeded in his endeavors.

There are other forms of esteem given by companies such as titles, keys to the executive washroom, parking places with names, executive hours, company cars (larger and higher priced according to status), expense accounts, time off to participate in social and club activities, stories and pictures in company publications, appointments to civic and charitable organizations, promotions, and other things which lead to respect from one's peers, subordinates, and superiors.

These external signs of esteem, recognition, and respect, can encourage a person to have respect for himself. He can feel that he has succeeded where others have failed, or achieve less success. He can know that he is good in what he is doing because of the rewards, because of the evaluations of his superiors. There is a high probability that the man who achieves this esteem, this satisfaction, likes the work he is doing, but there is a possibility that there is something more, something he would rather be doing although he has achieved the respect of others for his present work. This other work would satisfy his highest need.

This is the fifth and final, highest need of all, the need for self-actualization, self-fulfillment, the need to achieve the most that one is capable of achieving—the need to become the best, the greatest. Often, what satisfies the need for esteem, will not fulfill the need for self-actualization. Some people who have succeeded in their jobs and gained the esteem of their fellow men feel that they have been successful, but are not doing what they would like to do. Most of these people continue to work in their jobs and find outlets for their self-actualization in hobbies, in church work, charitable and educational outlets, philanthropies, or in something other than their regular work. The need for self-actualization may have nothing to do with the need which requires the acquisition of money. A man might want to grow the biggest and best tomatoes or the most perfect roses in the country. He may be willing to give up everything to grow tomatoes or roses, not in quantity, but in quality. He would want to do his very best at gardening. He might do it as an in-season sideline, or he might invest in a greenhouse and continue with his self-actualization the year around. He may not get the respect from others for growing these tomatoes or roses. In fact, he may even be held in contempt for people feel he should be working harder at his given occupation, making more money. But, Maslow feels, that to find satisfaction in this area of self-actualization, a man must be true to himself and do what he must do. Maslow felt a man did not have to satisfy a need completely before moving to a higher need, but he would have to satisfy most of his need before going on to the next level. There are people who skip certain needs to reach the ones most meaningful to them. For instance, an actor might have a great need for esteem, to be respected by others, and to gain self-respect. To him, this need might be so intense that he would forgo the satisfaction of his physiological need, going hungry just to pursue his career. Others might have a strong need for self-actualization and spend their entire lives in a hermit-like fashion doing what they want to do, oblivious to all others needs. Maslow also felt that man, in general, when confronted with two needs (the security and social needs, for example), would choose the lower of the two. If a manager told an employee he would get recognition (the esteem need) if he did more work than the others, and his fellow workers told him he would be ostracized if he did more work than they did (the social need), he would probably go along with his peers, forgetting the esteem, and settling for the social satisfaction.

By following Maslow's hierarchy of needs, a manager can adjust his rewards and punishments to the needs his subordinates are seeking to satisfy. For instance, an employee who is in good standing with the company, can become a member of the bowling team, but if his unexcused absences exceed three percent, he would be dropped from the team. If he works hard, his salary will be increased in a show of appreciation by management, but if he does not work hard, his salary will be held at its present level, reduced, or he may get fired and lose it altogether. If the employee does as he is instructed, his job will remain his, but if he should be constantly at odds with the manager, then his job will be in jeopardy, and his security will become non-existent.

MOTIVATORS AND SATISFIERS

Frederick Herzberg, another behaviorist concerned with motivation, proposed the two-factor system of motivation.[2] He said that all attempts to stimulate the worker could be divided into two categories: those which maintain or satisfy him (the hygienic factors) and those which actually stimulate him (the motivational factors). The maintenance factors in the Herzberg theory can be compared with the first three needs of the Maslow theory—physiological, security, and social. Herzberg said that attempts to motivate using these physiological, security, and social stimuli fail to motivate, and only maintain those who are to be motivated, keeping them from becoming dissatisfied. (See Figure 13.2.) This means that to pay people might not motivate them, but to withdraw the pay would dissatisfy them; to have job security will not motivate people, but to deny or withdraw job security will disturb them; to work with others in a group will not motivate people, but to isolate someone would dissatisfy that person.

It was only in the top two steps of Maslow's hierarchy that Herzberg said that man would be motivated. These steps are those of esteem and self-actualization. Herzberg said that man was truly motivated if he had a chance to be recognized, to advance, to achieve things, if he had inputs to work, if the work was satisfying, if he could accomplish something, and if he could grow within that work.

It might be more meaningful to you if you note the similarities between Herzberg's maintenance or hygienic needs and the hygiene course you might have had in elementary school. Washing your hands, brushing your teeth, getting plenty of sleep, and other such activities do not make you healthier, but they do help you maintain the

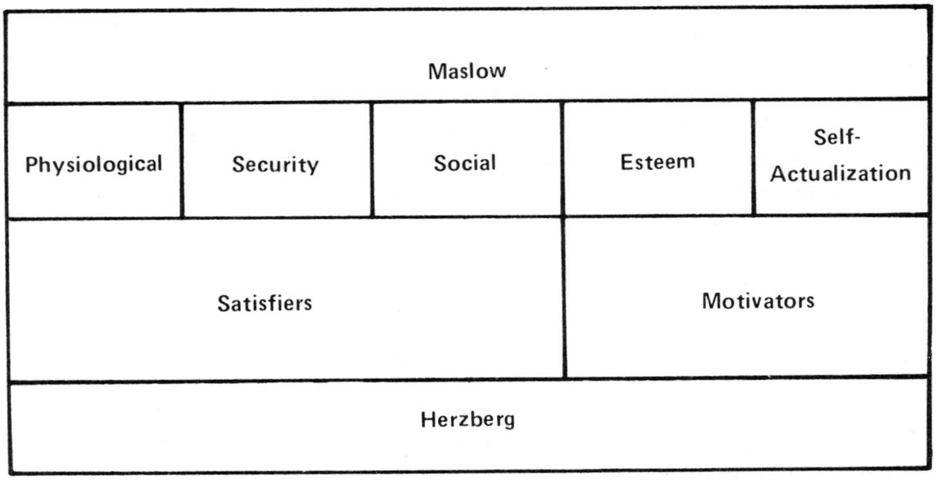

Maslow				
Physiological	Security	Social	Esteem	Self-Actualization
Satisfiers			Motivators	
Herzberg				

FIGURE 13.2. *Comparison of Maslow's Hierarchy of Needs and Herzberg's Two-Factor System.*

health you presently enjoy. These things preserve your health, just as pay, fringe benefits, and security keep you satisfied on the job, but do not motivate you to do more or better work.

A researcher from Texas Instruments, M. Scott Myers, elaborated on the Herzberg theory of motivation and said that physical, social, status, orientation, security, and economic factors are maintenance factors or those which keep the workers healthy, while those which provided chances for growth, achievement, responsibility and recognition are the motivational factors.[3] Included in these motivational factors (most of which relate directly to the work itself) are delegation, access to information, freedom to act, atmosphere of approval, merit increases, discretionary awards, profit sharing, company growth, promotions, transfers and rotations, education, memberships, involvement, goal-setting, planning, problem solving, work simplification, performance appraisal, the work itself, utilized aptitudes, inventions, and publications.

X'S AND *Y*'S

Douglas McGregor, another management writer, divided all workers into two classifications: those perceived to be approaching Theory X, and those perceived to be approaching Theory Y.[4] He also divided managers into the same classifications. Advocates of Theory X feel that all workers—

1. inherently dislike work and will try to avoid it.
2. must be coerced, controlled, directed, and threatened to keep them working adequately to achieve organizational goals.

3. want to be directed, do not seek responsibility, have little ambition and, above all else, want to be secure in their jobs.

At the other extreme would be the Theory Y advocates who feel that workers—

1. feel that work is as natural as rest and play and do not try to avoid it.
2. like to work and do not need to be watched or threatened. If they enjoy the work and are committed, they will direct themselves toward their own goals.
3. accept and seek more responsibility.
4. can be imaginative if given the opportunity.
5. have intellectual potentialities which are only partially used.

If a manager feels that his subordinates are Theory X people, he will react to them in that fashion and watch them, coerce and threaten them to get the job done. If a manager believes that his people are Theory Y, he will take a hands-off approach and allow them to grow as fast and as much as they can. A manager who is a Theory X believer will find that his subordinates who lean toward Theory Y will be dissatisfied with being treated like Theory X people, but might actually turn into Theory X workers, doing no more than what they are required to do, resenting the controls management puts on them. However, if Theory X people are treated as if they were Theory Y, then they may also become frustrated in not knowing what is expected of them and will probably do nothing until directed to do so.

Hardly anyone is totally a Theory X or a Theory Y person. Almost everyone is somewhere in between, tending toward one or the other.

OTHER MOTIVATIONAL THEORIES

Most modern motivational theorists feel that the more a person is allowed to participate in planning his destiny, the more he will be motivated to achieve it. There is a theory called management by objectives (MBO) advocated first by Peter F. Drucker.[5] In this theory, Drucker suggests that the manager and his subordinate get together and allow the subordinate to form objectives (with the concurrence of the manager) which will lead to the accomplishment of the individual's personal goals as well as company goals. The manager and the subordinate should get together at frequent intervals to discuss the subordinate's progress toward these goals. Finally, at the end of the evaluation period, the subordinate should compare his progress with his projections to determine if he did accomplish what he set out to accomplish. The proponents of MBO feel its success lies in giving subordinates inputs into the job—involvement, goal-setting, planning, problem solving, growth, achievement and other motivational forces.

Management by objectives has some drawbacks at the lower levels, because a subordinate who has no managerial skills or ambitions will have a hard time constantly improving his performance. However, insofar as management is concerned, MBO has an unlimited application toward growth.

Robert R. Blake and Jane S. Mouton derived a theory of management and motivation called the "Managerial Grid."[6] In their theory, they try to do away with the concept that a manager must have concern for either people or production, but not both. They say that a manager can have a high regard for people and in having this high regard, motivate them to greater extents than ever. They define their managerial types as those who have no concern for either people or production (1,1), those who have a high concern for people and a low concern for production (1,9), those with a high concern for production and a low concern for people (9,1), those with a moderate concern for both production and people (5,5), and those with a high concern for people and a high concern for production (9,9). This theory corresponds somewhat to McGregor's Theory Y in saying that all people want to accomplish a lot and will work hard if given the opportunity, growing as people as well as producers.

There is one other area which we should talk about concerning motivation and that is sensitivity training which continues to be advanced by proponents of truth in management. The idea of sensitivity training is that people, because of their rank or titles in an organization, act and react in a predetermined, but not normal, manner. They play the role which they feel is expected of them. In sensitivity training which may be conducted either within the company or away from the company, participants are encouraged to be themselves, to react as they feel, not as they think they ought to react.

People are taught to be sensitive toward others, toward their problems and feelings, and not to block out attempts to communicate because of preconceived ideas. Sensitivity training is often conducted between subordinates and managers, giving subordinates an opportunity to level with their managers in a face-to-face interchange, as well as the managers having the traditional opportunity of confronting subordinates. The idea is that this confrontation should "clear the air" and people should act in a positive, truthful fashion. A problem which has occurred in sensitivity training is that many people are not able to cope with the true feelings others have for them and many react negatively. For example, if a subordinate tells his supervisor that the supervisor is "two-faced" (telling the subordinates one thing and the superiors something else) then the supervisor should be shocked initially, but the whole matter should lead to a better relationship with a solid foundation. However, many participants never get over the initial accusation and spend their time trying to figure ways of getting even with the subordinate, rather than how to overcome the problem. They set up a barrier to that person rather than improve themselves. This makes sensitivity training (T-group training) extremely volatile and potentially explosive when people who work with each other engage in a session of direct confrontation.

SUMMARY

In summary, we might say that people are motivated by work itself and by their participation in it rather than by the pay or fringe benefits that they receive. This is not to say that pay and fringes are useless because as Herzberg and Maslow stated, the fringe benefit program makes the worker feel secure and satisfied in his work and get off-the-job satisfaction so they can reach toward the higher goals of esteem and self-actualization. MBO, Theory Y and "9,9 management" all suggest that the person who has an ability to determine his work, goals, to receive recognition, achievement, and advancement will be the one who is motivated to succeed in accomplishing his goals and the company goals.

MORALE

A manager is evaluated by morale, asked to improve morale, overcome and destroyed by morale, or successful by morale, so we will begin this section by defining morale. Morale is the state of mind of an individual or a group of people with regard to a specific topic or a general feeling about the work, the manager or the company. Morale represents a composite attitude, a total sentiment of a person or group toward something. Morale is further defined as being high or low, good or bad. When morale is high, workers do as management wants them to do. When it is low, anticompany feelings come into play, and production usually drops. All managers must be concerned with the morale of the workers. It is up to each manager to encourage high morale by his own attitude toward the work of his fellow man, and by eliminating any causes of low morale if he has the authority to do so. There are many cases in which the manager cannot affect the subordinates' feelings. This is typical in the case of an external cause. For example, an employee might have a sick child which has caused the worker to lose a great amount of sleep, or he might have a relative in the hospital, an automobile which needs repair, or some other external problem that causes despondency or discouragement. The manager might encourage the subordinate to discuss his problem with him, but he probably would be unable to take any positive steps toward eliminating or even lessening that problem.

Internally, the manager would have some authority to deal with, to take action to help overcome difficulties caused by problems which, in turn, cause hard feeling or a bad attitude toward the company. For instance, if an employee or a group of employees is being underpaid, the manager might be able to grant higher wages. If the employees are dissatisfied because of the structure of a job, the manager might be able to restructure the job, enrich or enlarge it to the satisfaction of the subordinates. He might restructure the job so that many subordinates would work as a team to accomplish the goal, and thereby give each participant a social outlet as well as an opportunity to achieve group and self-esteem. When people feel good about their work, morale is high and, normally, production will be high, too. The reverse is true if the morale is low. However, there are some occasions when not having a job to do, or other similar conditions which would be contrary to the well-being of the company, would cause nonproductive, high morale, but these incidents are few in number when compared to the total incidents.

Morale is elusive and difficult to measure. In fact, we cannot measure morale itself, only the effects of it. When morale is low, there will be a rise in the number of absences, tardiness, the number of turnovers, the number of accidents and the number of grievances filed. When morale is high, absences and turnovers will decrease, accidents will be on the downswing, and grievances will taper off.

Morale is the result of management's attitude and efforts to make the employees like their work and their work place. Low morale would indicate a need for change. Morale is only a symptom and it is up to the manager at some level to investigate the cause of the low morale and to recommend some positive action which would improve it. A morale survey, formal or informal, would give management the information it would need to make changes to boost low morale. An attitude survey is given to all members of the organization and returned to the personnel department to be tabulated to determine specific causes of low or high morale. Such morale surveys would be left unsigned to encourage the respondents to be truthful without fear of reprisal for having indicated those things about the company which caused him to be upset.

In conclusion, motivation is what a person will do to satisfy his needs, and morale is the state of mind in which he finds himself as a result of management's concern. It is, therefore, up to management to provide employees with opportunities for high motivation and high morale.

FOR DISCUSSION

1. *Define motivation.*
2. *What are positive and negative motivators?*
3. *People are (are not) motivated by money. Discuss this statement.*
4. *Discuss Maslow's hierarchy of needs.*
5. *Discuss Herzberg's two-factor theory.*
6. *Discuss McGregor's X and Y people.*
7. *Would you want to be involved in sensitivity sessions in your company?*
8. *What is morale?*

ENDNOTES

1. A. H. Maslow, "A Theory of Human Motivation," *Psychological Review*, 50, no. 4 (July 1943) : 370–96.

2. Frederick Herzberg, Bernard Mauser and Barbara Snyderman, *The Motivation to Work* (New York: John Wiley & Sons, 1959).

3. M. Scott Myer, "Who Are Your Motivated Workers?" *Harvard Business Review*, 42 (January-February 1964) : 86.

4. Douglas McGregor, *The Human Side of Enterprise* (New York: McGraw-Hill Book Co., 1960).

5. Peter F. Drucker, *The Practice of Management* (New York: Harper & Brothers, 1956).

6. Robert R. Blake and Jane S. Mouton, *The Managerial Grid* (Houston: the Gulf Publishing Co., 1964).

CASE 13–1

The Elected-Rejected Course

"This is an elective," Instructor Pete Chilton told his small business management class, most of whom were freshmen at Wilson Community College. "And, frankly, I don't know why most of you took it. You don't want to put forward any effort. You won't read enough to keep up. You show no incentive whatsoever.

"I've done everything I know to help you. I've prepared handouts and given them to you, dictated the notes to you word for word and still some of you don't get them. I don't require you to do any homework except read the chapters. There's no term project due. There's no role play or anything like that which would make you feel uncomfortable.

"I chose the speakers, invited them here, and made all the arrangements. I introduced them to you so you wouldn't have to do that. I got the films and ran them myself just to keep you from being distracted from the films because you had to run them. I even guaranteed you a grade, a minimum of a C just for coming to class. Better grades to those people who participated and worked hard. But I don't see many of you working for better grades.

"Now, why is it, when I knock myself out to help you, why is it that you won't take the first step to help yourselves? I'd like to know. I'd like your honest reaction. Why is this class slipping when you were so enthusiastic to begin with? I think I know. Because you thought business was a snap, and, after you got into it, you found that it was going to be hard, so you don't want to take part in it? Is that what it is?"

There was silence as Chilton looked around the room from person to person. Finally, one of the class members raised his hand. "Mr. Chilton, I'm reluctant to speak, but—"

"Go ahead, Ryan, say what's on your mind. I want to know."

"Well, Mr. Chilton, I don't think we've had a chance to participate, and—"

"Participate?" Chilton interrupted. "You must be kidding. You, of all people. You're going to tell me how I've failed. This isn't the first time you've done this. You had a "D" in the last class you had with me, and you'll be lucky if you get one this time. And you've got the gall to tell me in front of this class that you didn't get a chance to participate. I've stopped plenty of times in class and asked if anyone had any questions. Or to see if anyone wanted to make any comments. You never had anything to say. Now you want to try and blame the whole thing on me. I don't want to hear any more out of you. Just keep quiet. I think that's about the extent of your capabilities anyway. Now, does anybody who has any sense have any constructive comments to make about the class?"

No one said anything.

"You see? I give you a chance to participate and none of you do. I don't know what's happened to students now days. They sure don't make them like they used to. Now, get out your notebook. I have some notes I want to dictate."

GUIDE QUESTIONS

1. *Was Ryan right?*
2. *Does it seem that Mr. Chilton will ever solve his problem?*
3. *Is a person always happier when someone else does his deciding for him?*

CASE 13–2

The Splitting Seamstress

Pres Jones, general manager of the Blue Bonnet Dress Company, his assistant to the general manager, Ward Spivak, and the personnel manager, Ken Palmer, were holding an informal meeting in Jones' office and Pres said to the others, "Gentlemen, you know why we're here. We've got to find the answer to the question of why Viola Smith left our company. If we can determine why she left, then maybe we can cut down on this turnover problem. Ken, did you bring your records on Viola?"

"Yes, Pres, according to her file, she's fifty-two years old, a grandmother, with no kids at home. Her husband is a salesman for a pharmaceutical company and he's on the road quite a bit. From the address, I'd say he was a fairly successful guy with a better than average income. This is the first job she's had in about twenty-five years. She worked prior to her marriage, but in the first year after she got married, she had a baby. A couple more followed rather quickly, so she never got back to work. She, you know, is one of the old-fashioned kind who believes a woman's place is in the home, at least as long as there are kids there. She learned to sew through several classes offered by Singer and improved her skill by doing. She made her clothes, clothes for her kids, her husband, and lots of relatives for more than twenty years. After knocking around the house for better than a year after her last kid left home, she decided to go back to work. She was good at sewing and enjoyed it, so she came to us. As far as I can determine, she was excited about her job, happy to get it. Her induction was good. We gave her top dollar, and, of course, all the fringes. She seemed to like her work and, to tell you the truth, I was really amazed when I heard she was going to leave.

"I had her come in for an exit interview, but I got very little out of her. What she said was that she just wasn't happy. She didn't know why. She just wasn't happy. I thought maybe she just didn't like the regimentation of work and that she was going to go back home and take it easy. I asked her about this and she said no. She's going to work for the Darnell Company, doing the same work for less pay. And, with a shaky organization like Darnell. . . . That guy is late with his payrolls about twice a month. Still those people stick with him. Beats me why. I can't understand it, or Viola."

"What about you, Ward? What did you find out from her fellow workers?"

"Very little, Pres. I went around and tried to find out something from the people she worked with, but I couldn't find anybody who had been very friendly with her. Not that they didn't like her. It's just that she normally didn't work and break with anyone else. According to her forelady, Viola was assigned to zippers since she said she'd done quite a bit of that kind of work, and at the time, that was the only job open. I don't know whether it has any significance or not, but her job starts a half hour earlier than the other jobs, breaks for lunch a half hour earlier, and she goes home a half hour earlier than the other girls in the department. It seems that the zipper she has to insert has to go into the dress before the other girls can do their work, so therefore, she has to start the ball rolling every day and stay ahead of the other seamstresses. She worked faster than any girl we've ever had in that position and I think she enjoyed getting off early. She always seemed anxious to leave.

"Actually, Viola worked for two groups, with a girl serving her, bringing the zippers and dress parts to her and taking the finished products to the foreladies of the two departments. I checked with both her supervisors, since they were equally responsible for her, and neither of them had had to say anything much to her. She did her work, so they spent their time working with the other girls who were having problems. They were as surprised as we were when Viola gave her notice. One of them said she was thinking about putting Viola on another job which would have paid her more, but she never got a chance to work it out."

"Well, Ken, Ward, it looks like we've got a lot of facts here, but not much interpretation of them. Why don't you guys hash over the details some more and we'll meet back here at nine o'clock on Friday. At that time, I hope you'll be able to give me some recommendations for a policy change or a get tough implementation of what we've got, or something. We've got to get this turnover business stopped or its going to show up as big trouble when it comes to the overall financial picture for the year."

GUIDE QUESTIONS

1. *According to Maslow's hierarchy, what need do you think Viola was trying to satisfy?*
2. *Can you think of any reasons why she might have gone to the Darnell Company?*
3. *If Viola had been offered a substantial increase in pay, do you think she would have stayed? Why?*
4. *"She did her work, so they [her superiors] spent their time working with the other girls who were having problems." Evaluate this statement.*

At the conclusion of this chapter,
you should be able to—

- Determine some factors which influence a manager's style.

- Differentiate between the many styles of management.

- Understand the sociometric technique of choosing leaders.

- Know what a manager should do when faced with disciplinary situations.

14

Direction and Discipline

Remember our school superintendent? He's a manager. He gets things done through other people. The objective of a school system is that students learn. The students are taught by teachers, but the teachers are directed and controlled by managers, and those managers are the principals, who, in turn, are directed by our school superintendent. The school superintendent is a coordinator of people, a director of people. What we want to discuss in this chapter is the way the managers go about leading their subordinates.

LEADERSHIP INFLUENCES

We all know different managers, and we know that they act differently in similar situations. Some are nice. Some act crabby all the time. Some seem interested in subordinates, while others could not care less. Some are excited about their work, while others seem to be looking forward to retirement. Some even act as if the people working for them are more a problem than they are a help. Before we get into a discussion of the different styles of leadership, let us first think of some of the influences which would make a manager act in a particular way.

A manager's organizational level influences him to some extent. As a general rule, the higher the manager is in an organization, the more liberal he is in his direction, the more he allows his subordinates to work independent of him, making many of their own decisions. He has more experienced, better educated, and usually fewer subordinates than the entry level manager, the foreman, or supervisor, who is much more likely to feel a need to be aware of each move his subordinates make. He will likely give full directions and look for total compliance on the part of his workers.

This first level supervisor is the only manager supervising nonmanagerial personnel, and his expectations from his subordinates will be far different from the expectations of a president managing his vice-presidents.

A manager's regard for people, his feelings toward their leaning in the direction of Theory X or Theory Y as discussed in the previous chapter, will influence his style of leadership. If he feels that other people are objects to be used, then his leadership will reflect this. He will try to manipulate his subordinates to get them to do exactly as he wants, for his good, without regard for what is good for them. He will "play" with his subordinates, with the end result in mind of his getting ahead. If the manager feels that other people are his equals, or that they at least have had the same opportunities which he has had, then he tries to control them through a superior ability, bringing about a management attitude of matching wits with the subordinates and keeping one step ahead of them at all times. He would use his subordinates cautiously, always working to keep ahead of them. A third attitude that a manager might have toward his subordinates is that the subordinate is an individual, a unique item, which must be handled in a unique manner, and so this manager would respect his subordinate as an individual and try to direct challenging work toward him, rather than impossible or inconsequential work.

Another influence would be the superior's attitude toward his job. If he has a poor attitude toward his work, he will expect and maybe encourage his subordinates to be displeased with their jobs. The manager's own leadership might influence his attitude toward his subordinates, or his subordinates general attitude toward their work might influence the manager's style. If the subordinate's morale is low because of some particular incident, then the manager may change his leadership style to meet that situation, to help the individual recover from his depression.

The general level of the economy is a predisposing influence on a manager. If the economy is in high gear and there is full employment with no surplus of good talent, a manager might find himself getting soft in his manner of leadership because his subordinates don't have to take it because they can go somewhere else and get as good a job, or an even better one, with no problem. And so, when conditions are such, managers often carry on a relaxed style of leadership. However, if the economy is tight with high unemployment, with good men out of work, then often managers are inclined to be much more demanding of their subordinates with an overriding attitude of "if you can't do it, I'll get somebody who can."

Another influence on a manager's style is the situation itself. If the high school catches fire, the principal probably will act in a very dictatorial manner, commanding people to move out quickly. But on the last day of school, he may allow seniors to take liberties which would have been unthinkable during their whole school career. A foreman might be extremely tough when business is good and the shop is running behind schedule, but he may be inclined toward leniency when the shop is down to a low work backlog and hurrying is just another way of working oneself out of a job.

So there are many factors involved in leadership style. Managers normally adopt a style because it is the one which works best for them, the most effective method. Or sometimes, managers adopt a style because it is the only style they are aware of, because their only boss or all their bosses have used the same method, and the managers know of no other style.

STYLES

Remember Theory X? Remember the boss who thought all his people were slackers, not wanting to work and had to be coerced and watched? When the leader thinks his subordinates have to be watched, then he watches them. Then he becomes a "boss," an autocrat, an autocratic manager. This boss believes the workers are hired to do what they are told to do. He assumes full authority and full responsibility for the work. He is not concerned with input from the subordinates. He makes all the decisions and expects his workers to be the kind who get "paid for doing, not for thinking." Subordinates under this kind of leadership often work in an uninformed atmosphere, feel quite insecure, and are afraid of the boss and of what he might do to jeopardize their livelihood. The autocrat seldom, if ever, gives anyone a compliment. His feeling toward his subordinate is that the subordinate is paid to do a good job and therefore his check should be the "thank you" he gets. The autocrat is quick to criticize, but seldom compliments.

The benevolent autocrat, the "nice boss" gives praise and pats folks on the back when they do a good job. Like the "boss," he gives orders and expects people to obey them. He normally has the plan of action thought through, but often he asks subordinates what they think of the plan so that he might reassure himself, or give them the illusion that they are participating in the decision-making process. He does not, in fact, allow them to make the decisions, although many times the workers feel that they are working for a participative type of manager. The benevolent autocrat likes people, will work hard to help and please them, but he feels he must make all the decisions.

There is another kind of benevolent leader who acts like a "big daddy" and he is called a paternalist. This kind of a boss makes decisions about and for his subordinates and acts in a manner which he feels is best for his people. Like a father, he has his subordinate's or "children's" best interests at heart. When he punishes them, he is often in a position of "this hurts me more than it hurts you, but. . . ." Paternalists are almost out of style because the more intelligent, better educated subordinates have rejected them in favor of making their own decisions.

Even so, there is plenty of evidence around to show how paternalists work when they are on the scene. In almost any small town or in the older sections of large towns, we can find rows and rows of company houses, built by the paternalistic companies for their workers. In some of these communities, we would find a company theater; a company store; a company clinic with its doctors, nurses, and dentists; and a company hospital; a company recreation center; and possibly company schools.

In larger paternalistic companies, management even ranked the employees socially by building different types and styles of houses in various areas of the community so that those on a certain business stratum would occupy certain houses, and those with a higher or lower rank, would occupy comparable company houses in the community. These company communities are typical of textile manufacturing communities.

A fourth type of leader is the participative leader. This type of manager talks with his subordinates about decisions to be made to see what they think about the problems and asks their advice when there are questions about projects in which they have an interest and might be able to contribute. The participative type of manager tries to develop a sense of responsibility in his subordinates, giving them an opportunity to share their abilities and ideas with management. As we saw in the prevous chapter concerning motivation, when the subordinates are allowed to contribute to the overall plan and help set the goals and directions in which they and the company are headed, then those individuals are much more likely to work hard to accomplish the goals they have set. Participation, according to almost all behavioral researchers mentioned previously, is a motivator, not a satisfier.

A participative manager is not a manager who allows his subordinates to make all the decisions based on what they think is right. No, he makes decisions which he thinks are right, but he has an open mind when he asks them to participate, and if he hears an idea better than his own, he will change.

A fifth type of leader is one who might be characterized as a situational manager. This is the manager who has no style, at least none which he uses consistently enough to merit a label. The situational manager is one who adjusts to individuals and the circumstances at hand and acts accordingly. Under certain conditions, he acts as an autocrat. He gives orders and expects immediate compliance with no back talk. At other times, he is a democratic manager, allowing his subordinates to make their own decisions on how they want to do something. He gives them the authority to make the decision themselves, and then he abides by that decision. Sometimes he may get the input of the subordinates and make the decision himself, as a participative manager, or he might have the decision made already and then ask for input of the subordinates and make the decision his way (as would a benevolent autocrat), regardless of how his subordinates feel.

This situational manager must know his subordinates well to determine what to do under various conditions. Some people, the situational manager feels, do not respond to a Theory-Y approach. When given an opportunity to make their own decisions and set their own courses, they do not feel secure. They would rather be told exactly what to do and how to do it, and even watched to see that they are doing it right. These people must be administered under a Theory-X or an autocratic approach. There are others, he realizes, too, who like to work and can be trusted to do anything they are supposed to be doing, never need to be overseen, and for them, he adopts a Theory-Y posture.

The situational manager is the manager who falls in the middle of the scale, between the autocratic and the laissez-faire, between the X and Y, between the "hands-on" and the "hands-off" approaches.

We said that the participative manager did not allow the group to make the decisions, but rather to give an indication of how they felt concerning a problem or situation. The sixth type of manager is the kind who lets his subordinates call the shots. This one, the democratic manager, when confronted with any decision of consequence, will not make the decision himself. He will call a meeting of his subordinates, explain the situation to them, indicate how various decisions might affect the long range goals, and then he will let the subordinates make the decision on how they will do something or, sometimes, even if they will attempt to do that something. The business of being democratic has its drawbacks in that many times subordinates will elect to do something for their good, but not necessarily for the good of the company. In fact, what they choose to do might even be detrimental to the objectives of the company. However, the democratic manager, rather than risk the anger of his workers, could even let something go through which would not be for the good of the company, but would be good for him because his men would like him for letting them do what they wanted. On the plus side, the democratic method has the same thing in its favor that the participative method has—more dedication to goals through participation in setting those goals.

A final type of manager is the laissez-faire, the free-rein, or hands-off manager. This is the type of leader who does not interfere in any way with his subordinates. The style can be used effectively in a highly motivated professional group such as a group of research scientists or engineers who are dedicated to their profession or are extremely interested in accomplishing results which are beneficial and advantageous to themselves and to the company, in terms of recognition, pride, and prestige. This can be a poor type of leadership, too, when used by a manager who is "on his way out," who is about to retire, a person who is only managing until he can find another job, or a person who has given his resignation notice.

The laissez-faire manager can inadvertently train other managers by shutting his doors to his subordinates, causing them to turn to their peers for help or rely on themselves to accomplish whatever goals have been set. This peer becomes a manager of sorts, a natural leader rather than one appointed by higher management. This causes a phenomenon seldom used in the business world although constantly used in social, religious, and educational situations, and that is the choosing of a leader by the group itself.

If you join a political party, a church group, or a civic or fraternal organization, you and your fellow members would elect a leader. You would choose the person you wanted to direct you. The person that most of the members wanted and chose would become the leader, the elected leader. This technique of choosing leaders by subordinates, called the sociometric technique, is seldom used in business although studies have shown that allowing people to work for leaders whom they have chosen or elected, or allowing people to work with persons whom they have chosen, their friends or acquaintances, leads to more productive and efficient work.[1] We re-emphasize that, for the most part, businessmen retain the prerogative of choosing a manager for subordinates rather than allowing the men themselves to choose their leader.

What kind of leadership is best? The kind that works for the leader, the kind that gives the follower what he wants, the kind that provides the motivation each of the subordinates needs and causes him to strive to accomplish objectives for his good and the good of his company—autocratic when necessary, situational when possible, democratic when appropriate. There is no right or wrong type of management although there is a tendency to characterize the Theory X's, the autocrats or the bosses, as being the bad guys, and the Theory Y's, the participatives and situational managers, as the good guys.

Leadership styles have the same qualities as alternatives in any problem-solving situation. Any of the alternatives may be right. Some may be better than others under given conditions.

We have discussed the subordinate acceptance theory of authority in a previous chapter. We allude to it here again by mentioning that leaders without followers are not leaders. So, if an attempt to lead men by an autocratic approach by demanding that they do something leads those men to rebel and not follow the dictates of the manager, then that Theory X, that autocratic system does not work. It is not the right system to be using. If it does work better than any other system, then it would be right.

Figure 14.1 shows a graph of the various forms of leadership which we have mentioned in this chapter. It goes from the domineering autocratic on the far left to the laissez-faire on the right, and is compared with McGregor's theories X and Y.

FIGURE 14.1   Leadership Styles.

DISCIPLINE

When we speak of leadership, we speak of a manager who through some philosophy, some style, gets his followers to work toward accomplishing a goal that the company, or the subordinates, or the two in concert, have decided would be a good one for their mutual benefit. If the men accept the leadership of the manager, the morale is good and they will work toward doing what the manager wants them to do.

There are occasions when something happens which causes a subordinate to refuse to work toward that goal, to refuse to do as he is asked or instructed, to cease to follow the dictates of the manager. When this happens, the direction of activities has changed and everyone is no longer moving positively toward a goal and there are some who are moving away from this desired direction. When this happens, the normal discipline is disrupted and the manager must take some action to reinstate the direction and the discipline. Disciplinary action is an attempt on the part of the superior or the manager to redirect the activities of an erring subordinate back toward a desired goal. Disciplinary action should be positive, not punitive. Punitive action would be taken to make someone suffer, to make him hurt, to make him sorry he had done a certain thing, to punish him. It is not a positive act unless that sorrow, that punishment, causes the wayward subordinate to commit himself to a more positive direction and away from what caused his initial downfall.

RULES

Earlier we talked about rules being plans, special kinds of plans which have remedial actions for persons who do not comply with these rules. Plans say that we will do this, that, or the other. Rules say that everyone will do something or not do something and anyone who does not follow the rules will be subject to certain types of disciplinary action. Rules are plans for human behavior. All companies must have rules, and these rules should be set forth in writing. They should not be undefined, nor ill-defined, nor so general that they are not rules. They should be specific enough for a common interpretation by all who are governed by them. Rules with such wide-open interpretation that no two people would view them in the same light lend themselves to squabbles and arbitrations.

An example of a rule which confounded managers and personnel administrators in recent years concerned the dress length of female employees. If a rule were made that all female employees would wear dresses of "reasonable length," it would be vague and subject to any number of interpretations. Reasonable to one person would not be reasonable to others. Some companies tried to overcome this vagueness by saying that hems of skirts should be a maximum of x inches above the knee. This gave specific guidelines, and those people who objected to the rule could object *before* anyone violated the rule and had to suffer the consequences. If the rule said reasonable and the term reasonable was attacked by all members of the company community, then, through discussion, there could be general agreement as to what was reasonable and that feature could be inserted into the rule rather than the vague term of reasonable. Immoral is another word sometimes used in rules. Again, it is a word which lends itself to many interpretations.

Rules are standards of acceptable behavior and managers can best show their subordinates what they expect from them in terms of behavior by setting the behavior example through self-discipline. Following rules is a matter of self-discipline by the individuals involved. If the manager can discipline himself well, then he can reasonably expect his subordinates to discipline themselves. If the rules are so harsh, so complicated, and so demanding that the manager himself cannot understand or live up to them, then he cannot expect his subordinates to live up to them either. If a manager cannot subordinate his personal needs to the desires and needs of the company, then he should not expect his men to subordinate their needs.

If the rules state that all people should report to work on time, then the manager also should be on time. If he comes in a half-hour or an hour late, he cannot expect his men to be conscientious about punctuality. If management feels that smoking in a particular area of the plant is dangerous and no-smoking signs are placed there, then the manager must observe these signs as well as the subordinates. If he smokes, they, too, will smoke. If the rule says that there will be no fighting, no physical contact, and the manager is a big guy who pushes people around to get compliance from them, he can expect that his subordinates will, from time to time, push each other and perhaps even him, in defiance of company rules.

The manager must set the pace for his subordinates. He must show them self-discipline, and then he can expect self-discipline from them.

INITIAL REACTION TO RULE VIOLATORS

But even with this example of self-discipline, even if the manager is the pinnacle of rule observance, there will be some subordinate who at some time for some reason will disobey the rules, and who will become a disciplinary problem. When this happens, it will be up to the manager to take the disciplinary action mentioned earlier.

If a man violates a rule, is insubordinate, refuses to do as he is told, is fighting, loafing, or destructive, then the manager must take some action. Let's discuss the action he should take when discovering or being confronted with the disciplinary situation:

1. The manager should investigate the situation before he takes any action. There are many trite phrases which say the same thing such as "look before you leap" or "think before you act," but regardless of how trite the phrase is, the message is the same. It still has validity. It is much easier for a manager to review a situation with deliberation and then take the action he deems necessary, than it is to take action and then have to back down after he finds that he has made a great mistake. It is this shoot-on-sight approach that gets most managers into trouble.

For instance, there may be a rule which says that anyone fighting would be subject to immediate dismissal. The manager comes upon a fight between two men. He separates them, stops the fight. Then he fires them both, telling them to report to the personnel office and wait for their checks. The manager has acted in haste and has taken action which he feels is consistent with the rules of the company. However, it may be that one of the men was simply defending himself and was not the aggressor. He was forced to either defend himself or take a severe beating. In this base, the equal treatment for both participants in the fight is unfair to one of them. If this man belongs to a union, or can get a higher-ranking manager or a group of his fellow workers to intervene, then the manager who fired him might be forced to reinstate him and back down from his previous decision.

2. The manager should not become a participant in a battle with his subordinate. He is the manager and he should not forget his station. He should not lose his temper and get into a shouting contest with his subordinate. This is not simply a matter of "I'm the boss and you'll do what I say," and therefore the manager should not engage in any interchange with a subordinate. It is more a matter of not losing one's temper and arguing with the subordinate. The manager should answer his subordinate's questions as to why he should do the work or how he should do it. In the final analysis, the manager is the manager, the leader, the authority, and if the subordinate does not or will not accept the authority of the manager, then the manager must look to some other method of obtaining the subordinate's cooperation other than by beating him down orally or even physically, which leads us to number three.

3. The manager should not engage in physical contact with his subordinates. He should not put a hand on them except if it is to help a subordinate, to save his life, or to prevent one person from doing bodily harm to another. To get excited and lose one's temper and hit a subordinate is, in most cases, grounds for the dismissal of the manager who does the hitting.

4. The manager must decide what disciplinary action must be taken, appropriate to the incident and consistent with company policy. If the company policy is spelled out, the incident well defined, and the action to be taken specifically well documented, then the manager can follow the outlined procedure. In other cases where things are not so well defined, the manager must decide what action should be recommended or taken. It may be that the rule states that a person fighting would be subject to immediate discharge, but the manager realizes that what appeared to be a fight was simply horseplay and he might recommend a disciplinary measure more in keeping with the action rather than strict adherence to the letter of the law. We see this happening daily in courtroom activities where judges and juries not only decide the guilt of the defendent, but also decide upon the disciplinary action depending upon the severity of the offense and the circumstances surrounding it. Managers, too, must make these decisions. Once a manager decides on what action he must take, then he should move to the next step.

5. The manager should strive to discipline in a private setting. As we mentioned before, the act of discipline should be a positive measure leading the employee toward the objectives of the company. Public humiliation of the employee seldom brings about this result. It more often embitters the employee toward his superior and the company for the humiliation he has had to suffer.

As in any other interview, the disciplinary interview should be conducted in a private setting with a minimum chance for interruption. The employee should be told of the offense he is accused of committing and the disciplinary action which is to be imposed. If the employee agrees with the action, the the discipline should be administered quickly, without fanfare and without any publicity. If he disagrees, with either the accusation or the disciplinary action to be taken, then the manager should listen attentively and objectively and, if he feels it necessary, suspend the disciplinary action pending a further inquiry into either the offense or the subsequent action to be taken. This would be in keeping with step number one which tells the manager to get all the facts before he takes any action. For instance, it may be that the subordinate had been with the company for ten years, had abided by the rules in effect when he was employed, and, by administrative error, had not been made aware of a change in a rule or an action to be taken in regard to an infraction of a rule. If the employee does not know the consequences of his act, then those consequences should not be imposed until the employee is first made aware of them. The first person committing an infraction may have to be allowed to get by without disciplinary action because the imposition of that action would be contrary to the reason for that action in the first place—to redirect the employee toward company objectives.

If this disciplinary measure had been taken in front of a group, the suspension of the action might make the manager look bad. If the manager fails in his efforts to get the action he says he will get, or even if he succeeds in getting the action, the manager nevertheless has failed because he has humiliated his subordinate in public and has left him with a negative feeling toward the company and probably left all his co-workers with similar negative attitudes.

The only exception to this rule would be in a case where a subordinate challenges his manager in front of a group. Then the manager must retaliate in front of that same group. This would, again, require the manager to go back through the same provisions of disciplinary action outlined earlier. First, find out all the facts, then not lose his temper or physically contact his subordinate, and finally, determine the action to be taken and take it.

DISCIPLINARY ACTIONS

In companies which have written regulations concerning the personal activities of the employees, there is usually a set of disciplinary actions which appear appropriate to the specific incident outlined in the rules. The regulations also might give a disciplinary action depending upon the severity of the infraction or the number of times the rule was broken. For instance, being late once would not bring about a suspension or discharge of an employee, but fighting might, or stealing might, or smoking in a restricted area might. The severity of the infraction might alter the nature of the action taken. We said that being late should not cause the man to lose his job, but how about being late twenty or thirty times?

A typical company would require its managers to follow a sequence concerning disciplinary action. An example of an often tardy employee and the action to be taken might be as follows:

First tardiness—Nothing to be said by manager. (Situation to be regarded by manager as an isolated incident with probably acceptable excuse).

Second tardiness—Informal talk by manager. (Slight chastisement and warning by manager with emphasis on avoidance of habitual action).

Third tardiness—Oral reprimand by manager. (Manager to have a formal talk with subordinate outlining, previous violations of rule and emphasizing the subsequent steps if subordinate continues being late. This third step is a reprimand, not a simple discussion).

Fourth tardiness—Written warning by manager. (Manager "writes up" incident, stating exact nature of infraction, recalling previous infractions and outlining steps which will follow if subordinate continues to be late. One copy of written report will be given to employee, another sent to personnel for inclusion in employee's permanent file, and a third to be kept by the manager for his file. At this point it should be made perfectly clear to the employee that the manager is serious about taking action against him).

Fifth tardiness—Disciplinary layoff by manager and personnel manager. (Manager has compiled a file, noting the previous infractions of the tardiness rule, has advised the employee of the steps to come if he continues to violate the rule, and on the fifth unexcused tardiness, the manager, with the concurrence of the personnel manager, sends the employee home, usually for one to three days without pay. At the end of this period, the employee is reinstated to his regular job at full pay, but warned that another infraction will lead to more serious consequences).

Sixth tardiness—Demotion by manager. (At this point, there are only two things left to do to reprimand the employee—demote him to a lower position or fire him. Most companies do not use the former as a disciplinary measure, feeling that the pressure brought about by this action would be so severe that a negative attitude would result both in the reprimanded employee and his fellow employees to the extent that the sought after positive turn toward company objectives would be unattainable. The military service, however, is an example of an organization in which a man can be reduced in rank and pay for an infraction, but allowed to continue in the employ of the service without a loss of time toward retirement. Most companies do not demote. They favor the next step.

Seventh (or sixth) tardiness—Discharge by manager, personnel manager, and plant manager. (At this time the manager should confer with the personnel manager and the unit manager, get their concurrence, and fire the employee because he has proven, over a period of time, that he cannot or will not comply with company rules and regulations, that he cannot work toward the goals of the company.)

All companies will not have such a long sequence. Some may have shorter inputs, others even longer. Most companies will try to overlook offenses which have occurred in years gone by, if the recent activities of the employee indicate that his attitude toward the company rules has changed. Managers might also overlook cases in which some particular incident would cause a normally good employee to be absent or tardy several times within a short period, possibly to take care of some personal business which had never come up before and may never come up again.

Managers have to be decision makers just as judges must be. Every instance cannot be provided for in a rule or regulation. Managers must use their discretion. To treat everyone equally, in all probability, is to treat some unfairly. In an earlier instance, we mentioned that two people were fighting, one the aggressor and the other defending himself. If the manager simply assumes both are fighting and therefore both must be discharged, then he has treated them equally, but not fairly.

SOME GUIDES FOR DISCIPLINE

When a mother promises a child that "your father will take care of you when he gets home" she is missing a key ingredient in discipline—immediacy. If the child is small enough, he will more than likely forget why he is to be disciplined, and if his father comes home, confers with the mother, then whips the child, the kid might begin to fear the father's coming home. If the child is older and can be aware of what is happening, then he might spend the rest of the day worrying about the father coming home and whipping him, but have no remorse or thought of improving his action, which should be the basis of disciplinary action. Children, too, should be disciplined so that they change their direction toward a desired goal.

If a child does something wrong, he should be disciplined immediately. An adult, too, should receive immediate discipline if there is to be a positive result from the discipline. An adult who waits for days or weeks for a disciplinary action loses his effectiveness as a worker because of his preoccupation with the pending action to be taken by his superior. The manager should be fully aware of all the mitigating circumstances surrounding an act by a subordinate, but he must reach a conclusion and take action, without holding it over the head of a subordinate like the sword of Damocles.

Disciplinary action is a control device which we will speak about in a later chapter. In any control device there are three parts: (1) the goal or standard, (2) the comparison of actual against the goal or standard, and (3) corrective action if necessary. If any of these three parts are missing, there can be no control. If, for instance, the party who violated a rule did not know that such a rule existed, then to punish him for the violation would be the wrong "corrective" action. Proper corrective action would be to inform him of the existence of the rule.

If there is no way to measure a person's performance and compare it with a standard or a goal, then there can be no meaningful corrective action. If a rule states that anyone who is more than eight minutes late for work will suffer the loss of a quarter-hour's pay, but there is no time clock to verify the tardiness, then there can be no meaningful corrective action. If there is a rule which states that a certain action will be taken if an employee does or does not do something, and when that violation occurs, nothing is done about it, no positive corrective measures are taken, then there is no control.

Finally, in this area of disciplinary action, we should point out that a manager should deal with his subordinates in the most consistent manner possible. This does not mean that everyone who commits the same infraction should get the same penalty. No, it only mean that those persons who commit the same infractions *under similar circumstances* should get the same penalty. The manager must evaluate the circumstance under which the infraction occurs to assure his men that he is dealing fairly with all other subordinates.

As far as discipline is concerned, we can summarize by saying that a manager should, first, know what has happened, next, keep calm and not get involved physically with subordinates. He should make sure those subordinates know the rules and regulations in advance. He should be objective and make disciplinary action decisions based upon a goal of positive action rather than on a punitive basis. All his decisions should be as objective as possible, but with an appreciation for the circumstances under which the offense occurred.

FOR DISCUSSION

1. *What are some influences on a manager's leadership style?*
2. *Name and describe the seven leadership styles.*
3. *What is the difference between participative and democratic leadership?*
4. *What is the sociometric technique? Where is it used?*
5. *What is positive discipline?*
6. *How can a manager set the standard for behavior?*
7. *What action should a manager take when confronted with a disciplinary situation?*
8. *What are some disciplinary actions available to managers?*

ENDNOTE

1. Raymond H. Van Zelst, "Sociometrically Selected Work Teams Increase Production," *Personnel Psychology* (1952): 175–85.

Counselor's Counselors

"Gentlemen, I'm happy that you have found time to meet with me tonight," said Tom Bowers, the new guidance counselor at Washington Heights High School. "As you know, I've just completed a Masters Degree in counseling at Hopeful College and, since I'm new here, I thought that rather than impose my personal set of assumptions about sixteen-year-old boys on your children, with your help, I'd draw a profile, a composite profile of your boys and adopt a leadership style which would be appropriate to all of them at the same time. I'm sure there are many common characteristics which your boys share, and therefore, we should be able to come up with some sort of a style which would enable them to be treated exactly alike when they are called in for counseling. Let's start here with Mr. Carlwilde. Mr. Carlwilde, sir, if you would, please, describe your son and tell us how you have been able to handle him and what recommendations you would make to the rest of us in adopting a style for every boy his age."

"Well, Howard is a pretty headstrong boy," said Mr. Carlwilde. "He's sixteen. I guess all the boys we're talking about are, and he wants his way. He doesn't stand for too much advice from me so I've quit giving it to him. We don't go in for much small talk. It's all business. When I really want Howard to listen to me, I talk to him in about as tough a way as I can. I hate to admit it, but that's the way it is. When I try to be cheerful or joking, he just walks away, saying things under his breath. So, if you want my advice, I'd say that you'd better make it clear to these guys from the beginning that there'll be no funny business and any straying from the straight and narrow will result in an immediate disciplinary action."

"Thank you, Mr. Carlwilde. Now, Mr. Bean, how about your boy?"

"Jimmy's sort of strange. Not really strange, but he's big, well over six feet, but as shy as a little kid. He never has been able to overcome being too sensitive. He hardly ever talks to me unless I coax him. I think he's afraid he'll make a mistake and be embarrassed. He doesn't like any attention. Any of you who know Jimmy, know he stoops, and I feel this is because he doesn't want to be any taller than anyone else so that he doesn't stand out. He wants to be right in the middle of the crowd, almost anonymous. To deal with Jimmy, I'd say you'd have to take him to the side and reassure him that you are no threat to him or you'll not get any cooperation from him at all."

"Thank you, Mr. Bean. Mr. Puckett. . . ."

"Tony's one of these kids who says, 'Fool me once, shame on you; fool me twice, shame on me.' He trusts everybody unless and until he gets the shaft. After he once is done dirty, then he's sort of cautious of that person. But really, it amazes me, even then, he's not put off completely with that person. He will continue to work with the guy, but maybe be a little more careful. I try to play it straight with him all the way. I try not to take advantage of his gullibility. We've talked about drugs, girls, drinking, and all these things that will tempt a guy today. I've tried to level with him on every count, because I know that once I try to make something seem worse than it really is or say something is not any fun when he knows that it is, then he'll begin to lose his trust in me. My advice to you is to not threaten the guys, not comfort them, not play any favorites. Play everything straight across the board. Tell them, it's here for them. If they get it, okay. If not, okay."

"I object to that approach to the problem because I feel that most guys will be able to make it all right without counseling," said Mr. Wilson. "It's the exception, not the rule, that should get the attention. My boy, for instance, has been a discipline problem to me at home and at school. I believe that if the counselors had called him in several years ago and told him that he was a special case rather than a trouble maker, had encouraged him to be right rather than threaten him if he did wrong, that he'd be a good student now. But no, I've found that counselors want to deal with good students, the ones who don't give them any trouble, and give them the honors, the scholarships, and everything. But the ones who need the attention get very little except negative attention. I'd say that you should look for the people in trouble and work with them and let the majority of the guys take care of themselves."

"Encourage the boys to say what they want to do," said Mr. Martinelli, "That's what you ought to do. I believe my boy has a lot of good ideas if someone would just encourage him to bring them out or show him how he can put his ideas in a logical package. I've tried to encourage him, but you know how it is with a boy and his father. I think if you get guys to commit themselves, to make their own plans, to say where they want to go, then they're much more likely to do it. If you tell them where they should go, where their future lies, or where they're best suited, then they'll be turned off. "He's not going to tell me what to do," he'll say. I say, let them make up their minds. Let them speak their piece. Let them do their own thing."

"Do their own thing! I've heard enough of that to last me a lifetime. My boy has told me he wants to do his thing until I'm sick of it," said Mr. Moore. "His thing is nothing. His thing is to drive a car and run around. No, I can't go along with that. I say test them, find out what those tests say, and tell them what they are best suited for. Then lead them, guide them, push them into that occupation. Coerce them. Make them go into that field. What do they know at this point? Make them do it. That's the only way they're ever going to make it in this world, the only way they're ever going to be happy."

A short while later, after the men had discussed the opinions and descriptions the fathers had made of their boys, Bowers closed the meeting telling the fathers that he would study what they had said and come up with a recommended profile for the next meeting.

GUIDE QUESTIONS

1. *What do you think of Bowers' "profile" idea?*
2. *If you were supervising only one boy at a time, which style of leadership would you use for each of them?*
3. *What value might this meeting have?*

CASE 14–2

The Search for a Research Leader

"Gentlemen, the hour is late, and we've interviewed several men from outside our organization as potentials for the research director's job," Harold Hobson told the members of his personnel selection committee. "But, there is one guy here in our plant whom I would like you to meet. He is Van Toppin, a man from our production department. He has had excellent results with his subordinates. He is dynamic and energetic. He's excited about his work and excited about getting production out. He's a man who has gotten results. When he went into his present job as a first level supervisor in the production department, the men in the department were barely able to make their minimum quotas. After the first week, he had shifted them into high gear and they were all making their minimums and many were making bonus money. He got that production up fast. He lost some guys, but those were men who probably should have gone long before. Van got results, something we hadn't been getting before, and he is the only man that I recommend that we consider for an internal promotion to the research director's job. I want to call him in now and I wish you would question him and get an opinion on whether or not you think he'd be suitable for this job."

Hobson disappeared and shortly reappeared with a bright looking fellow about thirty, with a quick smile and an excited and energetic appearance. "Gentlemen, here is Van Toppin, the man I mentioned to you a while ago. Van, these guys are here to interview and select a manager for the research department. They'll ask you some questions. Just relax and tell them exactly what they want to know. Go ahead, men."

"Mr. Toppin, Harold said that you had had extremely good results in the production department. May I ask what you attribute that to?"

"Yes, sir, I have had good results and I'm proud of those results. What do I attribute these results to? Well, frankly, I just told the guys that they had to produce or get out, that my predecessor had been lenient with them, and that he had lost his job because of it, and that I wasn't going to put up with that. I had my job on the line, and it was either them or me and they knew by the way I told them that it wasn't going to be me, so they produced."

"Would you carry this policy to the research department?"

"Yes, sir. We all know that people are paid for their results, not for their good intentions. I'd check the track records of those men in research to

241

see who was producing and who wasn't. Then I'd lean on those who weren't. I would feel that it would be my responsibility to get rid of the deadwood, just as I felt we should get rid of it in the production department. I'm sure, gentlemen, that you'd be pleased with the results, once we got rid of a lot of idea men who don't have any ideas."

"You mean, Mr. Toppin, that you'd threaten people? And that's all?"

"Oh, no, that's not the only thing I'd do. I'd like to set up a bonus system so that we could pay these guys for their good ideas. Everybody could use a few extra dollars. It's been my own personal experience and the experience I've observed by watching others, that men work harder when you wave some money in front of their faces. We should have a system where we pay for good ideas, and I think this system should be a secret one, so that everybody knows he is competing with everybody else, but no one knows who is winning. That way, it keeps the pressure on to keep those guys thinking and working and producing ideas."

"We've had somewhat of a free wheeling atmosphere in research up to this point, Mr. Toppin, so far as I know. Would you continue this policy?"

"No, sir. In no way would I do that. I would try to determine what our major problems are and direct our researchers to solve those problems, concentrating on them and nothing else. I think that if men are allowed to think about anything and everything they want to think about, they come up with lots of impractical ideas, lots of junk which has no commercial value. Management ought to specify the problems for them to solve. That's the only way we can keep ahead of our competition. We've got to get our problems solved."

After a short pause, Hobson asked, "Are there any more questions, gentlemen? Well, if there aren't, then we'll excuse Van. Thanks, Van, for coming in. We'll let you know something as soon as we've made a decision."

As Van left the room, Harold said to the members of the committee, "What do you think of my candidate? Sounds pretty good, doesn't he? Let's talk about him."

GUIDE QUESTIONS

1. *Do you think Toppin's style will work in the research lab? Why?*
2. *Do you feel the bonus system proposed by Toppin will produce results? Why?*
3. *What would you recommend to Harold Hobson?*
4. *How do you think the researchers will react to Toppin, should he be appointed?*

At the conclusion of this chapter,
you should be able to—

    ·   **Give the meaning of good communications.**

    ·   **Describe the communications process.**

    ·   **Know some of the barriers to communication and how to overcome them.**

    ·   **Itemize several upward and downward means of communication.**

    ·   **Define the grapevine and show how it might be used by management.**

15

Communication and the Lack of It

Communication is the transfer of an idea of any kind from one person to another. Good communication is the accurate conveyance of this idea so the receiver would understand the idea just as the sender meant. Bad communication is just the opposite —the inability of the receiver to grasp the idea that the sender hoped to convey.

THE PROCESS OF COMMUNICATION

The process of communications is depicted in Figure 15.1. The initiator of the communication conceives an idea or perceives an idea, grasps an existing concept or becomes aware of an existing phenomenon. He or she puts the idea into some sort of a code, not necessarily a code like the Morse code or some other special code known only to a few, but puts the idea into any given set of signals for sending messages. These symbols are words, pictures, actions, graphs, or a multitude of other coding methods.

Transmission is a method by which the coded message moves from the sender to the receiver. It might move as a private talk. It might be by radio, television, or telephone. It might be a performance or an exhibit, but the message would be transmitted in some way so that the receiver receives it through a sense organ. Once he or she senses the coded transmission, then he or she must decide to decode the message, to translate the coded message into a comprehensible, understandable, intelligible idea. The hoped for result is that the idea received is the same idea the sender had transmitted.

Almost anyone in any business, or any organization, will say that the greatest problem an enterprise has is one of communications. Managers do not understand the subordinates, and the subordinates do not understand the managers. The men do not understand the women, and the women do not understand the men. The subordinates do not understand the goals of the company, and the company managers do not understand the worker's needs. Managers are moving in a direction and trying

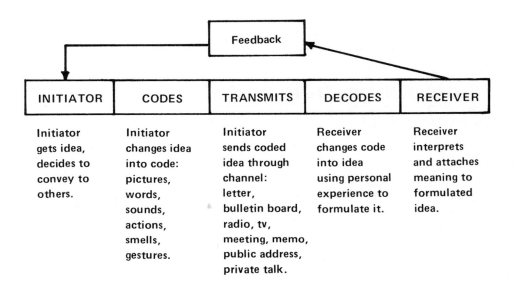

FIGURE 15.1 The Communication Process.

to communicate that direction to the subordinates, and the subordinates are interpreting what they hear as something which will affect them personally, not something which is good or bad for the company. And so we have a communications problem, a breakdown in communications, an inability of a receiver to grasp the idea sent by the initiator, or a barrier to the reception of those ideas because of a preexisting or predisposing condition.

Good communications is extremely important. It brings about better teamwork, higher morale, more productivity in the organization. It brings about a unity of purpose when everyone knows what he is doing, why he is doing it, and what he can hope to gain for both the company and himself by doing the job at hand.

Good communications does not mean that the receiver has to accept the idea or agree with the sender of the idea. Rather it means that the receiver gets an intact idea, just the same idea the sender had. When this happens, even if the receiver rejects the idea of the sender, he and the sender at least are talking about the *same* idea and can move from that point forward, hammering out a compromise if possible.

HUMAN RELATIONS IN COMMUNICATIONS

A study has shown that one of the most important conditions of the job, for the employee, is to feel "in" on things. The same survey which indicated this also showed that letting the employee know what was happening was about the *last* thing managers felt would be meaningful to the worker.[1] If a worker feels it is of prime importance for him to know what is happening, then he looks forward to finding out what is going on in the company. If, on the other hand, this is one of the least considerations of the manager, the manager will find little time to try to communicate with his subordinates. What normally happens is that the manager "tells" the subordinate what he feels the subordinate ought to know. The worker rejects what he is told and tries to find out what is really going on or makes up a story based on what he sees.

By observation, we should note that most managers spend more than half of their time communicating face-to-face, on the telephone, or by their actions. If the actions of the managers indicate a disrespect for the subordinates, the subordinates receive this communication.

Production employees view situations from a different point of view than do their immediate supervisors, middle or top managers. The men at the top have the responsibility for the entire company, for its profitability, its growth, for everything about the company. They also have the authority to make decisions which influence and change the direction of the company and make it run in the desired manner. The man on the bottom of the organizational structure has little or no authority to make decisions and is responsible for only a very restricted activity defined to him in his job description. He cannot make lots of things happen. He can only do what he is told to do. He is not responsible for the profits of the company. He does not see profit as a part of his job. Since he does not see it as part of his job, often he is unaware of what makes his company profitable or unprofitable. Communications downward which emphasizes the role of the production man, and leadership which allows the production employee to have a role in the decision making of the company, can make the employee aware of his overall responsibility toward the company and the part he plays in making it successful.

THE PROCESS IN DETAIL

Let's go back to Figure 15.1 (page 246) and go through, step by step, the components of the communications process:

Step 1   The person who is to send the message gets an idea. It could be an original idea, an idea from someone else, from a book, from any source. He may have had several ideas which he combines into one, or he may have chosen one idea from several. He may be taking an idea exactly as someone else has transmitted it to him, and he is preparing to send it along to another person. Once he gets the idea, he decides to communicate this idea to someone else for some particular reason. As we mentioned in a previous chapter on selling ideas, the sender wants to stimulate some action or reaction from the receiver of the message, either an immediate action or one in the future. Many communications are sent for the general knowledge of the receiver so that the receiver may apply that knowledge at some later time.

Step 2 The sender chooses a code by which he will send his message. It may be in the form of words, pictures, actions, gestures, signals, dots and dashes, sounds, or any kind of code possible, and its form will depend upon the audience, the persons who will receive the message and their backgrounds. The sender may choose a combination of codes, such as words and pictures, to convey the meaning to the receivers.

Step 3 Once the sender has determined the code he will use, he must determine then the method or channel of transmission he will use to convey the message to the receiver. Suppose a supervisor wants his men to be made aware of a change in working hours in the summer months. He might use a picture showing a man clocking in at seven o'clock instead of eight o'clock. Or he may use a picture of a man clocking in at seven-thirty with a boss figure gesturing that he is a half hour late. He might decide to use words and he could call his men together in a meeting during which he would talk with them, or he might decide to send a letter to each of the members, or he may even use words in a memo which would be placed on the appropriate bulletin boards.

Step 4 The receiver of the coded message decodes that message attaching his own personal meaning to the code. For instance, he may look at the bulletin board and see the picture of a supervisor shaking his finger at a subordinate and immediately attach a negative connotation to the message, a kind of a "how are they going to harass me this time" connotation to the new company policy. The receiver could just as easily attach a positive connotation to the message if the ingredients of the message have been good for the receiver in the past. It is in this step that much emotional feeling can take precedent over any logical message and defeat the intent of the communication. If the communicator tells a hundred truths and only one half-truth, and the receiver is aware of this one half-truth, he might attach the half-truth connotation to all the communications from the sender. Or, if he has no reason to doubt the sender's integrity, then he will assume that the message he is getting will be factual, accurate, and truthful.

Step 5 The receiver of the message unites the decoded message with his predisposed conditioning and interprets, formulates, and attaches meaning to the idea. He may understand the company message which will require all personnel to come to work an hour earlier in the summer, but he may find this to be to his benefit or to his detriment depending upon how he interprets the message. Even if he feels that going to work an hour earlier will be to his benefit, he may let feelings that it will be to the company's benefit override his good feeling for his own personal benefit, and have negative feelings about having to go to work an hour earlier. In a situation like this, participative management will go a long way in helping the receiver develop a positive feeling toward the change that management seeks to impose.

We can see easily from this step-by-step review that there can be a breakdown between the sender of a message and the receiver of that message, depending upon preexisting conditions of both the sender and the receiver. There are many receivers in industry—many workers who feel that any message from higher management is a negative message, always benefiting the company and always taking more from the employees. When this is the case, those employees will seek out a reason, *the* reason, that the company is doing something and find how the company is going to take advantage of the employee. At best, they will be skeptical until time shows that the company does do things which are helpful to both the company and the employees.

COMMUNICATION BARRIERS

Before we get into the upward, downward, and lateral forms of communications, let us consider for a moment the barriers to communication—those conditions which keep the receiver from getting the message the sender intends to convey.

The first of these that we will mention is language. This is a problem not only of the Frenchman speaking English or the Italian speaking Spanish, but it is a problem of two people who speak the same language, yet attach different meanings to words. It may be two people from different socioeconomic levels, two people with different educational backgrounds, people with experiential variances. It is a problem of semantics, of language, of the meaning of words.

It may also be that the receiver of the words is not at all familiar with those words used by the sender. When either of these occur, there is no effective communications.

A second barrier to communication is the indifference of the receiver, usually caused by a preconceived idea of what the sender is going to say. The receiver has the idea that nothing the sender is going to transmit is of any value or importance, so the receiver turns off his reception device, or just doesn't pay attention. If he does receive the message, he will assign a negative meaning to whatever the sender transmits. He may have a preudice against the sender. For example, a representative of the Red Cross is seeking contributions, and the would-be receiver says to himself, "I was in the war and I know that the Red Cross doesn't help the foot soldier," then there will be no meaningful communication. If, on the other hand, the receiver's experience with the sender has been good, the receiver's attitude will be good, possibly to the extent of overlooking obvious faults in the attempted communication.

A third barrier has to do with the relative positions and status of both the sender and the receiver. The subordinate might listen very carefully to every word his superior says to him, attaching meaning to each word, each gesture, each inflection in the speaker's tone of voice. However, the speaker may not see any significance to what he, himself, says. He might feel in a joking mood and say something to a subordinate which would indicate a lack of trust, a lack of respect or a lack of confidence in his work. The subordinate may not see the joke, but might take it as a direct affront. He may feel deeply humiliated. There are many cases in which a subordinate quits a job over what a superior thought was a harmless joke. Managers must be keenly aware of everything they say, every message that they send to subordinates. Managers control the destinies of subordinates—their raises, promotions, transfers, their very jobs—and so subordinates generally place an abnormal amount of meaning to whatever a superior says to them.

A fourth barrier to communication is an absolute resistance to change on the part of the receiver. Any message sent to him from management will fall on deaf ears because the receiver can never attach any positive connotation to a message and reacts negatively to messages which indicate a need for any kind of change whatsoever.

OVERCOMING COMMUNICATION BARRIERS

There are some ways to overcome the above listed barriers and these ways fall under a general, how-to-communicate-better heading. The first thing communicators might consider is the use of simple language, using words with which most people are familiar. If the sender is trying to communicate with a specific group, then he might use words that people in that group normally use to communicate with each other. Receivers do not like to be talked down to, as if they are first graders instead of adults, but most receivers would rather hear simple words and terminology and easily understood phrases and sentences, rather than an extensive vocabulary, esoteric terms, and incomprehensible dialogue. We often hear students say things like, "He must be smart. He has a tremendous vocabulary. And he must know what he's talking about. But I don't know one thing he said or one thing he was trying to get across."

This leads us to a second method of overcoming barriers, and, that is to be specific where possible, using simple words with specific meanings. Rather than say that the patient has "a fever" or "a high fever," the nurse might instead say that the patient has "a fever of 101.2 degrees." Rather than say "I talked with him on the telephone for a long time," the sender might say "for approximately twenty minutes." Rather than say "We have to increase production, get more out of these machines," the sender might say, "We need to get 17 percent more production or 22 more items per day out of these machines."

A third method of overcoming a barrier is feedback. Feedback is the technique a sender uses when he asks the receiver to send the message back to him, the sender. If the sender sends a message, the receiver receives it and returns it, and it comes back just as it was sent, the sender knows that it was received intact. If the idea comes back deformed, unclear, or in any way other than the one which was intended, the sender can resend it, using different words, different pictures, or a different channel of communication. He can continue to use this feedback until he receives the message he originally sent. To do this he must pay strict attention to what he is saying and to the meaning which is being attached to what he has said. He has to listen to the receiver's feedback to him. He must be an effective listener.

A fourth step a sender can take to overcome communication barriers is to repeat the message not in its original code but in a different code. For instance, he might explain something to a receiver and the receiver not understand. Then the sender might draw a picture of the message and send it in another form so that the receiver has this second code he can work with to interpret the message. The phrase, "Do you want me to draw you a picture?" is normally used in a derogatory manner, but it is quite meaningful to the receiver if he does not understand the word pictures drawn by the sender.

Downward Communications

Despite the fact that researchers say participation in decision making by subordinates is helpful to companies in terms of better morale and productivity, the bulk of communications is downward, from management to subordinate, from superior to underling. We will discuss the other two types of communications, upward and lateral, in the next sections, but for now, we will concentrate on methods of downward communications.

1. Face-to-Face This is the most often used form of communication. It is usually a one to one situation with a superior telling a subordinate something to do, giving him an order, explaining something to him, and the subordinate listening to the superior tell him what to do. In this instance, there is a good chance for feedback which does not occur in most other forms of downward communications. This method gives the sender of the message an opportunity to ask the receiver to repeat what he has been told, and in that way clarify whether the message has been received intact. The face-to-face form of communication usually follows the chain of command, from president to vice-president, from vice-president to superintendent, to supervisor and down to the person at the lowest level who is to be made aware of the contents of the communication.

2. Bulletin Boards should be placed strategically throughout the plant or store so that employees will be drawn to them daily. Near the time clock, the main entrance, or close to rest rooms are effective places for bulletin boards. Messages posted on the boards would include memos, bulletins, announcements, rosters, awards, notices of meetings, minutes, posters, and other forms of written communications. Often a party is designated to control the downward flow of information appearing on bulletin boards so that erroneous information, negative or anti-company information will not be posted on the board. To enforce this, a message stating that "no notices can be placed on this board without the approval of _____." can be posted on the bulletin board, or the board may be enclosed in glass and locked with only that person responsible for it having the key.

3. Letters to Employees This is a private form of communication from management to the employees to talk about a situation in which that employee might be involved. Letters directly to participants are used sometimes to involve the employee's spouse and family. For instance, a sales oriented company might write to its salesmen at home offering big prizes for more sales effort, bonuses and trips for quota breakers, hoping that this knowledge will cause the wife to add some incentive to the salesman's motivation. Sometimes, companies facing grave circumstances such as a plant closing might want to get the entire family involved in an employee's decision to walk off the job or take a cut in pay or take some action which would affect the company's staying open or closing.

4. House Organs Company newsletters, newspapers, bulletins, and magazines are called house organs and are used both for the downflow of information to their employees and for public relations with their customers and stockholders. These periodicals have features, tell about company progress and expansion, list births, deaths, and changes in the status or the status of the employees and their families. They give the president a chance to speak with the employees and customers. They also give the employees a chance to speak (upward communications) through letters-to-the-editor sections. Such periodicals help to satisfy the security, social, and esteem needs of the employees. They are usually sent to the homes, just as are letters to employees, to incorporate the whole family in company business.

5. Annual Reports Many companies want their employees to know everything that is going on in the company and send out annual reports to them to show exactly what the company did during the previous year, how that compared with years gone by, and what is projected for the coming year and years. This report lists earnings, earnings per share, dividends declared, taxes paid, investment per employee, new products and research, the sales volume, the number of employees, and other information about the company. It usually contains an opinion of the chief executive about the state of affairs of the company. This annual report gives the employees a feeling of being "in" on the plans of the company and they can see better how their individual efforts serve the whole company.

6. Group Meetings Most companies of any size have daily, weekly, or monthly meetings of supervisors and subordinates to discuss problems, projects, policy, or any number of things. This is a face-to-face situation, but it differs from number one because there are groups of people involved rather than a one-to-one situation. It still provides the potential for feedback as does the one-to-one, although the opportunity may not be as great because of the reluctance of many people to speak, to show their true feelings, to show their lack of comprehension, in front of a group.

7. Other Methods There are many more different methods of downward communication such as meetings with a labor union, stuffers in a pay envelope, public address systems with speakers in every department of the company, employee handbooks which would be available to new employees from the personnel department, and informational racks for material the company wants to dispense to the employees which may or may not be company related. Some companies provide pamphlets on such things as how to file your income tax, how to avoid accidents, boating, repairing your automobile, and other publications of this nature. In this last method, the company is not only dispensing things to the employee which benefits the company, but is also building an image of the company by attempting to show the employee that the company is interested in his individual well being as well as making more money for the company.

Upward Communications

When the sender of the message is the subordinate and the manager is the receiver, then this is called upward communications. There are many upward channels of communications and we will discuss some of them.

1. Face-to-Face Again, this is the most common form of communications, with the subordinate talking directly with his superior. Communication can be initiated by either the manager asking for a response from the subordinate or the subordinate initiating the conversation to tell or ask the manager something. The greatest advantage to this method of communication is that the receiver can question the sender immediately to confirm what he is receiving, and the sender can get instant feedback. The receiver can also hear inflections in the voice of the sender and see his facial expressions, just as the sender can see the receiver's expressions. Face-to-face communication does not eliminate all problems of communication, but it is the most direct, the most effective of all forms.

2. Group Meetings Group meetings are probably a better means of downward communication than upward. When management wants to tell a number of people something face-to-face, a group meeting is called. Group meetings sometimes polarize the members of the group if there is anything controversial about the subject. They can cause the participants to take sides immediately rather than be open-minded about the subject. Group meetings also inhibit people, keep them from making any statements at all because of the fear of some repercussion from their peers or superiors, even if only in the form of ridicule. Some people will never speak in a group meeting, while others jump at the chance to appear before any group to demonstrate their talents for speech making.

Two final advantages of group meetings are: (a) as we saw in the chapter of creativity, group sessions allow participants to build on each other's ideas, to rapidly reach conclusions to problems; and (b) group sessions can be used most effectively by a democratic or participative manager to get subordinate input and involvement.

3. Grievances Grievances are formal, upward communications from employees and their union representatives concerning actions taken by management which, in the eyes of that employee and his or her representatives, are questionable in view of the contract. The communication is a step in a predetermined procedure which would probably call for a response from management stating what management proposed to do about the situation at hand. A grievance is not a free-wheeling form of communication designed to get new ideas and suggestions from the worker to management as are most other forms of upward communication. It is a subdued, formal notice of discontent.

4. *Suggestion Box*   This is an upward form of communication used by a large number of companies which allows subordinates to put in a box their suggestions for improving the company or some aspect of it. They can either sign the suggestions or make them anonymous. Many suggestion systems offer cash or prizes to those participants whose ideas are used by the company. The suggestion box can be useful to management in allowing everyone to have an input into the operation of the company, but it can have a detrimental effect if those suggestions are not taken care of expeditiously. There must be a fair and immediate hearing and the authors of those suggestions must be contacted and given the results of the evaluation. If a person enters a suggestion to management and he does not hear about it in a reasonable time, his or her attitude toward the company takes a nosedive, and he or she is not likely to enter a second suggestion no matter how good it is. Sometimes the suggestion box becomes the complaint box, but this gives employees an opportunity to air their differences and gives management an opportunity to solve these problems. If management is unaware of the specifics of a problem, then complaints from employees can clarify problems. Maybe half the suggestions in a suggestion box are worth following up (the others being obscene, humorous, or inconsequential and anonymous), but they all must receive the attention of management. If management cannot get around to reviewing the suggestions and replying to their originators, it would probably be in the best interest of management to do away with the system rather than antagonize the employees.

5. *Letters to the Editor*   If the company has a paper, a magazine, or some publication which is used in downward communication, then the same publication can have a letters-to-the-editor column so employees can address questions and comments to the editor which concern the whole company, whether or not that particular employee reveals himself to management. These questions and comments give management personnel opportunities for further downward communications concerning certain actions and activities. If management has no real reason for actions which seem to annoy employees, then it might be in the best interest of the company to refrain from this action or abandon the activity which is causing the irritation.

6. *Morale Survey*   This is a survey undertaken by management usually through its personnel department or an outside consulting group to try and get a reading on the morale of the employees and the conditions which cause this morale, either good or bad. This should not be limited to the production employees and clerical workers, but should be open to the management personnel as well. Questionnaires are devised which management hopes will lead to an awareness of the feelings of the employees.

The respondents are given an opportunity to complete the forms, being anonymous about it, and then turn the questionnaires in to a central collection agency. The responses are tabulated and sent to the planners of the survey for study and interpretation. The result of the morale survey is to direct management's attention to those areas which are causing problems within the company so that steps can be taken to eliminate these causes. The morale survey is like the suggestion box. If management is not going to respond to the people surveyed, not going to make the results known to the people in the company, not going to take any action as a result of the survey, then it would be better not to have the survey, just as it would be better not to have the suggestion box.

Horizontal Communication

The third form of communication occurs when peers exchange information with each other. This is not normally a formal process, but more of a bull session, of informal talks between people on the same levels within the company. In both the upward and the downward forms of communication, there is a barrier of rank, a subordinate-superior relationship barrier which does not exist in the horizontal form of communication. With that barrier removed, peer managers can afford to be more honest and devote their efforts to solving problems rather than playing politics or striving to maintain an image. Horizontal communications do much to speed up the communication process by cutting through the formal lines, by eliminating the language barrier with a face-to-face give-and-take exchange of information and by the absence of "games" which people feel compelled to play because of their rank. Horizontal communications can easily be the most successful form and produce the best results.

THE GRAPEVINE

A boss tells his secretary something off the record; then she tells her friend in the lounge. Next, the friend tells the mail room clerk who tells it to the engineer in the upstairs office. This has a familiar ring! This is the grapevine, that informal, face-to-face, spoken form of communications which moves messages rapidly, either accurately or distorted, without feedback. Grapevine material can originate from facts or from the absence of facts. It can be an offhand opinion which quickly takes on the cloak of truth. It thrives best when people feel insecure and are ready to believe anything they hear.

Possibly the most important thing a manager should know about the grapevine is that the grapevine does exist and even though he may try to destroy it, it will continue to exist. This grapevine is constantly active and spreads facts and non-facts, truths and rumors throughout the organization. The manager should know this, and take any action he feels necessary to clarify stories which are inaccurate and might harm the company and its plans and policies.

Even though the grapevine is often an unreliable form of communication, it does carry formal messages from management to subordinates and from subordinates back to management, and often carries truths which are shunned in formal communications. For instance, a directive might be issued by management to subordinates asking, "Do you have any problems?" The answer might come back as "No." Yet, the grapevine might contradict this by bringing tales of woe from the subordinates to management, many of which may be true. Managers should listen to the grapevine in much the same way they would listen to a morale survey, to find out why the workers are unhappy and in what ways management might correct situations and make the employees more content.

The grapevine brings rumors from people who are afraid of something they feel the company is contemplating, from people who are angry with the company, or people who naturally distrust all companies, and from people who appear all-knowing and yet do not know so create their own stories. In almost every instance, the best way for the company to fight the rumor is by letting the employees know the truth, by clarifying the matter.

Using the Grapevine

Almost always, managers are advised not to use the grapevine to disseminate any information because of the potential distortion of that information. Managers are told to control the downward flow of information so that the recipients of the messages will get the ideas exactly as the managers sent them. As was previously indicated, the grapevine tends to distort messages, making them fit the needs of the people involved, regardless of the accuracy.

There is one exception to this use of the grapevine which is highly prevalent in government and is used to some extent in industry. This is the use of the "leak" which refers to bits and pieces of information that flow either accidently or on purpose from the office of the superior. When this happens on purpose, when the leak is made for a reason, that reason is usually so management can get a response to a contemplated action before that action is announced. Suppose management is considering going to a four-day, ten-hour-a-day work week. Rather than announce this and get a favorable or unfavorable response from the employees, the plan or part of the plan would be leaked to someone who would start this message into the grapevine. In a short time the entire plant would be alerted to the possibility of the change. If the reaction of the employees was poor, then management could deny that there was a plan to change to the four-day week. If the plan got favorable reaction, then management could report that it was contemplating the move. This is a way of feeling the pulse of the employees. It can be done in other ways by group meetings, participation, and feedback, but there are situations which do not lend themselves to participation and management can use the grapevine method. It may be only to test timing, to see if the time is right for the introduction of a new idea or not, and management would not want everyone to be stirred up prematurely.

Politicians use this informal method to take the pulse of their constituency, allowing a leak that they will be voting for or against a certain piece of legislation. If the response from the electorate is strong in one direction, then the elected official might officially announce that he will vote in that direction without announcing that he had gotten a reading on the pulse of the electors through the grapevine.

COMMUNICATIONS SUMMARY

We have all been asked the old question, "If a tree falls in the forest and there is no one around, does the falling tree make any noise?" A similar question might be asked concerning communications, "If a sender transmits a message, and a receiver hears but does not understand it, does any communication take place?" Because they have sent a message, senders often take for granted that communication has taken place; but understanding is the essence of communications, not hearing or seeing. The communicator, the sender of a message, must endeavor to put his or her idea into a code which can be understood by the receiver, and transmit this code by whatever channel is most likely to reach the receiver. Only then can the sender reasonably expect to communicate effectively with the receivers.

FOR DISCUSSION

1. *What is good communication?*
2. *Explain the process of communication.*
3. *What are some barriers to communication?*
4. *An extensive vocabulary helps the manager communicate with the workers. Discuss this statement.*
5. *Face-to-face, downward and upward, one-to-one, or group communications allows feedback. Explain this statement.*
6. *Suggestion boxes are good for morale even though no one reads the suggestions because employees get a chance to blow off steam. Discuss this statement.*
7. *The grapevine is often erroneous and distorted so management should never initiate messages through it. Discuss this statement.*

ENDNOTE

1. W. C. Minninger and H. Levinson, *Human Understanding in Industry* (Chicago, Research Associates, 1956), p. 12.

The Moving to Higher Education

Mark Christopher, Scott Andrews, and John Mathews were excited about starting at Murray Junior High School. They had lived close to it all their lives and were familiar with the outside of the school, but they had never spent much time on the inside and had never come face-to-face with the administrators. The first day, they, along with all the other new students, were called to the auditorium for an assembly.

Once the students were assembled, a boy in a scout uniform led the pledge of allegiance, a girl called for divine inspiration for the group, and then a man stepped to the podium and introduced himself.

"I am Mr. Withers, your principal. I would like to take this opportunity to welcome you to Murray Junior High School. This school has a long history of which we are proud, and we hope you will be as proud of it as we are, and that you will hold it with the same esteem as we do. We have two new members of our staff and I would like to introduce them for a few words. First, we have Charlie Maynard, assistant principal for the seventh grade, and next, our assistant principal for the eighth grade, Jacques Bordeaux, our jolly Frenchman. We'll hear now from Mr. Maynard."

"Thank you, Mr. Withers," said Charlie. "I want to implore you new students to be aware of the obligations accorded you by the leaders of this political subdivision, never to deface, mar or disfigure, either literally or figuratively, the hallowed halls of this institution. You must never instigate, initiate, nor perpetrate deprivations of your peer's individuality, nor should you reciprocate or retaliate when deprivation prevails around you. When this occurs, you should initiate a dialogue with the appropriate authorities. Finally, we must insist upon a policy of no transgressions by deceptions, fraud, or trickery, on a code of purity of mind and action concerning one's literary endeavors. Thank you, Mr. Withers."

"Thank you, Mr. Maynard, and now Jacques, what do you have to say?"

"*Bonjour,* boys and girls, it is with pleasure that I stand before you as your assistant principal," Mr. Bordeaux said with an accent. "I ask you to cooperate with me and come to me with your problems. I will do my very best to help you."

"Thank you, Jacques. Now I would like to add one thing before we adjourn this session. While we do not condone the use of tobacco in any form, we insist that you smoke on the smoking block, at the rear of the school at breaks. Now, when the bell rings, go immediately to your assigned home room."

On the way to their home room, Mark said to Scott, "What did you think of that?"

"I'm not quite sure," said Scott. "That first guy said something about steaming up all the rooms, but I guess he was talking about the shower room or something. My mama raises Cain when we steam up the bathroom taking a shower."

"Yeah," said John, "That second guy was something, too, wasn't he? He said something about hollowing out the halls and rolly-polly guys, but I couldn't make it out."

"I don't think that had to do with us," said Mark, "But I'll tell you one thing I didn't like. That head guy, the principal, said we had to smoke out on the smoking block at breaks and I don't see why we should have to smoke at all. He said he was going to insist that we do it. If we don't, I think we're going to get condoned, whatever that is."

"I wonder why he called that guy jock?" asked John. "He must teach phys ed. I wouldn't think the principals should go around calling each other jocks, though. At least, not while they're up there in front of everybody. Anyway, I think he was speaking Spanish or something."

"Me, too," said Mark. "There's a lot of crazy stuff going on around here."

"Yeah," said Scott, "I heard junior high was hard and it looks like they start right on you the first day."

In the principal's office, Mr. Withers and his two assistants were talking about the assembly program.

"Well, what do you think?" Withers asked.

"I feel we pretty well covered the rules," said Maynard, "Now it's up to the students to follow them."

GUIDE QUESTIONS

1. *Will the students follow the rules as outlined by the principals? Why?*

2. *What barriers to communications did the principals encounter? What did they do to overcome them?*

3. *Had this been the first day on the job, rather than the first day of junior high, what kind of a reaction might the boys have had?*

CASE 15–2

The Show Biz Whiz

"I think I can do it," said Knute Eskridge, "I haven't ever done this exact kind of work, but I have been involved in advertising and public relations, and other promotional work."

Eskridge was talking to "Long John" Miller, lead guitarist and leader of the rock group, the Lead Balloon. "The last guy we had thought he could hack it, too," said Miller. "Let me show you the review of the concert he worked on."

Paristown "I Could Stay Here Forever," one of the Lead Balloon's hits, wasn't quite true for the group at the Paristown Civic Center Saturday night. With only fifteen people in the audience, they had no intention of staying forever. The Lead Balloon and their back-up group, the Rosebuds, tried to perform despite the small audience, but had a difficult time. Their sense of humor waned and their music became overpowering as their enthusiasm drained with the night wearing on.

"This is the worst turnout I've seen in ten years," said Arnold Harrison, civic center manager. "No advance sales were made at all for this show."

"Sometimes you just have to gamble," said Harold Wagner, public relations man for the group. "The Lead Balloon has only been together about a year. We're a new show and people don't know us yet."

The show consisted of three groups, the Lead Balloon, the Rosebuds, and another group called Fat City which didn't bother to play at all.

"If we had had more publicity," Wagner said, "We'd have done much better. I went to the newspaper and the radio stations and put up a few posters, but I don't think that was quite enough. I went on radio just today and told the audience that everyone had to start somewhere, and since Lead Balloon was just starting out, they ought to come on down and support them, but I guess the audience didn't heed my advice."

Wagner said he was sorry about the financial losses suffered by the groups and the civic center, but he wasn't about to give up on the groups. "Lots of groups don't succeed in the first year," he said.

"Wagner just thought he wasn't going to give up," said Miller. "We thought differently. He's canned and we're looking for a new man. We've got to have somebody who can really promote us. We know we have the music, we've got the songs, we've got the sound, but we haven't got the acceptance yet. If we hire you, how would you go about promoting us?"

"I'd like to think about it for a while rather than give you a quick answer," said Eskridge. "Why don't we meet again this afternoon at four-thirty, and I can give you an outline then of what we would do."

"That's fine," said "Long John" Miller.

GUIDE QUESTIONS

1. *Do things sell themselves?*
2. *How would you recommend that the band be promoted? Be specific.*
3. *Would this kind of a problem lend itself to brainstorming?*

part 5

_____

control

At the conclusion of this chapter,
you should be able to—

- Enumerate the bases for standards.
- List several areas which lend themselves to control.
- Describe some accounting documents used in control.
- Discuss the various types of control.
- Explain some of the problems associated with control.

16

Examining the Control Function

Control is the fourth function of management. Managers plan, organize, activate, and control. Control is closely linked with the planning function because plans which have been established in the beginning become the standards or models for controls. The actual results, when measured against these standards, become the basis for new plans, for changes in goals, or in methods of accomplishing these goals.

There are three steps in control:

1.   Establish goals and set standards.
2.   Measure actual performance and compare with standard.
3.   Take corrective action, if necessary, as a result of comparison.

Control without corrective action is not control, but only an observation of what is happening. If a manager sees that a subordinate is not functioning according to a standard of performance, but has no authority to fire the employee or require an upgrade in performance to minimum standards, the manager is not in control of the subordinate. He or she is simply an observer of that subordinate's activities.

Earlier we discussed goals, how they should be specific, and how they should be communicated to the managers and subordinates who were being held responsible for carrying out these goals. We said that these goals should be written in a quantitative manner, if possible, to insure understanding. For example, sales next year should be $4,525,000; the collection should amount to $2,250 per Sunday to keep the church financially sound; students should be able to score a minimum of 75 percent on a standardized test; the production worker should average twelve soldering connections per minute. These quantitative goals are much easier to measure than those of general qualification. For instance, if a job description said that an employee should work hard, perform well, make a goodly number of products during his or her tenure at the plant, and be amiable toward peers, subordinates, and leaders, it would be very difficult to measure that employee's performance against such vague goals or standards.

BASES OF STANDARDS

There are several bases on which standards can be set. For a new company, the most often used method would be to set goals based on what the manager expects the company to do if it progressed as hoped. The goals would put into quantitative terms or into specific terms of performance, and these hopes would become standards and the goals to which the manager should aspire.

A second basis for setting standards would be using past performance. This might apply to a company which had been in business for some time. The managers who were responsible for setting goals could say that the company did a million dollars in sales last year and with more effort in a certain area could do a million and a quarter this year. The standard would be based on the actual performance of the previous year with the added ingredient of new plans and efforts for the current year.

The third method of setting standards would be to base them on analysis. This is the most scientific of the three methods. Under this plan, a manager might say that if an employee could make one part in five minutes then he or she should make twelve parts in one hour and ninety-six parts in an eight-hour shift, allowing for coffee breaks and fatigue. The father of scientific management, Frederick W. Taylor, would have made all his future projections on this basis rather than on history or hope.

The Tangible Versus the Intangible

The goals that we set may be tangible and the method by which we appraise them also may be tangible. For instance, sales can be projected in terms of actual sales dollars measured against planned sales dollars. These would be tangible. Man hours would be tangible. Bolts of cloth and ears of corn would be tangible results and could be measured.

There are other results which cannot be measured in tangible terms. There are such things as the morale of the employees, the total learning of the students, and the effect of a company on the society of which it is a part. Many of these intangibles are put into tangible terms when possible, such as dollar effort, number of complaints, passes versus failures, or some quantitative measure which can be compared with the past and future to determine trends. A manager should do this as often as possible, but should not be bound totally by these tangible results when making final decisions. Occasionally the manager will find some unexplainable phenomenon, some intangible force, which causes things to happen or not to happen, and the manager must be aware that that force exists. The manager would have to take this intangible quality and weigh it right along with measurable, tangible factors. For instance, the mood or the morale caused by the presence or absence of an employee might greatly affect the productivity of a department. Firing the employee due to a poor record may cause the production, not to go up with the addition of a new, more capable employee, but to go down because of the drop in the spirit of the remaining employees as a result of the departure of their friend.

Budgetary and Non-Budgetary Control

Along with the tangible and intangible, we want to consider the budgetary and non-budgetary controls. There is no doubt but that the budget is the most often used formal basis of control. As we mentioned earlier, budgets are quantified plans of action. If a company is going to put forth more effort to generate more sales, then both the increased activity and increased results can be measured in dollars. Closer supervision requires more supervisors, who require more salaries and more benefits, which can also be put into numbers. More non-personal selling efforts (advertising) require more advertising people, more advertising programs, more time and space. These also cost money and can also be quantified.

But again we run into areas of company effort which cannot be quantified. For instance, a company might seek to make a favorable image in a community. That favorable image will not be made on contributions alone, on donations to worthwhile programs. Contributions will be helpful, but they will not be the sole determining factor. A good citizen image must be created by the work and dedication of the employees, by the stability of employment the company provides, by the promotions from within, by providing jobs for the sons and daughters of the community citizens so that those young people will not have to leave the community to find meaningful employment, by the type of jobs the company offers, and whether the company offers its employees the opportunity to maintain dignity in the work they do. These and many other factors all have a bearing on the public image of the company and these factors cannot be quantified or budgeted. A company cannot budget the hours its employees will spend working with the church, the community, the little league, the girl scouts. These are things which happen under the proper conditions, but they cannot be budgeted. However, management personnel can take time themselves and allow others some time off to participate in community affairs and involve themselves in those things which are meaningful to the community. Managers have to be flexible concerning community needs, keeping in mind the feedback coming from the community members in reference to the public image of the company.

AREAS OF CONTROL

There are many areas in which a company might be controlled, and we will talk only about a few of the more prevalent ones. First, let us talk about some of those which are both budgeted and tangible.

Return on Investment

A stockholder invests money in a company in hopes of realizing a return on his investment, a return greater than he could get by putting his money in a sock or under the mattress or in a more risk-free form of security such as government bonds. An investor can get a return on his investment in two ways: (1) a dividend from the company, or (2) growth when the value of his stock increases. A farmer is like a stockholder when he buys a calf at the livestock market. If he keeps that cow for a long period of time, he will probably get regular dividends in the form of milk daily and calves each year, and still hang on to his principal, the cow. Or, the farmer might choose to sell the mature cow in which case he will get more than he has paid for her. Such a gain would be through growth. A professional manager is hired to get the stockholder a return in dividends or growth, or both, just like the cow. If he cannot do this, then the stockholders will sell their stock, and take their money and put it into other companies which do show a return.

Return on investment should be no lower than returns of other companies in the same general line of business and should be higher than those forms of investment which have less risk involved. If the manager cannot meet these provisions, the investors will sell out and cause the price of the stock to drop, which will indicate a lack of confidence in the management.

Sales

A company, just like any other enterprise, must continue to grow or else fall behind. No company, no church, no club, no school, no country can be the same thing forever without some change in quality and quantity. Most companies seek increased sales as a standard, a goal and use this sales increase as a motivator for all the people of the company. The costs of effort can be budgeted and the amount of sales anticipated from the effort can also be budgeted. Sales are made on the basis of a personal effort (sales from a salesman to a client) or on a non-personal selling effort (advertising). The mix of these two comprise the total sales effort. If the sales generated by those efforts cannot measure up to projected sales, then there must be some revision in the method of acquiring sales or in the sales goal itself. The manager must make decisions and recommendations in this area to bring the budgeted and the actual sales closer together.

Costs

It costs money to make sales. There are costs for the materials, the ingredients going into the product, the direct labor, for the indirect overhead, the administration, the housing, advertising, electricity, the personnel manager, transportation, depreciation and other costs necessary to generate sales must be deduced from the sales figure to determine profits. If these costs exceed what is projected and sales are on target, then profits will be less than anticipated and can only be brought into line by increasing sales or reducing costs to the projected levels. If the costs cannot be held because of some external force, such as the price of flour to a bakery, then it is possible that the price per unit can be raised so that the relative proportions between the cost of sales and the price will be kept, and then the profit as a percentage of sales can be maintained.

Profits

Total profits is another area which can be budgeted. Company officials regularly set profits as a percentage of sales, profits as a return on investment, or profits compared with some other index as a company goal, and then issue periodic statements of progress to all managers. The statements, normally the income statement (see Table 16-1) and the balance sheet (see Table 16-2), are distributed monthly throughout the company so that those people responsible for the profits (or losses) of the company are made aware of their positions on a regular interval basis. This allows them to know the exact status of the budgeted versus the actual so that they might take remedial steps to insure the profitability of the company. Here again, the managers might elect to increase sales, reduce costs, change or improve sales efforts, lower or do away with minimum standards of quality, or take any number of other steps to alter the bottom line figure.

TABLE 16-1   MaGruder's Scooters, Inc., Income Statement for October, 1974

	This Month			*Year to Date*		
	Budgeted	*Actual*	*Over (Under)*	*Budgeted*	*Actual*	*Over (Under)*
Gross Sales	$10,000	$11,590	$1,590	$100,000	$93,500	($6,500)
Less Ret. & Allow.	200	150	(50)	2,000	1,850	(150)
Net Sales	$ 9,800	$11,440	$1,640	$ 98,000	$91,650	($6,350)
Cost of Goods Sold	$ 5,400	$ 6,000	$ 600	$ 54,000	$51,250	($2,750)
Gross Margin	$ 4,400	$ 5,440	$1,040	$ 44,000	$40,400	($3,600)
Adm Salaries	1,000	1,000	—	10,000	10,000	—
Sales Salaries	1,000	1,200	200	10,000	11,600	1,600
Advertising	200	200	—	2,000	2,400	400
Utilities	140	150	10	1,400	1,320	(80)
Depreciation	80	80	—	800	800	—
Rent	200	200	—	2,000	2,000	—
Taxes	50	50	—	500	500	—
Insurance	90	90	—	900	900	—
Other	200	340	140	2,000	2,230	230
Total Adm & Sell Exp.	2,960	3,310	350	29,600	31,750	2,150
Net Operating Profit	1,440	2,130	1,090	14,400	8,650	(5,570)
Cash Discounts	100	115	15	1,000	950	(50)
Net Profit	$ 1,140	$ 2,245	$1,105	$15,400	$ 9,600	($5,800)

TABLE 16-2   MaGruder's Scooters, Inc., Comparative Balance Sheets, October 31.

Assets	1974	1973	*Over (Under)*
Cash	$ 4,135	$ 3,750	$ 385
Receivables	8,215	7,540	675
Inventories	41,020	42,150	(1,130)
Total Current Assets	$53,370	$53,440	$ (70)
Fixed Assets			
Plant and Equipment	$19,375	$16,820	$ 2,555
Less Depreciation	4,280	3,540	740
Net Plant and Equipment	15,095	13,280	1,815
Other Assets	2,040	2,040	—
Total Fixed Assets	$17,135	$15,320	$ 1,815
Total Assets	$70,505	$68,760	$ 1,745
Liabilities and Net Worth			
Current Liabilities			
Accounts Payable	$ 7,240	$ 6,825	$ 415
Notes Payable	4,800	4,800	—
Taxes and Accurals	2,440	2,580	(140)
Total Current Liabilities	$14,480	$14,205	$ 275
Note Payable	24,030	28,160	(4,130)
Total Liabilities	$38,510	$42,365	$(3,855)
Common Stock	10,000	10,000	—
Surplus	21,995	16,395	5,600
Total Liabilities and Net Worth	$70,505	$68,760	—

Cash

Companies can show a profit and still not have the cash to pay debts, to pay employees their wages, and to pay accounts payable for goods and services received. It is, therefore, extremely important that managers have the flow of cash under their control at all times. This, too, can be brought about by using a budgeting statement, one known as a cash flow statement (See Table 16-3). This statement indicates the amount of cash on hand at the beginning of a period, the inflow of cash from sales, accounts receivable, sales of securities, or from any other source. It also lists the outflow of cash during that same period to pay salaries, accounts payable, taxes, dividends, interest, and so on, and finally the closing cash balance. If the cash flow statement indicates that there will be some time during the budgeted period in which the company will be out of cash, then this control mechanism will tell the manager that he or she must find some method of providing the company with cash during the interim, or some way of eliminating this cash need. For instance, a retail sales company will probably

TABLE 16-3   MaGruder's Scooters, Inc., Estimated Cash Flow July 1–Dec. 31, 1974

	July	*August*	*September*	*October*	*November*	*December*
Opening Cash Balance	$ 3,840	$ 2,175	$ 585	$ 3,875	$ 1,995	$ 1,455
Cash in from Sales	9,250	9,500	9,500	10,000	11,500	12,500
Other Cash Income	50	—	5,000	—	—	100
Total Cash In	$13,140	$11,675	$15,085	$13,875	$13,495	$14,055
Cash Disbursements						
Inventory for Resale	7,425	7,500	7,600	8,000	8,100	6,000
Direct Labor	800	800	800	800	800	800
Materials	250	250	250	250	250	250
Administrative Salary	1,000	1,000	1,000	1,000	1,000	1,000
Rent	200	200	200	200	200	200
Utilities	140	140	160	180	190	200
Travel	200	250	150	100	50	50
Shipping	400	400	500	600	600	700
Note Payment	400	400	400	400	400	400
Interest	50	50	50	50	50	50
Other	100	100	100	300	400	400
Total Cash Out	$10,965	$11,090	$11,210	$11,880	$12,040	$10,050
Cash Gain (Loss)	$(1,665)	$(1,590)	$ 3,290	$(1,880)	$ (540)	$ 2,550
Closing Cash Balance	$ 2,175	$ 585	$ 3,875	$ 1,995	$ 1,455	$ 4,005

have need of extra cash to build up its inventory in September and October for the Christmas season. It is possible that the company can do without the increased inventory build-up, but this may cut down on sales, so is not a viable alternative. The company might borrow money from the bank, it might "ride" its creditors and not pay its bills until after the December holidays, get merchandise on consignment, or take some other measure to see to it that it will have the money necessary to see it through the cash outage situation to keep the company from bankruptcy while in a profitable position.

Capital Expenditures

Capital goods are those items of production which will last for more than a year, such as a typewriter, a building, automobiles, trucks, production machines, office furniture, and other items of this nature. Most companies budget each year for capital acquisitions, but here again, the amount of cash or the non-materialization of sales or unforeseen costs might put the capital outlay program in jeopardy. For instance, if company plans call for new cars for salesmen every other year, and sales are down in a certain year, the sales manager might elect to have his salesmen keep their cars for three or even four years with the hope that the maintenance costs of the cars will be less than the costs of buying new cars. He also might elect to sell the existing cars outright to generate needed cash, and then lease cars for the next year. This would give the salesmen their new cars, but would also bring more cash into the company rather than have a cash drain for auto expenses. Capital purchases is often the first area management looks to when a squeeze on profits dictates budgetary cuts.

Now let us look at some non-budgetable, intangible areas in which control can be used:

Morale

There is no way to put a specific dollar value on morale. Good morale usually brings in more dollars and more profits, while poor morale drains dollars from the company, but there is no exact figure that can be attached to a level of morale. One method of ascertaining the level of morale is to listen to the comments of the employees. Another method is to have a formal morale survey and ask all employees to list the good and bad features of the company. A third way managers can observe morale is by observing production. When morale goes downhill, production normally follows closely. If production goes down without any apparent cause, such as a shortage of materials or a change in methods, then it might be assumed that morale is causing this downward trend and management people can look into this situation to find the root cause of the morale problem.

Social Needs

Feedback is the best method of control in determining whether or not the company is meeting the social needs of the employees and the needs of the community at large. Are there enough activities within the company in which the employees might engage such as dances, sporting teams and events, clubs and other organizations? Is this company a good citizen to both its employees and to those living in the surrounding community? Are fellow managers treated fairly? Is the health and welfare of the employees and other citizens exposed to risk because of polluted air and water? These things are not measurable quantitatively but can be judged on the basis of quality, and through the reactions of the employees and citizens. If there is much agitation on the part of these two groups, then it can be assumed that the company is not satisfying the people and, therefore, is not accomplishing what it hopes to accomplish in terms of being a good citizen.

Product and Service Quality

An area which often can be measured, if the product has exact specifications, is quality. But if quality is the manufacturer's prerogative or service is the company's output, then management must determine when the company is giving enough quality.

When the product is completed, does it fall within the specifications of the plan approved before making it? If poor quality occurs, are there enough checks along the line so that production workers do not take a bad product and add to it? Is the quality of the work area good? Is the quality of the life which can be expected by the employees good? Most companies make reference to quality control, but it is almost always in terms of products, never in terms of people. Seldom are company officials talking about providing a quality place for people to work, but merely a place to work where good products can be made. Employees find it difficult to take much pride in company products if their existence in that company is uncomfortable.

Personal Growth

Promotion from within, transfers, growth in responsibility, and rewards are areas a company might want to control. While there are no magic numbers for guidance, managers should be alarmed if most vacancies are not filled from within the company. This indicates a deficiency in the training program when a person leaves a job and there is no replacement ready to fill the vacancy. Of course, if there is no replacement available, then company officials must look outside to find a qualified person. Not only should we be concerned with promotions and growth in this area, but also with a high rate of turnover. If this occurs, company policies should be investigated. If the reason for the turnover indicates that the cause is within the company and within the control of the managers, then something remedial must be done. However, the policy itself might be designed to encourage turnover. If the policy of a company is to pay low wages (which encourages high turnover), then that company takes a calculated risk that turnover will occur, but, may feel that this risk is preferable to paying higher wages, not having the turnover, and having to charge higher prices for its products.

CONTROL POINTS

When we are working to control something, we must have points at which our control devices can be inserted so they will be most significant. For instance, if we want to control the quality of a piece of cloth, or a man's suit, we would want to have not only a final inspection but intermediate quality checks so that the piece of work would not be finished or in the hands of the customer before anyone was aware that it was imperfect. We would want to have these reviews at every convenient point. This applies not only to non-budgetary types of control (such as quality), but also to budgeted items with check points in daily, weekly, or monthly sales and costs figures. Managers can use these as needed and not wait for yearly auditors' reports before making necessary changes in problem areas. It is important to have these control points located strategically within the system so that once an error occurs, the operation can be stopped quickly and appropriate action be taken to remedy the situation.

TYPES OF CONTROL

There are many types of control and we will talk about a few here. The first one is inspection. Inspection can be made by the president of the company, by his appointees, or by quality control inspectors of the customer who would come into the plant and inspect their orders before the material leaves the plant. Normally, the inspection route is not one taken by top management people. Top managers usually rely on reports from others. However, first level supervisors spend most of their time going around, watching, looking, checking on subordinates, using this inspection method to make sure that what was planned and expected is really taking place.

A second type of control is reports. Top management people, who themselves do not inspect, require lower managers, supervisors, and production personnel to issue reports to them stating exactly what will happen or what has happened. This puts the responsibility of control on a subordinate who is closer to the activity and is then supposed to tell a superior what is happening. However, there are many occasions when subordinates keep things from their superiors because what they have to report reflects poorly on them and they are afraid of what the supervisor will say or do.

A supervisor has the responsibility of checking the accuracy of reports received from subordinates. He or she occasionally should go into the plant and actually inspect the product or operation on which the report was made. It is the manager's responsibility to make sure that control devices are really working and he or she should not rely on a third or fourth party to enforce control.

If a subordinate makes a mistake in judgment or action which might cost him his job, he is not likely to want to report this to the manager, thus jeopardizing his own future. He might want to allow this mistake to be moved along hoping that he will not be blamed for it if he can get it into the hands of another department or even into the customer's hands before the mistake is discovered. He might want this time delay so that if one of his subordinates resigns or is fired before the discovery, the manager can blame the mistake on that person and he, himself, the real culprit, will be absolved. The manager should be aware that this happens and should make every effort to keep on top of all control situations, watching subordinates and taking immediate and effective action when any irregularities in the control system are noticed.

Sometimes the manager will call in outside experts to make sure that things are as they appear. Probably the most often used outside expert is the auditor, the independent accountant who will come in and investigate the books of the company to make sure that those books are kept in accordance with normally accepted accounting practices and procedures, inspecting such things as the inventories, machinery and other capital goods, and the salary and tax aspects of the business. There are other kinds of outside experts who come in, such as the customers' quality control experts, the professionals who conduct a morale survey, experts who might evaluate specific programs and make recommendations for more effective and efficient administration. and technical consultants for specific and large capital expenditures and major expansions.

Another method of company control is through morale surveys. A morale survey is a survey of all the employees of a company to see if they are liking their work, how they feel management could make it a better place to work, how they like their fringe benefit program, what they feel about their ability to communicate upward and other concerns of the employees. This is an effort on the part of management to try and change anything which might be disturbing the work life of the employees, cutting down on production, and increasing turnover in the company.

PROBLEMS WITH CONTROL

There are many problems with control. It is not always easy to administer and we will list some of the reasons and problems below:

No Plans

As we mentioned earlier, if a company has no plans, if it is not headed in a specific direction, then there is no way to compare the actual progress with the projected plans. If people have no standards to aim toward, then they will not know whether they have hit or how far they have missed. Without standards there can be no control. If there is no sales budget and sales hit a million dollars, then there can be no corrective action because nothing is correct.

Vague Measuring Devices

Laws are specific. The comparison of a person's performance with the law, his intent compared with the intent of the law, his interpretation compared with other interpretations of the law, makes this comparison difficult and often vague. The same applies to business control. If the standard for a company is to require a 20 percent return on investment, then it might be a matter of interpretation as to what is to be considered the investment. Is it the investment of the initial investors? Is it the amount of money invested in a particular project? Capital? Par value? All of these things could be considered investments, but would have different returns if the profitability were the same. One production worker might make twelve items per hour with three rejected, while another might make ten and have none rejected. Two of the three rejected could be repaired in a short time. Who, then, is the most productive? One worker reports his scrap losses, while another worker hides his. Good workers are tied in with poor workers and projects. When the project productivity falls to what is considered below standard, who is to be blamed?

There are also other vague measuring devices, such as improper or imperfect measuring instruments. There are many objectives which do not have a tangible measuring method and must be measured subjectively by a person who could easily be biased for or against a person or project.

Failure to Recommend or Take Corrective Action

The project has been determined to be far enough from the standard to require changes and someone must make these recommendations and someone must carry them out. Failure to recommend or carry out remedial action would lead to a situation of no control at all. Most control devices are not self-regulating like the thermostat which shuts off when the temperature reaches a few degrees above its setting and cuts back on when it falls a few degrees below. (See Figure 16.1.) This is an automatic device for maintaining a balance between two opposing forces, hot and cold. The study of the constant battle to establish equilibrium in organic and inorganic systems is called cybernetics. Most control devices are not automatic and have the managerial element thrown in so that someone must make decisions about what to do when the actual is not going according to the plan. This goes right back to the managerial process again where corrective action leads to a new plan, a new organization possibly, which must be activated and controlled. It is the continuous cycle of plan, organize, activate, and control.

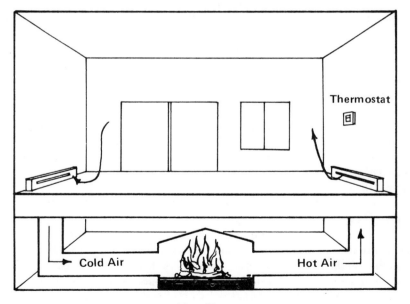

FIGURE 16.1   *An Automatic Cybernetic System.*

Dislike of Control

Employees, managers included, dislike control to the extent that they might rebel against it. Control, in their minds, represents an infringement on their freedom and a lack of confidence in their work. They want to be without any controls. Controls, they insist, lead to inflexibility on the part of the worker who is unable to react to situations instantly because of the necessity of reference to the controls involved. There are people who dislike controls because controls show them to be poor workers or poor managers. Few people want this to happen to them. Therefore, they resist controls, resist setting standards and measuring actual results, resist responsibility for actions, and try to avoid the consequences of control which would be some type of remedial action. Managers must fight constantly against this pressure to do away with control because without adequate controls there can be no meaningful improvement in the work situation.

Inability to Pinpoint Responsibility

Often it is possible to prove that a project is not on target, but it is difficult to determine whose fault it is. It may be that many workers and decision makers are involved in the project. To overcome this difficulty, a manager must go back to finding the root cause of the problem, not just the superficial cause. A production worker may fail to make his ten items per hour, but it is not necessarily his fault. It could be that the ten items were not delivered to him on time; that something had broken down prior to the worker's station, and he was only in a position to complete eight or nine items, not the ten he was expected to do. In a case like this, the manager must find the person who was first responsible for the mishap and take the action which he deems necessary to overcome the cause.

Changes in Basic Assumptions

Standards are set on the basis of things as they exist or as they may exist in the future. When there are many changes which are unforeseen and which occur between the time a standard is set and a measurement is made against that standard, then the standard might be incorrect. For instance, in an inflationary time, a machine is projected to cost a certain amount, but by the time the machine has been ordered and delivered, the final costs far exceed what had been projected. It was not poor projecting which caused this, but a drastic change in the national economy, far exceeding anyone's anticipations. An emergency situation such as a strike, a civil war in a foreign country, or a natural disaster can cause raw material to become short in supply in a matter of days, and cause plans based on the availability of that raw material to become non-functional.

Timing

The third part of control is corrective action. If the system is set up so that the corrective action is controlled by someone too far removed from the action itself, then the delay in the decision might cause as much or more harm than the original problem. For instance, in a quality control situation, the inspector finds an item slightly out of tolerance. His orders say he cannot approve it, and must report his findings to someone else. If the decision maker for the project is out of town and cannot make a decision as to whether or not the product would be acceptable to the customer, then control is nonexistent. The remedial action is delayed and possibly the machinery on which this product is being made will have to be shut down for days, or the set-up on which the part was being run would have to be torn down and reassembled at a later date. As mentioned in the section regarding control points, it is necessary that checks be made at appropriate places in the process, and once a measurable gap is found between what is anticipated and the actual, there must be someone close at hand to make a decision and keep the project moving.

MAINTAINING CONTROL

Control has a number of problems. There can be overcontrol, that is, the amount of money spent in the control function, exceeds the amount of money which can be saved as a result of control. A company which does not have any control devices is headed for disaster. Control is having a method of determining the effectiveness of the company and its employees. Without control, there can be no meaningful evaluation of this effectiveness.

FOR DISCUSSION

1. *What are the steps of control?*
2. *What are some of the bases for standards?*
3. *What are some of the major areas of control?*
4. *Why is a cash flow statement of value?*
5. *What are some tangible methods by which managers can check the morale of the workers?*
6. *What are some types of control?*
7. *Discuss the problems associated with control.*
8. *Can there be too much control?*

The Charismatic Character

"Look, Coach," said Martha Mitchell, self-styled, number one fan of the Gladstone and Johnson Junior College basketball team, "If you don't put Superguy Barnes back on that starting lineup, you're going to have a rebellion on your hands. Everybody—the guys on the club, the fans, and I— thinks he's the greatest. He's got what it takes. He's got charisma. He brings that team together. He's made it a winning team."

"That's where you're wrong, Martha," said Coach Bernard, "He hasn't made the team a winner. I've got all the statistics here. He's the tallest guy on the club and ought to be picking up the rebounds like crazy, but he's only got a little better than eight a game. And that's better than his scoring average. That's only seven. And he's played almost all of all the games. We've got reserves spending more than half their time on the bench who are going in there and making ten, twelve, or fourteen points a game. There's no way I can justify leaving Barnes in there when I have better rebounders and shooters on the bench. I had to pull him out."

"I don't care what your statistics show. There's something intangible about Superguy. Something that nobody else has. Something you'd better get with. He's got style. He's the guy people come to see. Not your ten-point men. Superguy has class. He's a character."

"Martha, this isn't a popularity contest. This is a game of basketball. It's not who's got the sweetest smile or who's the coolest guy around. It's the team with the most buckets, the most points, that wins the game. And we've been winning. You can't deny that."

"No, I wouldn't deny that, but until this game, you've always used Superguy. Now look where you are. Without him, you're losing.

About that time the buzzer for the beginning of the second half sounded. As the players were lining up for the jump, Coach Bernard wondered if Martha could be right about Superguy despite his statistics. He wondered if he should reevaluate his decision to put Mike Halsey on the starting team and bench Superguy Barnes.

GUIDE QUESTIONS

1. *Do you think Martha could be right?*
2. *Can all decisions, whether in sports or business, be quantified?*
3. *Is the player with the most points, or the worker with the greatest output, always the most valuable to the group?*

CASE 16–2

The Perplexing Promotee

"Well, I can't understand Wallace," said George Benson, superintendent of the machine shop, "He was, by far, the best candidate for the foreman's job, but I can't see that he's doing anything like we expected him to do."

"He sure isn't," said Bob Marshall, the personnel manager. "When you compare his results with the results of the other foremen in the shop, it just seems like we made a big mistake. He never should have been promoted. He just can't get the work out of these men."

"Apparently his men are happy with him," said plant manager John Burkeen. "The absentee record for his section is less than half of that of the other sections. This indicates to me that they either like him or they like their work or both. Since the work in his section is about the same as the work in all the other sections, I can't help but believe that it's him. Anyhow, we need the production that we would get if he did as good a job as the other foremen. I don't see how we can allow this situation to go along much longer. What did he say when you talked to him, George?"

"To tell you the truth, I really haven't sat down and talked with him about it," said Benson. "I felt he must know what's happening, that he's failing to get the work out. I thought he'd try to shape up on his own, but he just goes along, dumb and happy, friendly toward all his people, to me, and everybody else. He doesn't seem to have a care in the world. He treats his job like a game. Comes early and stays late, and has a great time of it while he's here."

"I have his personnel record here," said Marshall. "He's been with us for about ten years. He had the most seniority of anybody in the section. He gives all the appearances of being the natural leader and, in my mind, the natural choice for the job. He hasn't changed much since he got the promotion. He hasn't lost any of his friends. The men still continue to respect him as much or more than they did before he got the job."

"Maybe they're satisfied because he doesn't make them do any work," said Burkeen.

"No, I don't think that's right," said Benson. "They don't seem to be loafing. In fact, they seem to be as active as anybody else in the department. What brings the production down is the amount of scrap they report. Wallace's section reports more scrap losses than any section in the department."

"Then maybe it's a training problem," said Burkeen. "Maybe Wallace can't teach these guys anything."

"No, that doesn't seem to be it either," said Benson. "As a lead man [a working assistant to the foreman] he was the best trainer we had. No, that isn't it. The guys listened to him. They believed him and responded to whatever he said."

"Well, how do the men go about reporting losses?" asked the personnel manager.

"Each man reports his own," said Benson. "When he makes a mistake, kills a job, kills some parts, he calls a central number for inventory control and tells the inventory clerk what has happened so the clerk can make the proper adjustments. If the operator calls in a loss, the inventory control clerk takes the work out of work-in-process and transfers it to scrap. If nothing is reported, then the inventory clerk assumes the completed products have gone to finished goods inventory and he feeds this information to the computer."

"How has this been working so far?" asked the plant manager.

"We really don't know yet," said Benson. "We haven't taken a physical inventory. So far as we know, the physical inventory should be about the same as what we have on the computer. There may be some deviation one way or another, but we think it will work out just fine if all the men follow instructions and complete their reports. Anyway, this seems to be getting away from the main problem of whether or not Wallace is capable of getting out the production."

"Yeah, it does seem that way," said Burkeen. "Say, Bob, what recommendations do you have about what to do with Wallace?"

GUIDE QUESTIONS

1. *Do you think Wallace has failed?*
2. *Do you think his men trust him?*
3. *What do you think of a control system in which the worker is asked to report all his mistakes to a central inventory clerk?*
4. *What do you think a physical inventory will reveal?*

At the conclusion of this chapter,
you should be able to—

- Define ethics and legalism.

- Relate what occurred when businessmen failed to regulate themselves in their dealings with others.

- Know why a businessman might find himself in an ethical dilemma.

- Describe situations in which a businessman could act legally but unethically.

- Discuss what options are open to a person who discovers a wrong in a system.

17

Business Ethics

In the sixteenth century, Niccolo Machiavelli wrote that when the kingdom is at stake, the prince is justified in taking any action to save the kingdom. The end justifies the means. In business ethics, we would translate this Machiavellian concept to say that the manager can and must do anything which is necessary to save the business, for without it, there is nothing to manage.

A few centuries later, Henry Clay, one of America's leading statesmen for almost forty years, and a three-time loser for the presidency of the United States, said, "I would rather be right than president." He believed that he should do what he felt was right regardless of the outcome. To him, the means had to be right despite the end.

Today, many of our top managers, political leaders, and business giants are following the Machiavellian principle—the end justifies the means. Although Machiavelli wrote for princes, subordinates are also following this advice. "Everybody does it," is the byword of these Machiavellian disciples. "Everybody cheats on their income tax." "Nobody works any harder than they have to." "Take care of yourself first." "Do it to them before they do it to you."

Followers of Clay would respond with the Golden Rule, "Do unto others as you would have them do unto you."

Who is right?

ETHICS DEFINED

Ethics is the study of the voluntary human action of one individual toward other individuals and whether that action is right or wrong. Professional ethics is a code of action and of what is right or wrong for people involved in a particular profession. The members of that profession adopt a set of standards for their own actions in an attempt to strengthen the relationship between each other and to promote the general welfare of the community or the public which that profession serves. A minister would have a system of ethics for his profession. A school superintendent would be expected to abide by codes of ethics from the national, state, and local organizations to which he might belong. The businessman, however, will be in a different set of circumstances. There are many professional business associations, but business-men are not required to belong to these organizations, nor are they required to sub-scribe to a code of ethics which the groups espouse. This is in contrast to other profes-sional groups such as the medical profession where doctors of medicine must subscribe to the Hippocratic oath. Businessmen are not required to undergo any particular training or any rigorous testing to certify their competence in the field. And, business-men, in general, are much more loosely knit than are members of other professions.

The businessman, then, must be regulated in his ethical conduct by his own set of ethics and morals, and by law. The law is mentioned here because in the normal sequence, if the business community will not regulate itself, someone will suggest that a law be adopted which regulates the businessmen in that area where they are found to be negligent. In 1890, the Sherman Act was passed because businessmen were conspiring to restrain trade. Businessmen were working with other to control supplies, set prices, maximize profits, and minimize competition. Several other laws have been passed since then to prevent conspiring to eliminate competition.

The Food, Drug, and Cosmetic Act of 1938 was passed to require businessmen to show the accurate weight, the proportion of ingredients, and the use of colorants and preservatives in their products. Drugs, their uses, applications, and whether or not they are habit-forming also must be stated.

When managers refused to bargain with workers who supported or were mem-bers of labor unions, and refused to recognize and bargain collectively with the chosen representatives of the workers, Congress reacted by passing, in 1935, the National Labor Relations Act, or the Wagner Act as it is known. The effects of this act were to insure the rights of workers, encourage union growth and to spell out unfair labor practices by management personnel. Unfair union practices were spelled out in the Taft-Hartley Act of 1947.

When lending institutions took advantage of individuals who were forced to borrow money, usury laws were passed to prevent the charging of excessive interest. More recently, the Consumer Credit Protection Act of 1969, or the truth in lending act, was enacted to require lending institutions and other credit organizations to make clear what interest rate was being charged to the borrower in terms of simple interest. It would seem that we get more and more laws because businessmen find it difficult to regulate themselves.

HAPPINESS SEEKERS

Aristotle said that all men seek happiness. This, in itself, brings about many prob-lems of ethics, for the happiness of one man might be gained at the expense of an-other. If there were two men who had access to two cars, one a compact and the other a limousine, we might well run into a conflict. It would be convenient if one of the men would want the small car and the other, the larger one, and, while it might be convenient, it is not likely that this would happen. Because our culture places a high regard on material items, assigns esteem to the largest and the most, both men would probably want the limousine. There is the possibility again that one of the men would graciously accept the smaller car while giving the larger one to his associate, but again it is unlikely. In the showdown, one of the men would get the larger car and he would be happy. The other would get the smaller one and he would be unhappy. We might even see some unethical tactics used by the winner to get the larger car or by the loser, in a vain attempt to get even.

Getting even is an area where we find ethical conflicts. Literally billions of dollars are taken annually by employees who are just getting even with their employers. They are getting even because they feel the company works them harder than they should be worked, because the company does not pay them as much as they should be paid, because the company is not fair with them. Many of these employees, who are literally stealing, regard the taking of company property as just another fringe benefit.

If these employees are caught stealing, another ethical problem might be brought into play. This concerns self-preservation. Just as Machiavelli felt that the prince could do anything when the kingdom was in jeopardy, so do employees feel that when their positions or standing is in jeopardy, they can justify anything.

A business manager also might feel a threat to self-preservation when he and his fellow workers have spent many years of their lives, have invested their money, and have given up more than men should be asked to give up, all for the sake of the business, and then find that the business is failing. Where do they stand? Will they give up easily? Should they? Would they do things which would be considered unethical by an average man to save the business? Studies have shown that managers tend toward being pragmatic, rather than ethical or moral.[1] They lean toward what will bring satisfactory results, and they relegate to a second position the method of getting these results and what others think of the methods.

We might compare this pragmatic viewpoint of a businessman to that of a politician. Regardless of the good politicians might do for a constituency or their country, they can do nothing until they are elected. The businessman faces the same dilemma. He can do nothing for his stockholders, his employees, himself or society in general, unless his business is profitable and he can continue in business.

RESPONSIBILITY TO MANY PUBLICS

The professional manager has a responsibility to many publics. He must first be responsible to stockholders, to those persons who own the company and who have hired him to run their business. They have put up the necessary capital to begin or expand the business. They had an option of putting their money into this business or making some other investment, but they chose this business feeling that they would get a fair return on their investment. They chose the directors who, in turn, chose the manager to make this return come about. If the manager looks after himself first to the detriment of the stockholders, has he been ethical? If the manager gives erroneous information to stockholders or would-be stockholders to entice them to invest in the company, has he been ethical? If rumors and leaks started by the manager of a company cause the value of the stock to go up and then down again when the truth becomes apparent, has the manager been unethical? If the manager gets a great return to himself in salary and benefits while the stockholders get no dividends or growth, has the manager been ethical?

Stockholders are not the only public to which managers are responsible. They are responsible to the employees. The workers agree to give a manager a day's work for a day's pay. If the workers do not give the day's work, then this could be considered unethical, but if the manager fails to give the worker a fair day's pay, then he might be considered unethical. The part which is perplexing in this general situation is the consideration of what is a fair day's pay or a fair day's work.

It has been argued that stockholders should get all the profits because they are the ones who have made the investment, while the workers did not invest anything and were paid regardless of whether or not the company was profitable or successful. The workers, on the other hand, say that they did not put up money, but they did put up their time, their lives, and certainly their lives are worth just as much as someone else's money, and, therefore, they are entitled to a share of the profits although it might not be in the form of dividends. Higher wages and more fringe benefits would serve the same purpose.

If the manager has to pay dividends to the stockholder and wages to the employee, can he ethically get these dividends and wages at the expense of his customer? Can he give him a shoddy piece of workmanship and charge him a high price for it? Can he get together with other manufacturers and hold to an artificial price which gives him a better than average return on his investment with no concern for efficiency? Can a manager trick a customer into buying a product which is inferior to others, or less than it is proclaimed to be, and still be ethical?

To the businessman, the fair way to handle taxes, his debt to the fourth public he serves, the government, is to put off paying the taxes until he absolutely has to pay them. This means to take advantage of all the devices built into the tax system such as depreciation, investment tax credit, and deductions of legitimate business expenses. This is legal and ethical since those areas in which the government allows businesses to take advantage of situations are those areas in which the government want to stimulate certain actions. However, there are many areas of government relations where there are questions of ethical conduct. For instance, is the use of employee taxes and social security payments for working capital ethical? the deliberate underestimating of profits for tax purposes? wastefulness in cost plus contracts? being friendly with government inspectors so that they might overlook things for friendship purposes? Is it unethical not to follow government hiring guidelines?

And what about the manager's relationship to the community? He may make a profit with his paper mill and return that profit to his stockholders, pay his employees well, but what about the pollution to the air and water caused by discharging wastes by the cheapest method? Since businessmen are usually well educated, is it unethical *not* to serve on boards, committees, and citizens groups to make that community a better place to live? And even if the businessman decides that he is obligated to help his community, then he might have to face the question of whether or not it is ethical to draw a salary from his company while he is doing work for the community. Does the company derive any benefits from the salary it pays the executive while he plays golf with other community leaders and plans strategy for the community fund drive?

Is it ethical for a manager to overhire during good times only to lay off when the peak is over, or is he responsible to the community to maintain a steady employment situation?

The manager has all these publics and it is apparent that often he will be called upon to choose between his publics, to do something for one which may be detrimental to the other. His decision may profit one at the expense of the other, but still be legal. For instance, a businessman may pay his employees only a minimum wage because of the surplus of job seekers in a given locality, while returning an exorbitant profit to his stockholders. Or, he may bargain to pay his employees extremely high wages and have no profits from which to pay dividends or expand. It is up to the manager in these cases to decide what will do the greatest good for the most people in the long run, and these decisions are certainly not easy. He may decide to exploit the workers or take advantage of a situation against the stockholders. He may find that the stockholders are not unified enough to take any direct action against him so he would decide to favor himself or some other public he serves, at the expense of the stockholders.

THE MAGNITUDE OF THE MANAGER'S DECISIONS

Often we feel that managers make decisions which are internal and of little significance, but managers of large companies and political subdivisions make decisions which affect millions of people.

A first line supervisor, too, can affect the lives of many people. If he fires a subordinate, it is not only that person who feels the effects of the discharge. An entire family is deprived of an income. If he lays a person off because of over hiring, then it is that person laid off, his family, his creditors, and others who are affected. There is no implication here that supervisors or managers should feel totally responsible for all of a subordinate's obligations, but managers should clearly realize that what they do and what they say affects many others and their decisions should be made on a solid basis after considering the whole problem and all the ramifications of a decision.

A unique situation has developed in recent years where we find businessmen who are unethical, who not only take widow's and orphan's money, but the monies of retirement funds, trust funds and even the personal savings of bankers and other would-be astute investors, and who give nothing in return. They are considered as folk heroes and gain a certain amount of popular sympathy. If a person would assault an elderly lady and rob her of fifty dollars and he would be apprehended, there is a great likelihood that he would be given a prison term. But if a business-man, through stocks or loans or any other inducement, takes fifty thousand dollars from the same elderly lady, there often seems to be little regret on his part other than the fact that he has been caught, and a denial of any breach of ethics by saying that she deserved to be taken because she was so stupid to have believed him in the first place.

Union managers are also involved in decisions which involve large numbers of people and ethical considerations. If a union leader calls on his followers to strike because management fails to give him the respect he feels proper, or because he, personally, is unwilling to compromise on any point, is he looking out for the great-est good for the most people? If he asks his men to stay out another week or month over a principle involving union leadership, while he, himself, is being paid regu-larly, is he really looking out for the greatest good of the working man? Managers are entrusted with money, goods, and lives of people. They are morally and ethi-cally responsible for this trust.

LEGALISM

There seems to be a rising tendency in business for managers to skirt ethical issues by clinging to the doctrine of legalism, the doctrine of sticking to the letter of the law rather than the spirit of the law. This is accomplished through efforts to justify an action and allow a businessman to do something which would be considered un-ethical or immoral, but not illegal. Efforts on the part of lawmakers to protect the innocent often end up as devices to protect the guilty from any sort of punishment, allowing people to disregard the intent of the law.

It is often a matter of convenience that a manager adopts this stance of legalism. First, he decides what he wants to do. Next, he looks for anything which would legally keep him from doing it. If there is an obstruction, then the manager finds a method of going right ahead with his project without violating the letter of the law. The letter of the law is also the justification which allows a manager to look a per-son in the eye and say, "Gee, I wish I could help you, but that's the law."

It gives many managers the opportunity to evade the situation, evade the deci-sion which they might make for the good of the participants, by pointing to a law which may have been enacted for a completely different situation. Managers are not encouraged to go outside the framework of law, but to work within the intent of the legal structure.

THE SYSTEM

Akin to legalism is the skirting of an issue by saying that the system requires some-thing and if the system requires it, then it is impossible to go against the system. For instance, in government, it is felt generally that if a manager or a department head has not spent all the money allocated to him for the particular fiscal year, then he cannot get as much money the next year. So he spends money for anything which he can remotely justify simply so that the department can get more money the next year. When asked why he does this, the department manager replies "this is the way the system works. If I don't play the game, I won't get the money I need for next year."

Budgeting is another area in which the system is involved. The game of budgeting requires that a manager ask for twice as much money as he needs in the hope that he will get half as much as he requests. Here again, the manager will say that if he does not play the game, he will never get as much money as he needs. If anyone plays according to the stated rules, then he will find himself in a minority position without the funds he needs to accomplish his goals.

An ethical question which might be raised in connection with the system is what must the individual do when he sees that the system is wrong? Is he bound to try to change the system, or can he go ahead and play the game that the system requires? We can see from the example of a ratebuster that to do one's best is not always the ideal situation. The ratebuster does more work than anyone in his department. It is perhaps natural to think that his fellow workers might not like this because it makes them appear to be inferior producers, but the general tendency of management is also to dislike this person, not because of his production, but because of the disruption he causes to the system. By disrupting the system in this manner, he may not get the additional rewards he feels he has earned, but might even lose his job!

This same thing might happen when someone within a business makes known to the public an unethical practice and then the other members of the company rally against him and try to prove that he is the wrong one, that it is his sour grapes attitude, rather than their actions, which has caused the problem. We see repeated examples of men who blow the whistle on people they work for or with and soon find themselves without jobs and without any means of furthering their contentions of immorality or illegality. Even people who uncover mistakes are often treated in this manner, so we face the ethical question of what is a person to do when he or she uncovers or becomes a part of a situation which is unethical? There is no pat answer for this, of course. They must consider all the alternative courses of action, reflect on the outcome and the risk involved in each, and make the right decision based on knowledge and judgment.

CONFLICT OF INTEREST

When we consider the reasons why people do ethical or unethical things, we must consider their interest in the situation. If the person turns a criminal over to the police for a reward, then is his motive an ethical motive? Would he have done this same thing without the reward?

If a manager finds that his company is going to have a bad year and he anticipates that the stock will go down as a result of this fact becoming known, and therefore sells some of his own stock at the high rate in anticipation of buying it back after it goes down, is this good business or is it unethical? The person who is hurt is the one who buys that stock at the high rate in anticipation of continued success and has every right to assume this since he is not privy to the information the manager controls. The manager has taken advantage of inside information to help himself and has done a disservice to his stockholding public.

If a political candidate accepts money from a group to help him in his election efforts, then makes decisions which favor the group that helped him, but bases his decision on the merits of the case and feels that the decision will help the greatest number of people, then he has not compromised his ethics, but has done what he feels is right. It is not the action, but the motive behind the action, which shows the conflict of interest.

APATHY AND EXPERTS

Many businessmen, when confronted with ethical conflicts, are apathetic to them. If they see workers being exploited, they say that's a sign of good management. If they see stockholders continue to put money into the company, despite the fact that they are not getting dividends or growth, then they call this good public relations. If they see a company destroying the beauty of a community by the desecration of the local environment, then they say that trees are of no value until they are turned into saleable commodities, or that the rotten egg odor you smell is not sulphur but "bread" because without it you would have no bread. With these attitudes, the businessmen would not move for change.

Some philosophers have said that the opposite of love is not hate, but indifference. If you dislike your fellowman, you do not have to hate him, you just have to be indifferent to him. A businessman, when finding out that his fellowman is being exploited, would not have to hate him to allow this condition to exist, but simply be indifferent to his plight.

A businessman might seek to justify his position by turning to an expert, a person who is extremely knowledgeable in his field. The ethics of this move would be questioned when the businessman coaches the expert on what he should say, how he should recommend. There is some ethical consideration, too, on the part of the expert who may color his findings to suit his employer, the person paying his consulting fee. There is an area here for compromise, surely, but if the businessman gets his program, the consultant gets his fee, and the public of that businessman suffers, then there is a question as to the ethics of the situation. Here again, we are not speaking of legalism, but of what is good or bad for the people that the businessman is supposed to serve.

OTHER AREAS OF ETHICAL CONFLICT

Although we have mentioned some of the main areas in which ethical conflicts might occur, there are some others which we might consider:

Caveat Emptor

This Latin phrase means let the buyer beware, that is, let the buyer ask the questions, let him look into the situation, let him be responsible for what he buys. What the buyer buys is not the seller's responsibility according to this doctrine. In an era when all men are, at best, experts in their own business, it is unreasonable to expect that everyone should know what he is buying, that he be an expert in each product he must purchase. Therefore, there is some ethical responsibility on the part of the seller to make the condition of the product he has for sale known to the purchaser. There are laws against false advertising, but *caveat emptor* allows the seller to tell half truths, or omit truths entirely. An example would be a real estate agent who says, "If he asks me, I'll tell him that the basement floods, if not, I won't mention it."

Advertising

The Federal Trade Commission (FTC) is responsible to the public to see to it that advertisers do not make any false or misleading claims about their products. If the advertisers do, the FTC issues an order for them to cease and desist from this practice. But, even so, some of our largest businesses are guilty of untrue advertising at times. Some of them have been accused publicly of bait and switch techniques in which a product is advertised, but there is no intent on the part of the advertiser to sell this product. Instead, when a customer comes in to buy a product which is on sale at a low price, the salesman tells him that he should not buy the advertised product because it will not do the job, but—and then the seller tries to switch the buyer from the bait to a higher priced product. Often, the bait is not available to the customer even if he or she insists upon it!

Obsolescence

There is a matter for ethical consideration in manufacturing products which are made obsolete or are outdated by newer models, even though the product is still usable. This is quite evident in the automobile industry where almost all Detroit automobiles are changed every year. In many foreign automobiles, model differentiation is not so apparent, and owners keep their cars longer because they do not have the psychological pressure of having an old car. There are two questions of ethics here: (1) does the manufacturer have the right to use raw materials to support this change, and (2) does he have a right to force people to buy because of the stigma of owning an old model.

Compromise

President John F. Kennedy said that all politicians must make compromises so that they can get on with the business of making laws.[2] He felt that compromise gave balance to the lawmaking process. But while it seems necessary, there are areas where this compromise can become unethical if it tends to give favored treatment to some at the expense of others and is to the advantage of the politician.

Suppose a used car salesman asks a high price for his car and his customer, knowing the game, offers a low price, knowing he will go up just as the salesman will come down. But what happens when a customer does not realize that the used car salesman will come down and he agrees to pay the higher price? Has the salesman made an unethical sale? If the union negotiator asks for an unreasonable wage for his members and management extends an unreasonable offer, and then they work toward a compromise, is that unethical? Is it unethical for the union or management to make a flat offer and say that they will not bargain from that point on?

Discrimination

There has been much talk of discrimination in recent years, with particular reference to minority groups and women. White males still hold most of the executive positions in this country leaving one with the conclusion that women, blacks and other minority groups have been victims of discrimination. While businessmen must be cognizant of the potential discrimination aganst these groups, they must also guard aganst discrimination in favor of those groups which tends not to be for the greatest good, but for the good of that particular person or group at the expense of the majority. If this is the case, then we simply have more discrimination.

Gifts and Bribes

Many salesmen offer their clients small gifts as tokens of their appreciation and out of a genuine liking for their customers. Other salesmen offer their customers large gifts for their own personal use in an effort to "buy" their orders. There is a happy medium between these extremes and the businessman must be careful not to overstep this line of affection and appreciation into the unethical area of corruption.

Follow the Leader

If the boss makes a shady deal and gets by with it, should subordinates also get involved in the shady deals so that they can get more than they normally do? If a boss does something shady, and his subordinate finds out about it, can a boss compel his subordinate to become involved in it or be fired? And what should a subordinate do when he is asked to do something he feels is unethical or unacceptable? Does he do it out of loyalty? out of greed? out of fear? Or does he refuse to do it and become a hero? or a dummy?

Image Protection

If a manager feels that he has to maintain a certain image, how far can he ethically go in taking from his company to keep this "front" intact? If a man is elected to a position where his image would suggest that he drives a large, late model car, is he justified in passing these costs to his employer or in fact, taking money and goods from his employer or others in an effort to maintain this image?

SITUATIONALISM

These areas of ethical consideration are mentioned in an effort to point out to the businessman that he has ethical responsibilities to company owners, employees, customers, the community, the government, and himself, as well as having legal responsibilities to these groups. Businessmen are obliged under moral law to do their best for each of these groups at all times, so that the greatest good might result from their actions over the long term, and not have short term gains and long term losses. There is no set of rules for businessmen to follow in ethical decisions and to abide strictly by the law, always and without question, would be to place law above men and make no concessions for human needs.

Each situation is different in terms of ethics just as it differs in other ways. And, as was pointed out in an earlier chapter, businessmen must make decisions in areas, not of black and white, but of gray, when they are not sure of the outcome, or even if the chosen outcome is the right one. A manager must couple his business decisions with his ethical considerations, because he does not have a professional group to applaud him or chastise him for the right or wrong decisions and therefore he must be responsible to himself for the actions he takes when dealing with his many publics.

FOR DISCUSSION

1. *Discuss the concept that the end justifies the means.*
2. *What is the study of ethics?*
3. *Is there a code to which all business managers must subscribe?*
4. *Businessmen tend toward being pragmatic rather than ethical or moral. Discuss this statement.*
5. *To whom is a business manager responsible?*
6. *Should stockholders get all the profits from the business?*
7. *People who are "taken" by a scheme deserve what they get. Discuss this statement.*

8. *What is legalism?*
9. *The use of an expert can be and often is unethical.*
   How is this possible?

ENDNOTES

1. George W. England, "Personal Value Systems of American Managers," *Academy of Management Journal*, X, no. 1 (March, 1967), p. 61.
2. John F. Kennedy, *Profiles in Courage* (New York: Harper & Row, 1955).

The Boozed Accused

"Yesterday, I didn't know a discipline committee existed," thought Brenda Devons to herself, "And now here I am sitting in judgment of some guy I've never seen before."

Dr. Harold Small, a psychology professor who was chairman of the discipline committee, was concluding his examination of Ron Evans, a second year student who had been brought before the committee to answer to the charge of drinking on campus.

"Mr. Evans, do you deny that you were drinking beer on the tennis court, which is part of this campus, while you were a member of a physical education class?"

"No, sir, I do not."

"Did it occur to you that you were breaking the rules of this school?"

"It occurred to me, sir, that I might be breaking a rule, but I knew of no such rule then, nor am I aware of one now which prohibits drinking beer on campus."

"This is a state institution, Mr. Evans, and there is a state law which prohibits drinking on state property.

"There may be one, Dr. Small, but I've visited other state schools where beer is sold and served in the snack bars. I would assume from that that if there is such a law, it is not observed or enforced."

"Mr. Evans," said Dr. Small, holding up an official looking document, "Do you recognize what this is?"

"It looks like an application form, sir."

"Right, Mr. Evans. In fact, it is your application form and I'd like to quote from it. 'I agree to abide by the rules and regulations of this college.' Signed—Ronald A. Evans. You did read and sign this?"

"Yes, sir."

"Now, I'd like you to identify this book."

"The school catalogue, sir."

"Right, Mr. Evans. Now let me quote from it. 'The College refrains from making rigid rules regarding discipline, but reserves the right to take disciplinary action compatible with its own best interest when it is clearly necessary.' 'The student shall maintain a standard of conduct appropriate to membership in the college community.' 'Failure to meet standards of conduct acceptable to the college may result in disciplinary probation or even dismissal, depending upon the nature of the offense.' Were you aware of these passages in the catalogue, Mr. Evans?''

"To a certain extent, yes, sir, I was."

"And you drank beer despite these rules?"

"But, sir, they are not specific rules and since beer is permitted in other state schools. . . .''

"But, Mr. Evans," Small interrupted, "Those are four year residence schools. This is a community college. Certainly you can see the difference."

"There is a difference, sir, I suppose, but even here, we've been allowed to drink beer on campus on particular occasions."

"Yes, but those were functions sponsored by the student government, approved by the administration and occasions for which a special beverage permit was obtained. Certainly you were aware of this."

"I knew the beer was on campus and we were able to drink with no hassle, but I didn't know about the permits and things."

"I have no further questions, Mr. Evans," said Dr. Small. "Are there any questions from any of the other members? None? O.K. Mr. Evans, you may be excused."

After Evans left the room, Dr. Small said to the members of the committee, "It seems to me to be a simple case where Evans knew the rules, but chose to defy them. It is clear to me that he acted in a manner inappropriate to membership in this college. He even admits it. Therefore, I see no alternative but to find him guilty. Furthermore, I feel we should make an example of him and recommend to the president that Evans be dismissed immediately. We've got to nip this thing in the bud or we'll find ourselves teaching or attending classes with a bunch of alcoholics."

"I agree with you, Dr. Small," said Harold Keyser, instructor of biology. "We should stop it right now. What do the rest of you think?"

A pre-teaching student said people like Evans are bad examples for younger students and voted along with Small and Keyser. There were two other students to be polled and then Brenda would have to speak. She wasn't sure what she should do.

GUIDE QUESTIONS

1. *What rule did Evans break?*
2. *What options does Brenda have?*
3. *Could Evans be engaged in legalism?*
4. *If Evans is found guilty, would you recommend that an example be made of him? Why?*

The Right Bookkeeper in the Wrong Company

George McCallister was very much disturbed and unable to sleep. He had been visited earlier in the evening by his cousin, Amy Elizabethton, and she had asked him for advice concerning a problem at her office. At this point, George was unable to formulate a good answer.

Amy was in her first job since graduating from Southeastern Community College. She was an accounting major with twenty-four quarter hours in accounting subjects including introductory, intermediate, cost and tax accounting, and auditing. This gave her a good, basic working knowledge of accounting, but did not qualify her for, nor make her eligible to take the Certified Public Accountant (CPA) examination in her state.

In her job hunt during the four months preceding her graduation, Amy had three offers: one in the actuarial department of an insurance company, a second in the accounting office of a local dairy where she would process daily reports from the delivery men, and the third was as a one girl bookkeeping department for an intracity chain of four restaurants. She chose the latter because she wanted an opportunity to use all of her accounting theory in practical application before she forgot it. In this job, although she would make all the entries herself, she would have ready access to the company auditors, CPA's who could advise her in problem areas.

Amy was happy in her job, had pride in her work and pride in the company. Her boss, Richard Anderson, was a self-made man. He had worked in every conceivable position in the restaurant business from dishwasher to busboy, to waiter, cook, manager and finally, owner. At thirty-two, he had borrowed money to buy his first restaurant and at thirty-five, he owned four and was considering buying another.

All this had been accomplished, he said, because he had had confidence in himself and because he would not believe that the lack of a formal education should deprive him of a chance to succeed. When seriously questioned about his training, Richard said he was a graduate of the school of hard knocks.

The problem arose over the purchase of a new typewriter for one of the restaurants. When Amy received the invoice for the machine, she entered it on the books as having an eight year life. She chose sum-of-the-years'-digits method of depreciation in line with other similar purchases, and let the matter rest.

When Richard noticed the entry, he was quite upset.

"Why didn't you write this off as an expense?" he asked.

"We weren't suppose to," Amy said. "A typewriter is a capital item with an eight year life. I just thought that was the right thing to do."

"Well, you weren't right," he said. "We buy so little office equipment, we just write it off regardless of how long we keep it. That's a company policy and has been since I started the business."

"According to my accounting teacher, it's not the use itself that makes the difference," Amy said, "It's the useful life that determines whether an item should be written off or capitalized. And, since this typewriter will last longer than a year, I'm sure I'm right."

"You're not right because I say you're wrong. I didn't build this company by listening to some teacher. I did it with a lot of sweat and a lot of decision making which was best for the company. The way I figure it, what we write off now doesn't cheat the government, it just delays our taxes. In fact, it helps because we're using the money to expand and we'll pay more taxes later," said Richard.

Amy said, "I'll call the auditor and see what he says about it."

"I don't care what he says," Richard said, "I pay his salary, too. If either of you can't follow company policy, I'm sure I can find some people who will."

Richard stormed into his office and slammed his door. When Amy called the auditor, he told her that in theory she was right, but he would not advise her in her present predicament. As the company auditor, he said, he could live with whatever decision she made.

It was then that Amy decided to consult her cousin for his advice.

GUIDE QUESTIONS

1. *Do you feel Amy is right? Why?*
2. *What alternatives does she have?*
3. *What do you think of Richard's statement that "it just delays our taxes."?*
4. *What would you advise Amy to do?*

part 6

the future

At the conclusion of this chapter,
you should be able to—

- · **Define an ad-hocracy.**
- · **Take a position on the professionalization of professional managers.**
- · **Discuss the direction of leadership styles.**
- · **Contrast the present and future levels of automation.**

18

What's Ahead?

A study commission appointed by President Herbert Hoover in 1929, which later reported to Franklin D. Roosevelt, advised the president how to plot the course of this nation through 1952. There were thirteen volumes in the report prepared by some five hundred researchers. There was a two-volume summary of sixteen hundred pages, yet in this total report, there was nothing about atomic energy, jet propulsion, antibiotics, or transistors. At the same time, the people who were predicting the future most accurately were the science-fiction writers whose dreams were not encumbered by committee reports and whose imaginations were not limited to what was known at that time.[1]

Alvin Toffler divided the last fifty thousand years into eight hundred lifetimes and only in the last two lifetimes has there been any systematic study of management theory and principles.[2] During these same two lifetimes, more than half of the major events which have ever happened, did happen, and more than half of everything which has been discovered, was discovered. This should indicate to us that while the pace of life greatly increased in those two lifetimes, it will be much more accelerated during this lifetime and the next. Things which people only dare to dream about now will become history before those people themselves become history.

THE AD-HOCRACY

Toffler predicts that the future will bring an ad-hocracy, a business society where men come together in single purpose organizations to solve specific problems and then disband, once those problems have been solved. This is in opposition to our current bureaucratic form of organization where we form an organization and attempt to make that organization flexible to the extent necessary to solve the problems which come before it.

If this comes about, then man will not be ensnared by computers and dehumanized by electronic gadgetry, but will be freed from his day-to-day mundane existence, and be able to work on the projects he wants to work on and not have his desires subordinated for the good of the corporation. He will not have to give up doing those things he wants to do in order to make a living. He will be able to take more risks in the future because he will not feel he will face deprivation as a result of an unsuccessful venture. He and his family will be able to have food, shelter, clothing, and the other physiological needs without having to sacrifice meaningful work. Maslow's first two steps of physical and security needs will be met before man begins to work.

Some writers have characterized this ad-hocracy or single purpose organization as a matrix organization where managers go from project to project, and in a sense, coordinate the activities of specialists who also go from project to project.[3] The overall structure would look like Figure 18.1.

In this matrix organization, the manager picks the most qualified of the technicians available to him and co-ordinates their efforts in an attempt to accomplish the purpose of that organization. He bids against the other managers for the best talent available. In the future, there may be a super-management group which will do all the planning while other managers will be involved more in organizing, directing, and controlling projects.

One of the best examples we have of this matrix organization now is in the in-

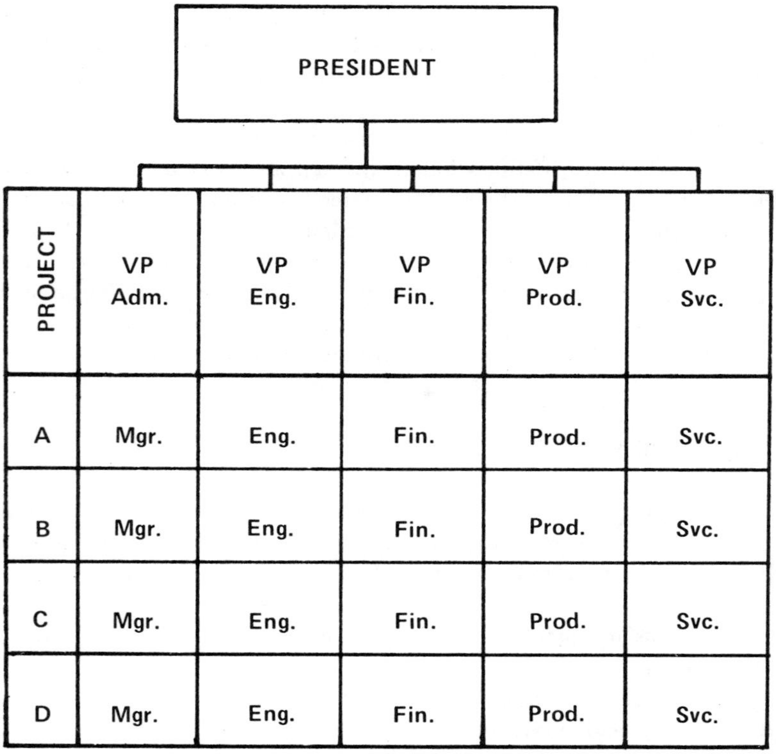

PROJECT	VP Adm.	VP Eng.	VP Fin.	VP Prod.	VP Svc.
A	Mgr.	Eng.	Fin.	Prod.	Svc.
B	Mgr.	Eng.	Fin.	Prod.	Svc.
C	Mgr.	Eng.	Fin.	Prod.	Svc.
D	Mgr.	Eng.	Fin.	Prod.	Svc.

FIGURE 18.1 *A Matrix Organization.*

vestment business where investment bankers get together in syndicates to underwrite public stock issues for large companies. Tombstone ads appear daily in our papers with the names of the participants in the syndicate. These firms work together in the initial sale of the stock, and, once all the stock has been sold, they disband. The purpose for which this syndicate was formed has been accomplished and its usefulness is over. Future projects will be much more attuned to this syndicate concept than they will be to continuous flow projects.

MULTI-NATIONAL MATRIX ORGANIZATIONS

While we are talking about matrix organizations, we should say that they probably will be made up of international members rather than national, regional, or local members. This will come about for two reasons

The first is that the space and distance between people and countries will grow smaller as distances are overcome by better and faster transportation methods. With people traveling from the United States to Europe and Africa in an hour or two, neighbors and business associates will be made up of people from a much wider geographical area. We will no longer be provincial in our organizations; we will have world-wide participation.

A second reason for working together is that as our nations become more independent, they, in fact, become more dependent on each other not to use armaments which are capable of destroying the world. The United Nations may eventually succeed in getting all nations to work together toward peaceful endeavors, toward solving world problems, rather than spending money and energy in finding new and more effective means of destruction.

Benjamin Franklin in reference to the unification of this country, said, "We must all hang together or assuredly we shall hang separately." This now has world-wide implications. The advanced nations are spending exorbitant sums of money on weaponry, while many problems go unchecked and unsolved. This will end as world leaders more and more realize that world security lies in cooperation and that mankind must find some common means of peaceful existence to prevent world annihilation.

MORE AND LESS RISKS

We mentioned earlier that man will be able to take more risks because of his ability to feel secure even though he might fail in one or more undertakings. Thus, people will work either to gain the respect or esteem of their fellow men or to accomplish something which they, themselves, feel must be accomplished. In the future, man will have a purpose more noble than providing himself with the necessities of life and the external symbols which are now required for status.

Until this time of noble purpose arrives, there will be a growing sentiment among workers to require managers to pass "tests of purpose." There are companies now which require their employees to take polygraph or lie-detector tests to determine if they might steal from the company. To follow this trend, managers in the future might have to take polygraph tests to prove to their subordinates their motives, their feelings toward the workers, and their tendency toward exploitation of people. They also might have to test their ethical responses to situations which might adversely affect any of their publics. Just as an employer would not want an employee who would steal from him, the employee would not want to be saddled with an employer who is determined to exploit him. And so it may well be that one of the demands of labor will be that managers be required to pass a test of intent and purpose.

PROFESSIONALIZED MANAGEMENT

It also may be that managers themselves will become more professionalized, institute licensing requirements, and form their own groups for professional competence and ethical considerations. Now, we have rules which require a hairstylist to prove his or her competency to cut our hair, but we do not require any proof of the competency of the president of our country who is the manager with the most responsibility of all the managers in the nation. We do not require a corporation president to pass any tests as a basis for making decisions affecting millions of people and billions of dollars, and yet, we say that the man who accounts for the money once it has been made (or lost) must have a college degree and pass a certified public accountant (CPA) exam. We say that a psychologist who counsels people must have an academic background, but we do not have any educational requirements at all for that supervisor who, because he does not care about people, or because he feels he must make someone suffer to prove his authority, may be causing the very problems the psychologist is trying to cure.

We require the licensing of people who affect our lives from time to time such as a dentist, doctor, nurse, barber, engineer, lawyer, plumber, accountant, or electrician, but we do not require certification or accreditation or professional surveillance of those people who affect our lives daily.

It would appear that in the future managers will gather together in an association and require that managers in companies of certain sizes, or those which have the greatest impact on humanity, must fulfill certain basic requirements or would have to experience certain situations before they would be allowed to become managers. Managers would not be required to make the same decisions, just as doctors are not required to make the same decisions, but all managers would have to be exposed to a study of alternatives so that they could make the best decisions in light of the circumstances, just as we expect a doctor to make the best decisions in light of his diagnosis. This would not be a way of phasing out free enterprise, but a way of strengthening it.

MANAGERIAL ORIENTATION

The educational gap between the manager and his subordinate is closing at a rapid rate. At one point in history, the manager was the literate person and the subordinate was the illiterate, and both parties knew and accepted their roles. Now, managers often have less education than their younger subordinates who have had better opportunities and more pressure to attend school. At present, this fact is causing apprehension among the lesser educated managers who fear the loss of their jobs to their academically better qualified subordinates, and a dissatisfaction among the subordinates with managers who have achieved their rank through a seniority system. In the future, when managers and subordinates alike will have basic material goods without working, the best qualified people will become the managers regardless of experience, age, or other factors presently considered.

There will be a shifting of emphasis in authority and responsibility. Whereas now, authority comes to managers from above, in the future, much more authority will be granted by approval from below. The responsibility of the manager, too, will be to those in the organization he manages, rather than to higher management.

We will see an invasion of business by the sociometric technique which is prevalent in non-business organizations such as social organizations and politics. The leaders will be elected by those in the business organization, just a political leaders are elected by those in the political subdivision. If the leader fails to measure up to the expectations of his constituency, then he will be deposed and another leader chosen.

This should bring about a better relationship between managers and their subordinates. Managers should become more people oriented, more behavioral oriented. In addition to seeking profits as they now see, managers will try to please their subordinates, expand their jobs, enhance their opportunities for self-fulfillment. Managers will have to make people happy, as well as productive, if they, the managers, want to continue to have a spot in the organization. The leaders, the managers, will be those people who willingly want to help their subordinates achieve greater personal success.

MOBILE MANAGERS

Through the matrix organization, managers will attain additional mobility, going from job to job, place to place, company to company, without fear of loss of status, pay or fringe benefits (which will be portable). The chief difference between this mobility and our present day mobility is that it will be more at the option of the manager than of his company. We see evidence now that the moves of present managers from region to region are disruptive to his life and the lives of his family, but to be a complete organization man he must accept the company as the number one force in his life, and relegate all other things to secondary positions. The manager of the future will be able to choose where he wants to go, the kind of work he wants to do, the kind of problems he wants to solve, and areas of work in which he feels he can do the most good.

This does not mean that the manager will have to disrupt his family life as he does now. Transportation of the future will make it possible for him to achieve this greater mobility while maintaining a stability of home and family. He will not have to disrupt their lifestyles while changing from project to project because he will be able to expand his commuting range. The husband and wife will be able to work at the job site and still be at home, in the area which they chose to live, and he or she will have as much or more time to devote to family, social, leisure, and educational activities because people of the future will devote less time to acquiring things and more time to enriching the quality of their lives.

RISING LEVELS OF ACHIEVEMENT

Much of what society now considers to be achievement is in terms of numbers—more dollars, more units, more profits, more customers—but, success in the future will be measured in terms of quality rather than quantity, in better rather than more. There will be much higher levels of aspiration. The level of work itself will move upward. Whereas we once had common labor to dig ditches, we now have mechanical devices to aid construction and the laborers have achieved higher positions in industry. This will continue as the educational level of mankind continues to grow.

College graduation will be the springboard to business and industrial jobs rather than the high school level of today and the elementary level of yesterday. The work itself will change radically as automation takes routine work *completely* from men. Our present level of automation has succeeded in taking only part of the routine work from the worker. Instead of making his job easier, automation has succeeded in making his job more boring. Instead of being completely automated, jobs are partially mechanized and people have become human machines instead of decision-making creatures. We can recognize those industries which automation has hurt rather than helped, and gauge the boredom by the record of absenteeism and turnover. Automation in the future will overcome this problem, allowing people to direct their efforts to challenging and stimulating work while machines do that work which can be totally automated. This complete automation will enable man to overcome his physiological and security needs without his having to exert any work effort.

As the lower level of achievement rises, so will the top level, and the manager will be responsible, not just for getting out more production, but for answering the "why" problems of business. Why are we making this product? Why is this man man doing this work? Why am I doing what I do?

In conjunction with the why questions, managers will be asked to cooperate with the development of, and subscribe to, a world system of business ethics, so that the members of the world society can eliminate their fruitless efforts of worrying about, checking on, and distrusting their neighbors, business associates, competitors, government officials, and leaders of foreign powers. For the world to reach its full potential, these problems of mistrust will have to be overcome through the adoption of some minimum acceptable standard of ethical conduct.

Future managers will be asked to solve problems in the area of social and people betterment rather than the making of more goods. There will be more effort directed toward improving physical and psychological health, toward the consideration of the ethical concepts of changes in nature which technology will make possible. Managers will become involved with the consequences of their products, instead of just producing them. They will be responsible for the social impact of the decisions they make. While these decisions may be harder, other decisions, which now require a great amount of a manager's time, will be eliminated through the improved predictability of quantitative methods and automatic data processing. More cybernetic systems will be employed, and the manager will be able to devote more of his or her time to other projects.

GROWTH OR NONGROWTH

As production becomes more automated and as work becomes more optional, people will have time and the need for more and continued education. Managers will have to spend more time keeping abreast of current trends and innovations in management.

Managers will face a different method of education in the future. They will experience more things first-hand. Travel will reach a state where people can go to places rather than read about them, can become involved in situations rather than view them on television or in motion pictures, can see and talk with participants in controlled experiments rather than just read the results of the studies. We will have a growth or nongrowth situation for both managers and subordinates. Everyone will be required to continue his education as long as he wants to be a producing member of society. The largest industry of the future will be that of education, of telling people what they want and need to know through books, periodicals, television, and all other media and means of education.

LIFE WILL BE BETTER

Since the measurement of success will change from that of net worth, of dollars, to a quality of personal achievement and results which benefit mankind, there will be much less pressure on the manager to be like his fellow managers. He will not have to "keep up with the Jones" of his block or plant. He will be more motivated to achieve results he deems beneficial to mankind. The pressure he experiences then will not be a negative motivation, a threat, but an internal pressure, a pressure to achieve, a pressure to do something for the good of others, a pressure which he will enjoy. He will have a positive incentive to do what he wants to do most, to work to the fullest extent of his abilities. If he feels the pressure is too great, he can take a break, enjoy leisure activities, travel and become more aware of other things, without losing face, without feeling the external pressure of failure.

Managers of today start as personal managers and move toward professional management as a career. In the future, the trend will be for professional managers to become more personal managers, again managing their own time and assets, to achieve more permanent satisfaction through the attainment of professional results.

FOR DISCUSSION

1. *What is a matrix organization?*
2. *Why will matrix organizations of the future be multi-national?*
3. *Discuss the professionalization of managers.*
4. *Has automation "freed" man from routine tasks? Discuss.*
5. *Discuss the need for education for the manager of the future.*

ENDNOTES

1. Walter B. Wriston, "The Trouble With Government Regulation," *Readers Digest*, 105, no. 627 (July, 1974), 93–96.
2. Alvin Toffler, *Future Shock* (New York: Random House, 1970).
3. Willaim E. Newman, Charles E. Summer, and E. Kirby Warren, *The Process of Management, Concepts, Behavior, and Practice*, 3rd ed. (Englewood Cliffs, N.J.: Prentice-Hall, Inc., 1972), pp. 104–108.

CASE 18-1

The Church That Change Built

"I would like for you to understand, Reverend Wilson, that the inquiry by this committee is not to persecute or prosecute anyone. We have been appointed by the board simply to look into the situation of our loss of membership and determine how that loss can be turned around so that we can get our church back into a growth posture."

"I understand," said Reverend Wilson, pastor of the Church That Change Built.

"Now," said Mike Robertson, chairman of the committee, "We would like to ask you some questions. First, how did our church get the motto "The Church That Change Built?""

"Well, ladies and gentlemen, when I came here thirty-two years ago, we had no church. We held services in Fred Perry's living room at first. Then we bought ourselves a tent when we got too big to meet in his home. And, finally, we built this church. Not from the dollars contributed from our people, but from the coins—the pennies, nickels, dimes, quarters and halves. I asked, particularly, that no one give us any money in bills, that all contributions made toward the building fund should be in coins. We wanted change—in our church and in our people. We wanted to change our worldly ways to religious ways and we got the change. Both changes, in fact. We built our church!"

"Did we continue to grow even after we had built the church and the novelty of the slogan wore off a little bit?" asked Peg Worrell.

"Yes, once the word was out that we had a church built on change, the people came around. People who could no longer contend with their churches or with nothing, came to our church. People who wanted changes in their lives came to our church."

"When did the church make the change from growing to losing?"

"Oh, I'd say it was only about five years ago that we began a steady downward trend," said Reverend Wilson. "We reached a peak and then began to lose some of our younger members and there were no older people joining to offset this loss. No younger people joining, either."

"What do you attribute this to?" asked Robertson.

"As you know, society, in general, began to accept things which I and, I'm sure, you and the other members of the church body felt were unacceptable. There was this sudden acceptance of scantily clad females enticing men, alcohol and drugs, and the drug culture. People accepted abortion as if it had nothing at all to do with life itself. Dress codes were relaxed. People wanted to come to church—that is, men wanted to come to church without coats and ties, women wanted to come in pants suits and shorts. No respect at all for the sanctity of the church or for what it stood. And I told them about it. My job, as I see it, no matter how the people react, is to do what I think is right, to say what I feel I should say. I could not accept the changes that they wanted to make and I told them so. I told them from the pulpit. I told them that we were not going to change our rules and regulations. We weren't going to be disrespectful. If they could not abide by good moral conduct, then they should not be a part of this church. I insisted that we continue as we had in the past, and many of the younger members objected.

"I realize you have a problem on your hands, trying to find the solution to getting new members and additional financial support for this church, but I would like to say one thing—this is the Church That Change Built, but, in my opinion, to go along with the whims of the world, the whims which each succeeding generation brings to this church, will make it the Church That Change Destroyed. Thank you."

"Thank you, Reverend Wilson, for your observations. I'm sure we'll give considerable thought to them in our deliberations. Thank you, again."

As Reverend Wilson left the room, chairman Robertson turned to his group and said, "Well, committeepeople, what do you think?"

GUIDE QUESTIONS

1. *If declining attendance is a symptom of a problem, what do you think that problem might be in this case?*
2. *Who has the problem? Who can solve it?*
3. *Could this be a problem in which the decision makers would agree to do nothing? Why?*
4. *If you were on the committee, what recommendations would you make to the chairman?*

The Disappearing Cavity

Bob Birmingham, senior editor for the *Dental Journal of North America,* finished reading an article he had taken from the Associated Press wire service. The article read as follows:

CHICAGO   Dental researcher, George P. Archer, says he has found a painless treatment that offers lifelong protection against tooth decay.

He says the treatment consists of first coating the teeth with a mild solution of phosphoric acid, temporarily removing the enamel. After two minutes, a solution of zinc chloride is painted on the teeth. The zinc is absorbed by the teeth and forms a protective wall against germs which cause cavities. The enamel grows back naturally within two weeks, enclosing the metallic barrier, which lasts for life.

The key to the process, says its inventor, is the fact that tooth enamel carries a negative electrical charge, allowing positively charged heavy metals like zinc to cling to it like a magnet. Zinc is the only heavy metal which turns white after application, so the treatment leaves teeth whiter than before.

The process takes several visits for all teeth to be treated.

At this time, no dental science journal has accepted the scientific report on this method.

Birmingham considered the impact of this story, the change it might make in the profession he represented, and he wondered whether or not he should try to contact the dentist who had come up with this process, or if he should even show any interest at all if the dentist, himself, tried to contact the *Journal.*

GUIDE QUESTIONS

1. *What obligation do you feel Birmingham has to investigate the story? To whom is he obligated?*
2. *What alternatives does he have now?*
3. *Do you feel this kind of a story might occur in many types of service industries in the future?*
4. *What would you advise Birmingham to do?*

Glossary of Management Terms

Absenteeism   The time employees are absent from their jobs, usually expressed in percentage. The average rate of absenteeism is 3 to 5 percent, but some industries experience a 15 to 20 percent rate.

Accountability   The extent to which one is held responsible for work he or she directs.

Accounting   The systematic collection, recording, summarizing and presentation of all financial transactions of an organization.

Achievement Tests   Test which indicate the level of skill or knowledge acquired in or for a particular field or job.

Acquisition   The purchase of one company by another company with the purchasing company assuming control.

Activating   Putting all plans and organizational procedures into motion.

Actuating   In the management sense, a synonym for activating.

Ad Hoc   Established for one situation only; temporary.

"Ad-Hocracy"   A system of temporary organizations created to solve specific problems and then disbanded.

Administration   A synonym for management.

Alternatives   Various plans and methods which might result in the solution of a problem or the accomplishment of a goal.

Anti-Trust Laws   Federal laws enacted to insure significant and fair competition.

Apathy   An attitude (usually existing in impersonal companies) evidenced in workers who have little or no interest in the organization or its goals.

Appointed Leader   A person assigned to a management position by his superior or the owner of the business rather than elected by those he manages. The authority results from the right of private property.

Appraisal   A systematic evaluation of a person and his or her performance.

Apprenticeship.   A formal method of training a person for a skilled position, usually a craft or trade, through on-the-job and classroom techniques.

Assembly Line   A production method by which the work is conveyed to a worker who performs a specific but routine task. The work is then moved to another worker, and so on, until it is complete.

Assets   Properties of a person or business, either real or intangible, which have value.

Assistant-To   The title of a staff aide to a manager. The assistant-to has no line authority over the manager's subordinates, nor can he assume this authority in the manager's absence.

Auditor   An accountant, either inside or outside, hired by a company to make an independent determination of the accuracy and propriety of the firm's financial records.

Authoritarian   A domineering manager who retains all decision-making rights. He is a boss who gives orders.

315

Authority The responsibility to make decisions and the right to command subordinates to carry out those decisions.

Autocratic Leadership An authoritarian approach to management in which the manager is a boss who expects strict adherence to his orders.

Automation A system in which work is accomplished by machines and actuating devices without the intervention of people.

Backlog An accumulation of unfilled orders.

Back Order To hold an order for an out-of-stock item until that item is available for delivery.

"Bait and Switch" An illegal method of selling by which an advertised item is either unavailable or severely criticized by the salesman in an effort to entice the customer to buy similar, higher priced items.

Balance Sheet A statement showing the assets, liabilities, and owner's equity of a business.

Behavioral Sciences Various sciences (psychology, sociology) which examine human activity in an effort to formulate rules and patterns of human behavior.

Benevolent Autocrat A "nice boss" who likes people, wants them to feel they are participating, but feels he must make all decisions and hold all authority.

"Big Picture" An overall view of a company's objectives, needs, and methods, primarily to determine the reason for or the suitability of individual isolated decisions.

Board of Directors A group of persons, usually an odd number, elected by the stockholders to make policy and major decisions, hire chief operating personnel, and oversee the activities of the company.

"Bogey" An arbitrary amount of work determined by the workers themselves, which they consider fair. This may differ from work quotas set by management.

Bonds Certificates of debt issued by a borrowing company in exchange for capital which is to be used in a predetermined manner.

Book Value The net value of a company, its assets less its liabilities, without regard for its potential earning ability. Often this book value is divided by the number of shares outstanding to get a book value per share.

Brainstorming A group activity in which the participants attempt to generate a large number of solutions to a given problem without regard to the feasibility of their answers.

Breakeven Point A point at which total sales equal total costs without profits or losses. (Sales = Fixed Costs + Variable Costs).

Budget A financial plan with estimates of needed income and expenses necessary to accomplish a predetermined goal such as a specific amount of profit or return on investment.

Bureaucracy A system of organization defined by Max Webber as having clearly stated relationships and hierarchy as found in governments or churches.

Capital Goods Long life, durable goods, such as machines or trucks, which are capitalized and then depreciated over their estimated useful lives.

Capital, Working A company's investment in current assets—cash, short term securities, receivables and inventories. Net working capital is the net of current assets less current liabilities.

Cash Budget A plan for the in and out flow of cash in a business, excluding such non-cash items as depreciation, with the objective of meeting all cash needs.

Cash Flow The amount of actual cash flowing in and out of a business.

Casual A person who applies for a job spontaneously, not as a result of a recruiting program.

Caveat Emptor Latin for "Let the buyer beware." A selling philosophy which places the entire responsibility of buying on the purchaser.

Centralization The policy whereby authority is retained by the leader of an enterprise or department, with little or no delegation of authority.

Chain of Command The line of authority which can be traced from subordinate to superior, from the entry-level worker to the top manager.

Charisma A natural leadership quality which inspires a great popular following.

Clique An informal group whose members are united in their support of a common cause.

Collective Bargaining Negotiations between management and a representative of the employees, usually a union, in an effort to reach agreement on an employment contract for all members of the particular union.

Committee A group of people chosen to work and act on specific matters.

Communications The flow of ideas and concepts by any method or media from a sender to a receiver.

Communications, Downward The flow of ideas from superior to subordinate.

Communications, Lateral The flow of ideas among peers.

Communications, Upward The flow of ideas from subordinate to superior.

Common Stock Shares of a company representing the ownership of that company and providing the basis for voting and paying dividends.

Compensation A person's pay, a total of cash, fringe benefits, and psychological fulfillment, which he receives for doing his work.

Conflict of Interest A situation in which personal well-being or chance for gain might unduly influence a business decision.

Consultant A specialist from outside an organization who is hired to study a situation and recommend a course of action.

Consumer Laws Laws intended to protect the consumer from unjust and unscrupulous acts on the part of the producer or seller.

Control The function of management which requires the superior to make sure that objectives and standards, set forth in the plans, are being met, or that appropriate remedial action is being taken.

Control, Span of The number of subordinates a manager supervises.

Cooperative Advertising The dividing of advertising costs between two or more members of a channel of distribution such as the manufacturer and the retailer.

Corporation A form of business ownership in which the business legally becomes a person with rights and obligations, and the owners of the business, the stockholders, are granted limited liability.

Corrective Action The action which must be taken when it is determined that existing methods are not accomplishing planned results, and without which, there can be no control.

Costs, Fixed Those costs which will remain essentially the same regardless of variations in output. Examples are rent, insurance, the president's salary.

Costs, Variable Those costs which rise or fall in proportion to the output of the company. These are primarily direct labor and materials costs.

Creativity An ability to generate ideas which are original, different, and unique.

Cybernetics A science of communications used extensively in self-regulating systems by the constant comparison of feedback information to set standards with automatic triggering of corrective measures.

Debt The money owed by a company or an individual.

Debt Financing Expanding the level of business by borrowing money rather than selling equity, or generating the money internally through profits.

Decentralization The tendency for top management to delegate authority and have decisions made at all levels of the company.

Decision Making Deciding upon and implementing a course of action after: (1) defining the problem or situation; (2) proposing alternative solutions; and (3) projecting these alternatives to a logical conclusion.

Delegating The granting of decision-making authority and responsibility by the manager to a subordinate.

Delineation The outlining of the duties, responsibilities, and authority attached to a particular job and to the person holding that job.

Democratic Manager A manager who allows his subordinates to make major decisions through majority vote.

Demotion A reduction in rank, grade, or status usually as a disciplinary device.

Departmentalization Dividing a total company or unit into separate divisions, usually functional areas, for better management control.

Depreciation An accounting device in which the value of an asset is decreased over the useful life of that asset rather than reducing its value to zero as soon as it is purchased.

Devil's Advocate A person who takes the negative point of view of every decision made in an effort to test the validity, the soundness, of the decision.

Dilution Making weaker or "watering down" a situation such as existing stockholder control weakened by the issuance of additional stock.

Directing Actuating a situation by giving authoritative instructions, orders and commands and monitoring the adherence by subordinates and their motivation to carry out assignments.

Directors, Inside Members of a company board of directors whose primary business activity is within the company for which they are directors, such as the president, vice-president or controller.

Directors, Outside Members of a company board of directors whose primary work is outside of that business for which they are directors.

Discharge To dismiss from employment.

Discipline, Negative Discipline with the intent of punishing the offender.

Discipline, Positive Discipline with the intent of improving the employee's behavior.

Dividends The share of the profit of a company paid out to the stockholders. The remainder of the profit becomes retained earnings.

Division of Labor The dividing of a job into components requiring specific skills so that workers become experts in their fields.

Dual Subordination (Also called *Unity of Command*). A principle which states that no employee should get his orders from more than one source at one time.

Earnings The compensation of a man or the profits of a company.

Employment Agency A business whose major service is securing employment for its clients, usually for a fee.

Entrepreneur One who organizes, manages, and assumes the risks of a business or enterprise.

Esprit de Corps   A group spirit of pride and honor which unites all the members in an effort to accomplish a particular objective.

Esteem Needs   The human psychological need for status, for recognition and respect from others, and for self confidence through achievement.

Ethics   The discipline dealing with what is good and bad and with moral duty and obligations. The principles of conduct governing an individual or group.

Exception Principle   The management principle of concentrating action on exceptional cases, those which fall outside of the control limits.

Expenses   Costs incurred to earn revenue.

Expenditures   Costs incurred to acquire an asset or service.

Exit Interview   An interview with a person leaving a company to find what he thinks of the company, its personnel, policies, and why he is leaving, if his departure is voluntary.

Faction   Those within an organization who support an idea or cause, usually different from that of the main body.

Feedback   A system in which the issuer (either man or machine) of a message, has a built-in method of communication to determine if the receiver of the message reacts as expected or if corrective action is necessary.

"Fighting Fires"   Solving problems as they occur, without a guiding philosophy or basic objective.

Fixed Assets   Company assets, such as land, buildings, and machines, which cannot be readily converted to cash.

Fixed Costs   Costs of operating a business which occur in spite of the volume of sales or production, such as executive salaries, insurance, and depreciation.

"Flat" Organization   An organization with only a few levels of management, but with wide span of control.

Flexibility   A built-in provision in a plan which allows adjustment and modification as needed without destroying the main thrust of the plan.

Forecast   A prediction of what will happen or what could happen.

Foreman   A first level manager, usually in a manufacturing type of business.

Formal Authority   The authority as outlined on a formal organization chart.

Formal Organization   The structure of a company with rigid relationships as set forth in an organization chart.

Fractionalization   The breaking up or splitting of a total job into smaller, specialized work units.

Fringe Benefit   Benefits for employees such as insurance, paid vacation, and paid sick leave which are not included in the basic salary and are provided free of charge or for a modest sum.

Function   Professional or official position; the action for which a person or thing is specially fitted or used.

Functional Authority   An authority granted to a person because of unusual competence rather than position in the organization. An example would be an attorney having authority over higher level persons in legal matters.

Functional Organization   An organization divided into groups by the kind of work performed.

Gantt Chart   A chart which gives visual representation of the progress of the parts of a project as it goes from step to step.

Grapevine   The unofficial, informal channel of communication which functions primarily by word of mouth.

Graphology   The study of handwriting to determine aptitudes and character.

Grievance   A formal complaint by a worker that he or she has been treated unjustly and or inequitably.

Halo Effect (or Error)   The tendency of an evaluating manager to give a total rating of a subordinate based on one incident or factor, whether good or bad.

Hawthorne Studies   Studies conducted at Western Electric's Hawthorne plant in the 1920s (under the direction of Elton Mayo) which helped form the basis of the human behavior school of management.

Hierarchy of Needs   A. H. Maslow's theory of human needs ranging from physiological needs to self-actualization.

House Organ   A newspaper, newsletter or magazine which is published by a company for its employees.

Image   The impression of a person or company either presented to or perceived by the public.

Incentive Wages   Payment to an employee for production above a quota.

Incentive, Positive   The offer of additional compensation for exceptional or additional work beyond the required output.

Incentive, Negative   A threat to withhold pay or some other desired benefit for failure to achieve a certain goal.

Income Statement   A financial report listing sales, costs associated with the sales, and the net results—profits or losses.

Incumbent   The present holder of a position or office.

Induction   The process of bringing a new person into an organization.

Informal Organization   The actual relationships of people within an organization which sometimes differs from the formal or stated relationships.

Innovation   The development of new ideas or new applications for existing ideas.

Inspection   An investigation or examination of a product, person, or other factor to be controlled.

Inspection Tour   A method of control by which the manager checks the people, products, and facilities on the site rather than through a report.

Intermediate Term   Planning or financing for a period of from two to five years.

Interviewing   A face to face meeting between people, usually a superior and a subordinate, to obtain or exchange information, to form a basis of evaluation, to hire or fire, to discipline, to elevate, or to advise.

Interviewing, Directive   An interview in which the interviewer asks specific questions to which direct, limited answers are expected.

Interviewing, Nondirective   Interviews in which the person interviewed is encouraged to express himself or herself freely rather than be required to answer specific questions.

Investment   An amount of money put into a business, a machine, stocks and or bonds, or some asset, for the purpose of obtaining a profit.

Investors   Those persons who invest money in a business or a project.

Inventory   Stocks of raw materials, work-in-process, finished goods and supplies.

Inventory Control   The management of inventory to prevent both shortages and excessive inventories.

Job   A task to be done by one person or the total amount of work under one grouping, such as a contract.

Job Analysis   Process of collecting information about a job through observation and interviews.

Job Description   A description of the authority, responsibility, and objectives of a job as well as the relationships of the jobholder to others in the organization.

Job Enlargement   The increasing of the variety of work done in a job.

Job Enrichment   Adding higher level, more responsible work to a job.

Job Satisfaction   The ability of the jobholder to find satisfaction through the work he performs.

Job Specifications   The human requirements and personal achievements needed to qualify a person for a particular job.

Journeyman   A person who is accomplished in his skill.

Labor   Work, indicating workers collectively, particularly those in industry who are organized by unions.

Laissez Faire Management   A management style of not interfering with the workers, letting them do as they want.

Last Critical Incident   The tendency for a manager to evaluate an employee based solely on the last significant happening, good or bad, in which that employee was involved.

Layoff   The suspension or dismissal of an employee or group of employees usually because of a lack of work or as a disciplinary measure.

Leadman   A worker who is not generally regarded as a supervisor but who aids the foreman in some management functions such as training and work allocation.

Leak   The accidental or intentional dissemination of confidential information.

Legalism   Strict adherence to the law or rule, without regard to the spirit of the law.

Liabilities   Claims against the assets of a company.

Line   Those activities and people concerned with accomplishing the basic objectives of the company, or used to express the command relationship between superiors and direct subordinates.

Linear Programming   A mathematic method of optimizing a total when the parts have linear relationships.

Line Manager   A manager of a line function, such as production, sales, or finance, directly related to the company objectives.

Lines of Communication   Channels through which information flows in all directions throughout an organization.

Line-Staff Concept   The dividing of management and technical people into those who command (line) and those who advise (staff).

Longterm Planning   Planning for five years or more.

Maintenance Factors   These factors of work which keep the worker from becoming dissatisfied although they do not motivate him.

"Making Scrap"   In production, the repetition of errors which results in unacceptable products.

Management   Those who strive to achieve goals through the planning, organizing, activating, and control of labor and resources.

Management by Exception   A style of management in which control efforts are devoted only to exceptional cases, those outside acceptable limits.

Management by Objectives (*MBO*)   A management technique in which the subordinate, in conjunction with the manager, sets individual goals to benefit both the company and her- or himself.

Management Grid Theory A management theory which encourages managers to have great concern for both people and production.

Management Principles Guidelines and theories for management behavior.

Manager A person who gets things done through other people by supervising and controlling their activities.

Man in the Middle A name given to foremen or first level supervisors who feel they must represent higher management to the workers and represent the workers to higher management.

Marketing All activities related to getting the product from the producer to the consumer.

Market Research Research activities designed to answer questions concerning the reception of the product and customer buying motivation.

Matrix Organization A system of organization in which the participants are combined for a single project, disbanded, and then, reassigned to another project.

Merger A combining of two companies through an exchange of stock.

Model A mathematical representation of a given situation in which solutions can be found where factors are changed through the assignment of different inputs.

"Monte Carlo Technique" Operations research techniques using probability.

Morale The mental or emotional attitude of a person or a group toward a particular subject or the tasks on hand.

Morale Survey An anonymous survey used to determine the general attitudes or morale of the employees of a company.

Motion Studies Studies to determine the most efficient method of physically doing a job.

Motivation An inducement to do more or better for the good of the company and or the individual.

Motivators Those things which tend to induce an employee to do a better job.

Negotiating Conferring or discussing specified topics with the object of reaching an agreement.

Nepotism A practice of hiring relatives of those persons already working for the company, regardless of competency.

Niche A place or position particularly suitable for a person or company.

Objectives Goals of the organization and of those people working within the organization.

Obligation Work for which a person is held accountable regardless of how that work is delegated.

On-the-Job Training Training a person by having him or her do the actual job.

Organization, Formal The official positions and the relationships of positions to others within an organization as outlined on the organization chart and in the job description.

Organization, Informal The unofficial or personal relationships of people within an organization which probably does not correspond to the relationships outlined on the official chart.

Organization Chart A pictorial representation of the formal organization of a company.

Organizing A manager's function of dividing the work or the organization into workable units; assigning authority and responsibility to these persons within the units, and providing a framework of formal relationships for the members of the organization.

Orientation The initial briefing session between a new employee and company representatives concerning general information and policies of the company as well as specific information relating to that person's assignment.

Overtime Work in excess of the normal day or week for which the worker, either by agreement or by law, is paid a premium, usually one and a half times the regular pay.

Owner's Equity The claims the owners have on the assets of a company.

Participative Leader A leader who involves his subordinates in decisions which affect them.

Paternalism A system in which the manager's relationship to his subordinates resembles that of a father to his children.

Paternalist A manager who adopts a paternalist approach to management.

Peer A person of the same rank, an equal.

Peer Pressure Pressure by one's coworkers to conform to the group's standards.

Phrenology The study of the shape of the skull based on the belief it is indicative of mental faculties and character.

Physiological Needs The human needs for elements which satisfy the body such as air, water, food, shelter, and sex.

Piecework A pay system whereby the worker is paid per piece of work accomplished rather than for time spent in doing the work.

Plan, Planning Setting objectives and determining the methods by which they will be reached.

Policy A general principle to guide the managers as they strive to reach company goals.

Pragmatic Workable, practical, a method that gets results.

Principles of Management Fundamental truths that should form the basis of a manager's policies.

Problem Definition First step in decision making in which the root cause of a problem is isolated from its symptoms.

Probability Decision Theory A quantitative method of decision making by assuming the likelihood of events.

Procedure A specified series of steps to be taken to accomplish a given task.

Production The producing of a product in a manufacturing company, the main line function of the company.

Productivity The comparison of production output to manhour input to determine efficiency.

Profit Surplus remaining after costs of sales have been deducted from total sales.

Profit and Loss Statement (Income Statement) A financial statement which shows sales, costs of sales, profit, taxes, and other related expenses.

Profit Sharing A practice of giving employees a share of company profits in addition to their regular wages.

Promotion The raising of a person to a higher position within a company.

Proprietorship A form of business organization in which the owner is the business, entitled to all the profits, and is personally responsible for all debts and losses.

Proxy A document appointing a person, or the person designated, to vote on or act in behalf of a stockholder.

Public Relations Activities of a company designed to secure a good public image.

Purchase Order An official document of a company authorizing the purchase of goods or services.

Qualifying an Audience   Making certain the listeners to an idea are able to both use and implement the idea.

Quality Control   Measuring a product or service against a predetermined standard to see if it is acceptable.

Quantification   Putting problems and situations into numerical terms.

Quantitative Analysis   Solving problems and making decisions based on the mathematical analysis of models representing these problems.

Queuing Theory   The quantitative method of determining optimums when dealing with problems involving queues or lines such as in a supermarket checkout.

Ranking   A method of evaluating people or jobs in a group by assigning the top grade to the "best" person, second grade to the "next best" and so on.

Recruiting   Various methods used to attract new employees.

Reliability   The ability to get consistent test results over a period of time.

Reports   Statements giving an account of a situation, often with recommendations, used for control and planning purposes.

Requisition   A document requesting necessary authorization to purchase a product or service.

Research and Development (R&D)   That part of the company and its budget devoted to developing and testing new products and processes.

Responsibility   The obligation of a manager or worker to do his or her job.

Retained Earnings   That part of profits retained by the organization rather than being paid out in dividends.

Retraining   Teaching employees new jobs and skills when their old jobs have become obsolete.

Return on Investment (ROI)   The annual yield, measured in several ways, which results from an investment.

Risk   The degree of chance for loss associated with a management decision.

Rules   Plans and regulations which concern the personal conduct of people within an organization and the penalties for noncompliance.

Salary   Compensation paid to an employee, usually refers to the cash portion only.

Satisficing   Selecting an alternative which exceeds the minimum requirements for completing a project but not the one which offers the optimum solution.

Satisfiers (Hygienic Factors)   Those factors which tend to keep people from becoming dissatisfied but do not provide motivation.

Scaler Principle   The chain of command principle, the superior-subordinate relationship existing in a direct line between the top and bottom people in an organization.

Scapegoat   The person or thing onto which is transferred guilt and blame for troubles.

Scientific Management   The management theory formulated by Frederick Taylor in which the emphasis is on more productivity through better, more efficient, scientific methods.

Screening   Interviewing and testing to find qualified candidates for a job.

Security Needs   The need to be protected and safe from both physical and psychological dangers.

Self-Actualization Needs   The need a person has to develop to his or her fullest potential.

Semantics   Having to do with the meanings and use of words.

Seniority System A system which gives preference to its members with the greatest length of service.

Sensitivity Training (T-Group Training) Group sessions in which participants are told what reactions others have to them and how they might improve negative traits.

Service Department Staff departments in a company, such as maintenance, stores, purchasing, and personnel, which render services to other departments.

Shop Traveler A procedural, step-by-step, plan which travels with a piece of work as it goes through the manufacturing process.

Shortterm Plan Plans which are for a year or less.

Simulation The use of mathematical models and computers to determine what will happen to outputs as inputs and mixes are varied.

Situational Manager A manager who adjusts his style to the needs of the subordinates and the situation at hand.

Social Isolation A job which isolates the worker from all contact with others, co-workers and customers.

Social Needs The needs people have to be accepted, to associate with others, to give and receive affection and love.

Social Responsibility Management's responsibility to the company employees, the community, and consumers.

Sociometric Technique A work technique in which the workers choose or elect their leader and choose those persons with whom they want to work.

Sole Proprietorship A form of business in which the sole owner of the concern is the business, entitled to all profits and being personally responsible for all debts.

Span of Control (Span of Management) The number of subordinates over which a manager has direct control and authority.

Spokesman A person who publicly announces decisions made and positions taken by the group he represents.

Staff Technicians and specialists who aid and advise line managers, and who have no direct authority to issue commands or make changes.

Staffing The management function of finding, hiring, training, and developing people for jobs within an organization.

Standards Guidelines of acceptable quality, value, size, or other measurable attributes.

Stockholders Those persons owning common stock in a company, the owners of the company.

Stock Options A right given as an incentive to certain executives of a company to buy a specified number of shares of common stock in that company at a fixed price within a stated period of time.

Stock Purchase Plans Plans devised by companies to allow the employees to buy company stock in installments through the company and without a brokerage fee.

Strategy, Grand The program of action for a company under normal conditions.

Strategy, Competitive A grand strategy which has been adjusted to counter moves made by competitors.

Subordinate A person who is below another in rank.

Suggestion Box A box strategically located in the company, for the purpose of upward communications and participation by all the workers within that company.

Supervisors Foremen, foreladies; first level managers who are between the workers and higher management.

"System," The   Usually a derogatory term used to express the actual way an organization operates, often in opposition to the intention of the designers of the organization.

T-Account   An accounting device, in which all increases in an account are shown on one side of the "T" and decreases are shown on the other. Also used to express the positive and negative aspects of a situation.

Tall Organization   An organization with many layers and a narrow span of control.

Temporaries   Temporary workers hired by the hour or day, usually through an employment agency.

Termination   A voluntary or involuntary quit, a removal from the payroll.

Theory X   Theory devised by Douglas McGregor in which a superior views workers as being lazy and unimaginative, and must be coerced into doing any work.

Theory Y   Theory which views workers as willing participants in a job who want to contribute and are capable of great achievements on their own.

Training   Teaching students or workers to do a particular task, usually a technical one.

Turnover, Employee   The percentage of the work force leaving the company and being replaced within a specified period of time.

Turnover, Inventory   The total amount of sales divided by the average inventory to determine the number of times inventory is replaced within a year.

Unity of Command   Oneness of command. The principle of subordinates being responsible to only one superior at a time.

Validity   The accuracy of a test or device to measure that which it is intended to measure.

Vendor   A supplier, usually one who sells goods and services to a purchasing department.

Vestibule Training   Employee training which occurs on the premises of the employer but in an area segregated from the main work area.

Wages   Compensation for work done.

Work   Physical or mental effort exerted to make or do something.

Working Capital   That part of capital which circulates from inventory to accounts receivable to cash and back to inventory.

Bibliography

Albers, Henry H. *Principles of Management: A Modern Approach* 3d ed. New York: John Wiley & Sons, 1969.

Anthony, Robert N.; Dearden, John; and Vancil, Richard E. *Managerial Control Systems.* Homewood, Ill.: Richard D. Irwin, 1965.

Argyris, Chris. *Interpersonal Competence and Organizational Effectiveness.* Homewood, Ill.: Richard D. Irwin, and Dorsey Press, 1962.

Barnard, Chester I. *Organization and Management.* Cambridge, Mass.: Harvard Univ. Press, 1948.

Bittle, Lester R. *What Every Supervisor Should Know.* 3d ed. New York: McGraw-Hill, 1971.

Bittle, Lester R. *Management by Exception.* New York: McGraw-Hill, 1964.

Crosby, Philip B. *The Art of Getting Your Own Sweet Way.* New York: McGraw-Hill, 1972.

Dale, Ernest. *Management: Theory and Practice.* 3d ed. New York: McGraw-Hill, 1969.

Drucker, P. F. *The Practice of Management.* New York: Harper and Row, 1954.

———. *The Effective Executive.* New York: Harper and Row, 1967.

———. *The Age of Discontinuity.* New York: Harper and Row, 1969.

Fayol, Henri. *General and Industrial Management.* London: Sir Isaac Pitman & Sons, Ltd., 1949.

Filley, A. C. and House, R. J. *Managerial Process and Organizational Behavior.* Glenview, Ill.: Scott, Foresman, 1969.

Flippo, Edwin B. *Management: A Behavioral Approach.* 2d ed. Boston: Allyn and Bacon, 1970.

———. *Principles of Personnel Management.* New York: McGraw-Hill, 1971.

Gantt, H. L. *Industrial Leadership.* New York: Association Press, 1921.

Gellerman, Saul W. *Motivation and Productivity.* New York: American Management Association, 1963.

Gilbreth, F. B. and Gilbreth, L. M. *Applied Motion Study.* New York: Macmillan, 1919.

Gulick, Luther and Urwick, Lyndall. *Papers on the Science of Administration.* New York: Institute of Public Administration; Columbia Univ., 1937.

Haimann, Theo and Hilgert, Raymond L. *Supervision; Concepts and Practices of Management.* Cincinnati: South-Western, 1972.

Haynes, W. Warren and Massie, Joseph L. *Management: Analysis, Concepts, and Cases.* rev. ed. Englewood Cliffs, N.J.: Prentice-Hall, 1969.

Hepner, Harry Walker. *Psychology Applied to Life and Work*. Englewood Cliffs, N.J.: Prentice-Hall, 1973.

Herzberg, Frederick. *Work and the Nature of Man*. New York: World Publishing, 1966.

Kleppner, Otto. *Advertising Procedure*. 6th ed. Englewood Cliffs, N.J.: Prentice-Hall, 1973.

Koontz, Harold and O'Donnell, Cyril. *Principles of Management*, 4th ed. New York: McGraw-Hill, 1968.

Likert, Rensis. *New Patterns of Management*. New York: McGraw-Hill, 1962.

Longenecker, Justin G. *Principles of Management and Organizational Behavior*. 2d ed. Columbus: Merrill, 1969.

McGregor, Douglas. *The Human Side of Enterprise*. New York: McGraw-Hill, 1960.

Newman, William H.; Summer, Charles E., Jr.; and Warren, E. Kirby. *The Process of Management*. 2d ed. Englewood Cliffs, N.J.: Prentice-Hall, 1967.

Odiorne, George S. *Management by Objectives*. rev. ed. New York: Pitman, 1970.

Reid, Allan L. *Modern Applied Salesmanship*. Pacific Palisades, California: Goodyear, 1970.

Sieloff, Theodore J. and Aberle, John W. *Introduction to Business, American Enterprise in Action*. 6th ed. Belmont, California: Wadsworth, 1972.

Sisk, Henry L. *Principles of Management—A Systems Approach to the Management Process*. Cincinnati: South-Western, 1969.

Taylor, Frederick W. *Scientific Management*. New York: Harper, 1947.

Whyte, William Foote, *Men at Work*. Homewood, Ill.: Richard D. Irwin and Dorsey, 1961.

Index

Achievement, rising levels of, 308
Activating, 9
Actuating, 189
Ad-hocracy, 303
Administrative management, 37
Advertisements, help wanted, 192
Altering forms, 119
Alternatives, 23
American Federation of Musicians
    (AFM), 194
American Management Association,
    179
Analysis of alternatives, 24
Annual reports, 252
Apathy, 292
Applicants, evaluation of, 198
Application blank, 196
Argyris, Chris, 4
Aristotle, 286
Action, methods of asking for, 135
Assistant, 153
Assistant-to, the, 153
Audience, qualifying an, 133
Authority,
   definition of, 172
   limits of, 174
   sources of, 172
Autocratic manager, 227

Babbage, Charles, 34
Balance sheet, 270
Barnard, Chester I., 39
Barriers to communication, 249
Behavior norms, 38
Benevolent autocrat, 227
"Big picture", 81
Blake, Robert R., 215

Brainstorming, 120
Bribes, 294
Budgets, 106

Capital expenditures, 271
Case presentation, 27
Cash flow statement, 271
Casuals, 193
Caveat emptor, 293
Chain of command, 39, 150
Change, reasons for, 132
Checking references, 198
Clay, Henry, 285
Clique, 160
College visitations, 194
Communication,
   barriers to, 249
   definition of, 245
   human relations in, 247
   overcoming barriers to, 250
   process of, 245
Communications,
   downward, 251
   horizontal, 255
   upward, 253
Compensation, 201
Compromise, 293
Conflict of interest, 291
Consumer Credit Protection Act, 286
Control,
   definition of, 265
   problems with, 275
   steps in, 265
   types of, 274
Control points, 273
Controlling, 10
Corrective action, 11

Creative process, 118
Creativity,
  aids to, 120
  barriers to, 115
  definition of, 115
  overcoming obstacles to, 116

Davis, Ralph C., 39
Decentralization, 177
Decision making,
  bases for, 19
  method of, 20
Delegate, manager's inability to, 178
Delegation, 10, 177
  reasons for, 177
Democratic manager, 228
Departmentation, 161
Dickson, William J., 38, 208
Directing, 225
Discipline, 230
Disciplinary action, 233
  example of, 234
  positive, 230
  punitive, 230
Disciplinary interview, 233
Discrimination, 294
Drucker, Peter F., 215

Employment agencies, 193
Esteem needs, 211
Ethics, definition of, 285
Evaluation, critical, 8
Experts, 292

Father of Scientific Management, 34
Fayol, Henri, 37, 148
Federal Trade Commission, 293
Flat Organizations, 180
Food, Drug and Cosmetic Act, 286

Gaming theory, 40

Gantt chart, 35
Gantt, Henry L., 35
Gifts, 294
Gilbreth, Frank, 37
Gilbreth, Lillian, 37
Goals, 67
  communication of, 74
  company, 68
  long and short, 74
  profit, 72
  non-business, 68
  non-profit, 73
  soundness of, 76
Grapevine,
  definition of, 255
  use of, 256
Grievances, 253
Group planning, 87
  advantages of, 87
  disadvantages of, 88

Hawthorne studies, 38, 208
Herzberg, Frederick, 213
Hierarchy of needs, 209
Hippocratic oath, 286
Hoover, Herbert, 303
House organs, 252
Human relations school of
  management, 38
Hygenic needs, 213

Ideas,
  presentation of, 135
  selling, 129
Implementing, 26
Income statement, 269
Induction, 199
Innovation, 6, 115
International Longshoremen's
  Association (ILA), 194
Interviewing,
  directive, 195

Interviewing, (Cont.)
  nondirective, 195
Interview,
  atmosphere for, 197
  disciplinary, 233
  physical setting for, 197

Job,
  analysis, 171
  description, 9, 171
  definition of, 171
  specification, 9, 172

Kennedy, John F., 293

Labor unions, 194
Leadership, 225
  best type of, 229
  influences upon, 225
  styles of, 226
Legalism, 290
Letters to the editor, 254
Licensing, 306
Line, definition of, 150
Line and staff, 149
Linear programming, 40

Machiavelli, Niccolo, 285
Maintenance needs, 213
Manager,
  definition of, 3
  educational requirements of, 309
  entry level, 52
  laissez-faire, 224
  middle, 52
  responsibilities of, 287
  top, 52
Manager's decisions, magnitude of,
  289
Manager's mobility, 307

Managers, professional, 5
Mangement by Objective (MBO), 39,
  71, 215
Management,
  definition of, 3
  professionalized, 306
  systems, 33
Managerial Grid, 216
Managerial roles,
  chief spokesman, 55
  communicator, 54
  control center, 54
  coordinator, 57
  figurehead, 53
  final decider, 55
  information center, 54
  liaison, 53
  negotiator, 55
  resource allocator, 55
  trainer, 56
  umpire, 54
Maslow, Abraham H., 209
Matrix organizations, 304
Mayo, Elton, 38, 208
McGregor, Douglas, 214, 230
Monte Carlo theory, 40
Mooney, James D., 39
Morale, 217
  as a basis of control, 272
  survey, 254
Moses, 33
Motivation, 10, 207
  history of, 208
  negative, 208
  positive, 208
  self, 208
  money as a, 208
Motivators, 213
Mouton, Jane S., 215
Myers, M. Scott, 214

National Labor Relations Act, 286
Nepotism, 194

Objectives,
  definition of, 67
  setting, 8
  as motivatiors, 70
Obligations, definition of, 176
Operations research, 40
Open-door policy, 152
Organizing, 9
Organization,
  dynamic, 181
  flat, 180
  formal, 158
  informal, 158
  line, 153
  line and staff, 153
  process of, 147
  tall, 178
Orientation, 10, 200
Osborn, Alex F., 119
Overcoming objections, 138

Participative leader, 227
Paternalist, 227
Physical examination, 199
Pigiron studies, 35
Planning, 6
  definition of, 81
  done by, 83
  group, 87
  pervasiveness of, 81
  reasons for opposition to, 84
  steps in, 82
  time span for, 84
Plans,
  dissemination of, 89
  failure of, 85
  written or unwritten, 86
  single purpose, 106
Precedence as policy, 101
Procedures, 98
  examples of, 103
Presentations, steps in, 130
Professionalized management, 306

Professionals, definition of, 5
Pseudo sciences, 197
Physiological needs, 209
Policy,
  definition of, 98
  examples of, 100

Qualifying an audience, 133
Quantitative management, 39
Queing theory, 40

Recruiters, types of, 189
Recruiting, 189
  means of, 191
References, checking, 198
Reich, Charles A., 4
Reiley, Alan C., 39
Relationships, delineation of, 9
Responsibility, definition of, 175
Responsibility for planning, 275
Roosevelt, Franklin, D., 303
Roethlisberger, F.J., 38, 208
Rules, 99, 231
  characteristics of, 105
  reaction to violators of, 232

Safety needs, 210
Satisficing, 57
Satisfiers, 213
Scaler principle (see Chain of
    command), 39, 151
Scientific management, 34
Screening, 195
Selecting, 199
Self-actualization needs, 212
Selling ideas, 129
Sensitivity training, 216
Sherman Act, 286
Single purpose plans, 106
Situationalism, 295
Situational manager, 228

Social,
  isolation, 211
  pay, 159
  needs, 211
Span of control,
  number of subordinates in, 179
  reasons affecting, 180
Staff, definition of, 150
Staffing, 10, 189
Staff personnel, problems with, 157
Standard operating procedure
    (SOP), 103
Standards,
  bases of, 266
  tangible and intangible, 266
Strategy,
  competitive, 98
  definition of, 98
  grand, 98
Subordinate acceptance theory, 174
Suggestion box, 254
Symptoms, 22
Systems management, 40

System, the, 290

Taft-Hartley Act, 286
Tall organizations, 178
Taylor, Frederick W., 34
Teamsters, 194
Temporary employees, 194
Testing, 198
T-group training, 216
Theory X, 214
Theory Y, 214
Toffler, Alvin, 303
Townsend, Robert, 157
Training, 200

Unity of command, 148
Urwick, L.F., 179

Wagner Act, 286
Weber, Max, 37